W9-CQC-428

The ANNOTATED CHARLOTTE'S WEB

The ANNOTATED CHARLOTTE'S WEB

by E. B. WHITE

PICTURES BY GARTH WILLIAMS

Introduction and Notes by
PETER F. NEUMEYER

hers

The Annotated Charlotte's Web

For information address HarperCollins Children's Books, a division of HarperCollins Publishers, 10 East 53rd Street, New York, NY 10022.
Typography by Tom Starace
1 2 3 4 5 6 7 8 9 10
❖
First Edition

Library of Congress Cataloging-in-Publication Data
Neumeyer, Peter F., date
The annotated Charlotte's web / introduction and notes by Peter F. Neumeyer. Charlotte's web / by E. B. White ; pictures by Garth Williams.
p. cm.
Includes bibliographical references.
ISBN 0-06-024387-2.
1. White, E. B. (Elwyn Brooks), 1899–1985 Charlotte's web. I. Williams, Garth. II. White, E. B. (Elwyn Brooks), 1899–1985 Charlotte's web. 1994. III. Title. IV. Title: Charlotte's web.
PS3545.H5187C536 1994 92-37470
813'.52—dc20 CIP
AC

The author has made every effort to locate all owners of material and to obtain permission to reproduce it. Any errors or omissions are unintentional, and corrections will be made in future printings if necessary. Thanks are due for permission to reprint the copyrighted material listed below:

Booklist, Vol. 49, September 1, 1952, p. 2. Reprinted with the permission of *Booklist*.

Eleanor Cameron, "McLuhan, Youth, and Literature," Part II. Copyright © by *The Horn Book* (December 1972). Reprinted with the permission of *The Horn Book*.

Aidan Chambers, *Booktalk: Occasional Writing on Literature and Children*, first published in 1985, Bodley Head, London. Originally from "The Child's Changing Story," copyright © 1982, first published in *Signal* 40, January 1983. U.S. edition published 1986 by Harper & Row, Publishers. Reprinted with the permission of Aidan Chambers.

John Henry Comstock, *The Spider Book: A Manual for the Study of the Spiders and their Near Relatives, the Scorpions, the Class Arachnida, Found in America North of Mexico, with Analytical Keys for their Classification and Popular Accounts of their Habits*. Rev. and Ed. by W. J. Gertsch, Ph.D. Ithaca, NY: Comstock, 1948. Reprinted with the permission of Cornell University Press.

Linda H. Davis, *Onward and Upward: A Biography of Katharine S. White*. Copyright © 1987 by HarperCollins Publishers. Reprinted with the permission of HarperCollins Publishers.

Scott Elledge, reprinted from *E. B. White, A Biography*, by Scott Elledge, by permission of the author and W. W. Norton & Company, Inc. Copyright © 1985, 1984 by Scott Elledge.

D. J. Enright, "A Mania for Sentences" in *Encounter*, April 1978. Reprinted with the permission of Watson, Little Limited.

Joseph Epstein, "E. B. White, Dark and Lite," *Commentary*, April 1986. Reprinted with the permission of *Commentary*.

Beverly Gherman, reprinted with permission of Atheneum Publishers, an imprint of Macmillan Publishing Company, from *E. B. White: Some Writer!* by Beverly Gherman. Copyright © 1992 by Beverly Gherman.

Marion Glastonbury, *Writers, Critics, and Children*. Ed. Geoff Fox et al. New York: Agathon Press, copyright © 1976 by Geoff Fox. Reprinted with permission of Agathon Press.

Fred Inglis, *The Promise of Happiness: Value and Meaning in Children's Fiction*. Copyright © 1981 by Cambridge University Press. Reprinted with the permission of Cambridge University Press.

M. F. Kieran, "New Books for Children," originally published in *The Atlantic Monthly*, December 1952, pp. 100–102. Reprinted with the permission of *The Atlantic*.

Ulrich Knoepflmacher, "The Doubtful Marriage: A Critical Fantasy," in *Children's Literature* Vol. 18. Ed. Francelia Butler. Copyright © 1990 by Yale University Press. Reprinted with the permission of Yale University Press.

Sonia Landes, "E. B. White's *Charlotte's Web*: Caught in the Web," in *Touchstones: Reflections on the Best in Children's Literature*. Ed. Perry Nodelman. West Lafayette, IN: Children's Literature Association, 1985. Reprinted with the permission of Children's Literature Association.

Jane Langton, in *The New York Times* Book Review, May 10, 1992. Copyright © 1992 by The New York Times Company. Reprinted by permission.

David McCord, "E. B. White," in *20th-Century Children's Writers*, ed. D.

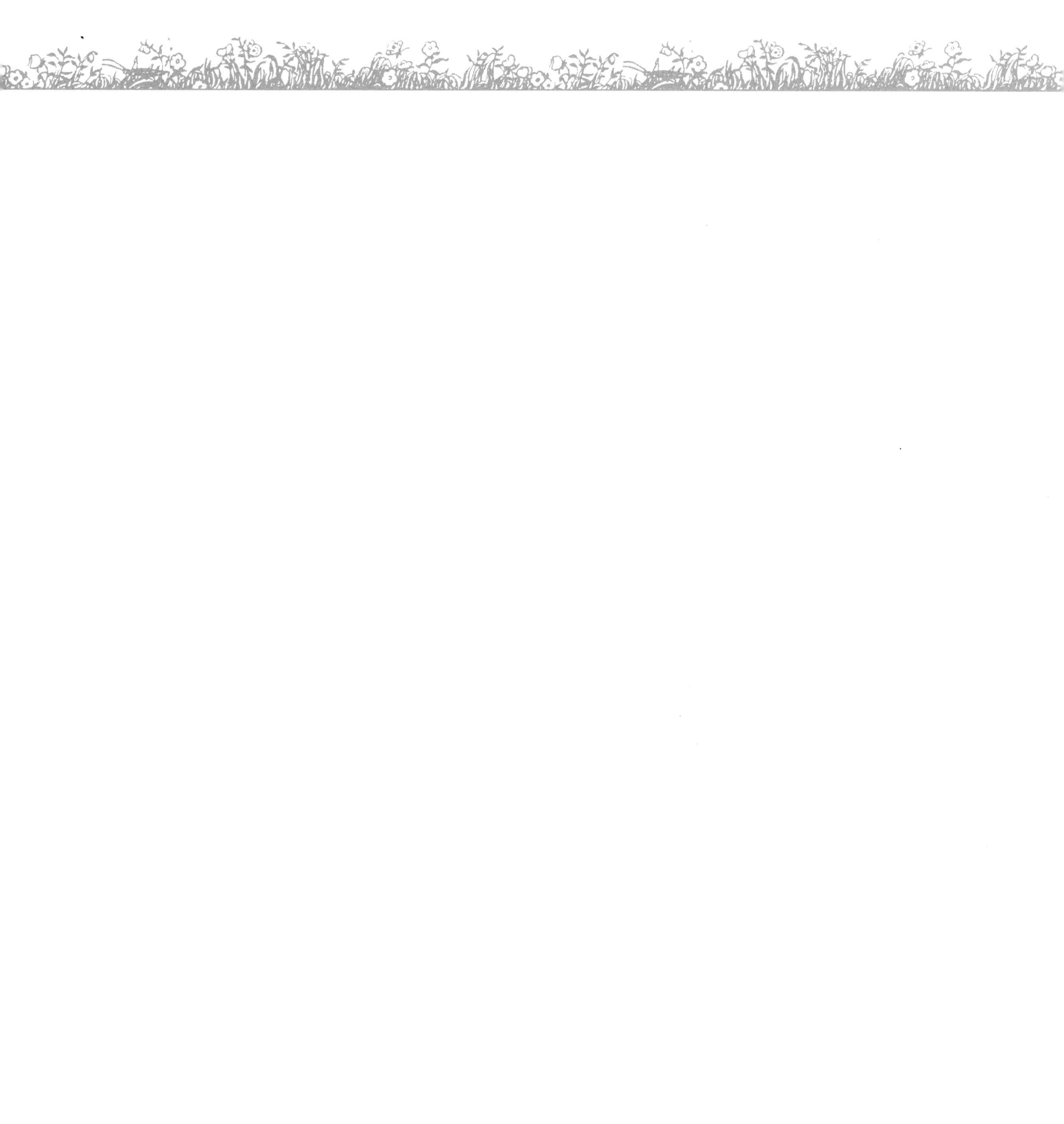

To the memory of my grandparents,
Karl and Anna Neumeyer

ACKNOWLEDGMENTS

My gratitude spreads wide and deep; it encompasses friends and mentors as well as bureaucracies with heart. Without the kindness and hospitality of Lucy B. Burgess and the staff of the Cornell University Library, Division of Rare & Manuscript Collections, this book would not have been possible. My sincere thanks to the Curator, Mark Dimunation.

Ethel Heins, then editor of *The Horn Book*, helped birth this project as she welcomed my first articles on E. B. White's manuscripts; her successor, Anita Silvey, has kept the tradition alive.

Among the many friends to whom Charlotte and I are beholden for their encouragement and counsel are Eleanor Cameron, Ulrich Knoepflmacher, and Ramon Ross. My colleagues Dan McLeod and Jerry Griswold helped, probably even when they didn't know they did. Conversations with Professor Scott Elledge have meant much to me. The chapter on *Charlotte's Web* in his biography of E. B. White remains for me a model of balance between fact and interpretation. I could not have had a more empathetic reader of the manuscript than Geoffrey Ames. My gratitude also to Corona Machemer, Nancy A. Stableford, Stephen Roxburgh, and Gary Piepenbrink.

The National Endowment for the Humanities assisted with travel grants to view White's manuscripts at the Cornell University Library, Division of Rare & Manuscript Collections, and the Pierpont Morgan Library in New York, as well as with opportunity to exchange views with colleagues in a 1984 Summer Seminar at Princeton University.

To San Diego State University—the Department of English & Comparative Literature, the College of Arts and Letters, and the office of the President—I am grateful for generously assisting me even in difficult years.

E. B. White always professed bemused wonderment at undertakings of this nature, and THE ANNOTATED *CHARLOTTE'S WEB* would have proved no exception. But just like E.B.W., Joel and Allene White have been generous, supportive, and patient through the whole long trip.

Thanks to Garth Williams for his lively account of the early days of his memorable collaboration.

To Antonia Markiet, my editor, friend, in-house advocate at HarperCollins, and to Judy Levin for her early labors on the manuscript, sincere thanks. For their scrupulous editing, I am grateful to Renée Cafiero and Katherine Balch. A good index may aspire to the condition of art, and for this one I am beholden to Laura Moss Gottlieb. Without the patience and keen diligence of my research assistant, Joni Mah, there's no telling how much longer this book would have taken.

Finally, I confess I was unable to follow my natural inclination to dedicate this book to my wife, Helen, because, in *every* sense, she is, in fact, the coauthor. And the editor. And the critic. And the bringer-down-to-earth in flighty moments, and lifter-up-of-spirits in sodden ones. Not every sentence here has passed her muster, but if any one shines in some way, it was touched by her.

Our boys, Dan, Chris, Zack, have tolerated all this for years.

—Peter F. Neumeyer, 1994

CONTENTS

List of Plates xii
List of Abbreviations xiii
What Is an ANNOTATED *CHARLOTTE'S WEB*? xvii
Introduction xix
Title, Cover, Endpapers, and Frontispiece of *Charlotte's Web* xxxii

Chapters I–XXII, Annotated 1

Plates 1–12 185
Appendices
- A. Garth Williams, the Illustrator 197
- B. The Manuscripts 204
- C. Spiders 210
- D. E. B. White's Letters and Comments About *Charlotte's Web* 218
- E. Readers' Responses 245
- F. Critical Appraisals 248
- G. Recommended Reading 257

Notes 259
Works Cited 268
Index 274

LIST OF PLATES

1. "Zuckerman's Barn," which White modeled on his own 185
2. E. B. White's handwritten chart of punctuation style 186
3. Half title page of E. B. White's first publication 187
4. Revised draft for *Charlotte's Web*, page 41 188
5. E. B. White's notes on spider anatomy 189
6. Revised draft for *Charlotte's Web*, page 56 190
7. Revised draft for *Charlotte's Web*, page 60 191
8. Revised draft for *Charlotte's Web*, page 66 192
9. Manuscript page in which E. B. White enumerates possibilities for Charlotte's web writings 193
10. E. B. White's drawing of the vectors of the web-spinning process 194
11. E. B. White's notes on web weaving 195
12. Second draft for the beginning of *Charlotte's Web* 196

LIST OF ABBREVIATIONS

ACW	*The Annotated Charlotte's Web*
CW	White, *Charlotte's Web*
D	Davis, *Onward and Upward*
E	Elledge, *E. B. White*
EBW	E. B. White
ES	Strunk & White, *The Elements of Style*
L	*Letters of E. B. White*
NYT	*The New York Times*
NYTBR	*The New York Times Book Review*
OMM	White, *One Man's Meat*
PC	White, *The Points of My Compass*
S	*A Subtreasury of American Humor* (ed. with Katharine S. White)
SL	White, *Stuart Little*
ST	White, *The Second Tree from the Corner*
TNY	*The New Yorker*
TS	White, *The Trumpet of the Swan*
WF	White, *The Wild Flag*
WNY	White, *Writings from the New Yorker*

I have attempted to keep the running text of the annotations as clean as possible. The endnotes for each chapter will afford citations for those who want to follow my tracks, but I have attempted to keep those, too, to the minimum necessary for responsible citation.

For complete bibliographical information for all books and all citations in the Annotations and their notes, see Works Cited.

For example, when "McCord" is cited in the annotations accompanying page 26 of *Charlotte's Web*, you will find page 1326 listed in the Notes for Chapter IV. From there, you would look under McCord in Works Cited, to find that the reference is to page 1326 of McCord's article on White in *20th-Century Children's Writers*.

"It is an extraordinary document, any way you look at it, and it makes me realize how lucky I was (when I was writing the book) that I didn't know what in hell was going on."

—*E. B. White, on reading a scholarly analysis of* Charlotte's Web

"I could have written longer notes, for the art of writing notes is not of difficult attainment."

—*Samuel Johnson*

WHAT IS AN ANNOTATED *CHARLOTTE'S WEB*?

The Annotated *Charlotte's Web* is intended to shed light on one of America's favorite children's books—its origins and its allusions. Obviously one should read White's lovely, musical novel unhampered by annotations several times first (preferably when one is seven or eight)—let it work its spell, relish its charm and its joy and its poignancy. But then, after such a purely appreciative reading, one may compound one's pleasure by an attempt to understand better the intricate construction of the book, as well as its relationship to the life of its author and to other books of its type. Moreover, it's both fun and instructive to glance over the writer's shoulder, to watch E. B. White wrestling with writerly decisions as he prepares this seemingly seamless tale for publication.

To give such understanding and insights, I've included four types of annotations:

First, there is information from White's eight manuscript drafts for *Charlotte's Web* that are deposited at the Cornell University Library, Division of Rare & Manuscript Collections. From these, we may obtain insights into the craftsmanship of a highly conscious and self-aware artist, and gain an appreciation for the difficulties of writing beautiful prose fiction.

Second, there are cross-references to other writings by E. B. White, as these shed light on *Charlotte's Web*. Some of these cross-references are, themselves, from secondary sources such as the excellent biography of E. B. White that Professor Scott Elledge completed after fifteen years' labor.

There are also references from the sourcebooks White consulted on the subject of spiders.

Third, there is stylistic commentary by the editor—by me, acting as a sort of tour guide—pointing out some of the felicities of the text.

Fourth, there are some general, "cultural," comments, such as references to the literary conventions within which White was working.

This great American children's novel has stood by itself without the aid of notes for over forty years. Certainly, it could continue to be read without. But if selected insights into the workshop of a thoroughly self-aware author enrich the reading for some, and help to establish the conviction that books for children are not a type of subliterature insufficient to nourish the mature adult, then this edition justifies its existence.

White's sense of style was demanding; one jots in his margins with trepidation. Still, as Samuel Johnson, that greatest of English annotators, said at the end of great labor, "I have indeed disappointed no opinion more than my own; yet I have endeavoured to perform my task with no slight solicitude."

INTRODUCTION

"Just about perfect," exclaimed Eudora Welty, one of America's most revered writers, when she first read E. B. White's *Charlotte's Web* in 1952, the year of its publication.[1] Pamela Travers, of *Mary Poppins* fame, echoed Welty's enthusiasm, as did the distinguished poet David McCord, the writer-editor Bennett Cerf, and countless other reviewers and commentators. Eight years later a *Publishers Weekly* poll declared *Charlotte's Web* the best children's book written between 1930 and 1960.[2]

Indeed, most of the reading world seems to have borne out those early judgments. Selling more than six million copies, the book has been taken to the hearts of readers of all ages and has been translated into more than eighteen languages, ranging from Dutch to Telugu. Urged from 1956 on to have the story filmed, the author didn't relent till 1973, when he felt himself in straitened circumstances.[3] And today, finally, the hitherto-scarce recording of the author's reading of the book is available from a major publisher.[4]

Let's try to see more closely what is the nature of this remarkable book that brings joy and tears of empathy and compassion to children and to hardened critics alike. In doing so, we will also catch a glimpse of the life and thought and preoccupations of the sometimes elusive author E. B. White, and of his fortunate relationship to the world of children's books.

Charlotte's Web, an American pastoral, is a hymn of praise, a glorious prose poem, a human and animal comedy in the old sense of the word "comedy," meaning a yea-saying, a celebration of life—and it is one of the first children's books to deal seriously, without sentimentality or condescension, with death.

Charlotte's Web was not, however, White's first children's book. That honor goes to *Stuart Little*—the story of a "small boy who *looks* very much like a mouse"—which had appeared seven years earlier, and which we'll consider in a moment.

By the time *Charlotte* took the children's-book world by storm, E. B. White was still known to most people primarily as the shrewd commentator of *The New Yorker* magazine's "Notes and Comments" section. To another audience he was the coauthor of that little writer's handbook *The Elements of Style*, usually eponymously referred to as "Strunk and White." After the appearance of Wilbur the pig, Wilbur's sophisticated mentor with the eight hairy legs, and the ingratiating little girl who, for a brief moment, loved them both, a whole generation who knew Charlotte and Stuart intimately, but who probably could not care less* about *The New Yorker*, came into being.

To learn how the venturesome Stuart and the idyllic farmyard and its denizens evolved from the life and imagination of the urbane (if not cosmopolitan) *New Yorker* journalist-essayist, we must go back to the beginning.

Born in 1899,** "of respectable people in Mount Vernon, New York," as he whimsically put it, Elwyn Brooks White first became a "published author" as a child, receiving his first literary award at the age of nine from *Woman's Home Companion* for a poem about a mouse, and continuing his winning ways with gold and silver badges from *St. Nicholas Magazine*.[5]

In college, at Cornell, White acquired the nickname he was to retain among friends and family—Andy, after that university's then president, Andrew D. White. He became the editor and a prolific writer for the *Cornell Daily Sun*, and from his graduation in June of 1921 until 1925, he contributed articles and poems to publications such as the *New York Evening Post* and Franklin P. Adams's column, "The Conning Tower," in the *New York World*.

For White, the two events that were to shape much of the rest of his life came in 1925: That was the year of his first contribution to the just-launched *New Yorker*; and that was the time, too, when he met his future wife, Katharine, who was assistant to and literary editor for Harold Ross, the founding editor (known to the New York literary world simply as Ross). Katharine, over the years, was to become White's "in-house" editor, screener of correspondence, and confidante.

Plans for the new magazine *The New Yorker*

*The lamb would have said "cared less than nothing" (*CW*, p. 28)

**When not extrapolated from White's own personal and autobiographical writing, biographical information about White comes primarily from Scott Elledge (*E. B. White: A Biography*, 1985) and from Dorothy Lobrano Guth (ed., *Letters of E. B. White*, 1976) and occasionally from unpublished materials in the White archives at the Cornell University Library, Division of Rare & Manuscript Collections. Linda H. Davis (*Onward and Upward*, 1987) is instructive primarily in matters concerning Katharine White.

had been announced in 1924 with something resembling a manifesto, setting forth its mission, promising that the magazine "would be more than a jester," that it would "hate bunk," and that it was not about to cater to "the old lady in Dubuque"—or "little old ladies from the Midwest," as one euphemistic biographer of White wrote recently.[6]

Nine weeks after White picked up that first issue of *The New Yorker* of February 19, 1925, there appeared his own first contribution—a parody of six examples of what an advertising copywriter might have to say if handed the "VERNAL" (i.e., spring) account. Sample selection:

> New Beauty of Tone in
> 1925 Song Sparrow
>
> Into every one of this season's song sparrows has been built the famous VERNAL tone. Look for the distinguishing white mark on the breast.[7]

Thereafter, and for the rest of his long writing life—even as he ventured in other directions—White continued indefatigably with *The New Yorker*, contributing more than eighteen hundred pieces to the magazine in his lifetime. As late as his eighty-third year, White still edited the "Newsbreaks" section.[8]

So intertwined, in fact, were the development of *The New Yorker*'s literary style and the evolution of White's own typical mode of expression that between the two there seems to have existed almost a sort of symbiosis. Whether White's "voice" became that of *The New Yorker* or *The New Yorker*'s that of White is a question that remains open for discussion. But according to Marc Connelly, a distinguished writer for the American stage at the time (author of, e.g., *The Green Pastures*, 1930), it was White who "brought the steel and music to the magazine."[9]

In *The New Yorker*'s Harold Ross, White found a man who treasured what White had to offer, a superb editor, a true original, passionate about the American language, and fully cognizant of the rare talents of the writers who were in his employ. Ross, White, and Katharine became, in a sense, a team. As White's biographer Scott Elledge states, "[S]omething deeper than their shared sense of humour bound Ross and Katharine and Andy. They all trusted each other's honesty and respected each other's gifts."[10]

When White, aged twenty-six, had first walked into the magazine's offices, Katharine was thirty-three years old, married and with two children. White's own recollection of the first meeting was sketchy: He recalled "that

[Katharine] had a lot of back [sic] hair and a knack for making a young contributor feel at ease."[11]

After their meeting, after Katharine had urged Ross to offer a position to the young writer, and following a rendezvous in Europe and a considerable period of well-documented soul searching as well as an earnest attempt to be apart, Katharine and E. B. White were married November 13, 1929.

In 1938, the Whites moved to the saltwater farm in Maine that they both had fallen irremediably in love with and bought five years earlier. Geographical distance notwithstanding, White continued, at variable pace, to send his pieces to Ross at *The New Yorker*. Katharine, too, maintained her position as part-time editor, in addition to writing the annual roundup of new children's books for the upcoming Christmas seasons.

And it was those children's-book columns, specificially the column Katharine was writing in the fall of 1938, that hastened not only *Stuart Little*, White's first children's book, but eventually, too, *Charlotte's Web* itself.

As White pondered Katharine's pre-Christmas avalanche of books for review, he wrote a humorous account in *Harper's Magazine* suggesting his serious ruminations about writing for children.

> Among the goat feathers which stick to us at this season of the year are some two hundred children's books. They are review copies, sent to my wife by the publishers. They lie dormant in every room, like November flies.
>
> The inundation of juvenile literature is an annual emergency to which I have gradually become accustomed—the way the people of the Connecticut River valley get used to having the river come into their parlors. The books arrive in the mail by tens and twenties. . . .

White went on to speculate:

> Close physical contact with the field of juvenile literature leads me to the conclusion that it must be a lot of fun to write for children—reasonably easy work, perhaps even important work. One side of it which must be exciting is finding a place, a period, or a thing that hasn't already been written about.[12]

"Easy work" surely was said in jest, for *no* writing was easy work for White. His own comments and even perfunctory glances at his manuscripts show that he sweated every line. It does seem likely, however, that the pile of children's books did start some wheels turning.

Actually, White had been working on *Stuart Little* off and on for years. Stuart had first appeared to White in a dream in the late 1920s, "not as a mouse, but . . . a second son,"[13] "a small character who had the features of a mouse, was nicely dressed, courageous, and questing."[14] White related that he had eighteen nephews and nieces to whom he occasionally told stories, and having no head for improvising quickly, "for self protection" he had jotted down some of the mouse-boy's adventures and kept them in a desk drawer, to be pulled out when occasion demanded.

Let White tell the rest:

> In 1938, having decided to quit New York, I began tidying up what I called my "affairs." One of these was the Stuart Little adventures, now grown to perhaps a dozen episodes. At the suggestion of my wife, I carried them to a publisher [not Harper][15] and left them, to see whether they might be acceptable if expanded. The answer came back No, and I left for Maine, taking my rejected child along.
>
> Seven years later, in winter of 1944–45, I returned to New York to spend a few months in a furnished apartment and do some work for *The New Yorker*. I was almost sure I was about to die, my head felt so queer. With death at hand, I cast about to discover what I could do to ease the lot of my poor widow, and again my thoughts strayed to Stuart Little. My editor at Harper's, Eugene Saxton, had been urging me to finish the narrative, and I determined to put it off no longer. Mornings I sat at a top-floor window looking out into West 11th Street and there I completed the story. I turned it in to Harper and then took the train to San Francisco. . . .[16]

Stuart Little was published in October 1945, and by December 1946 had sold one hundred thousand copies (half a million by 1975, not counting paperback editions), and had obviously taken the country by storm—save for some adults, parents and librarians primarily, who objected to the hero's unusual arrival.*

The story of *Stuart Little* would not be com-

*In the first edition, Stuart was *born*. Presumably, public pressure changed the first sentence to read, "When Mrs. Frederick C. Little's second son *arrived* . . ." [my italics].

White tells that when the book first came out, *New Yorker* editor Harold Ross poked his head into White's office, shouting, "God damn it White, at least you could have had him adopted." *NYT*, March 6, 1966, Sec. 2, p. X 19.

White's amusing account of the response to *Stuart Little* appeared in the same (March 6, 1966) *New York Times* article as the story of the book's creation, and is reprinted in E, pp. 263–64. Also, D, 140.

In the HarperCollins files there is a copy of an extraordinary cable sent by Cass Canfield, Sr., White's previous editor at Harper, in which Canfield dissuades the British publisher, Hamish Hamilton, from attempting to get White to alter the ending: "HAMILTON WE ALSO WERE DISSATISFIED ENDING STUART LITTLE & APPROACHED AUTHOR W/O ANY RESULTS STOP AS E B IS DIFFICULT PERSON OUR ADVICE WOULD BE AGAINST YOUR RAISING QUESTIONS ESPECIALLY AS HE WOULD PROBABLY NOT AGREE TO ANY CHANGE STOP OUR ADVANCE SALE IN EXCESS OF 50,000 COPIES." Whether Canfield agreed with whatever Hamilton's concerns may have been or actually meant the concluding sentence as a Whitean put-down depends on how you read it.

plete without mentioning two other people who played significant roles in his creation: Anne Carroll Moore and Ursula Nordstrom.

Anne Carroll Moore (1871–1961), head of the Children's Department of the New York Public Library, an articulate woman of influence and power, was widely regarded as a sort of doyenne of children's librarians in the United States. In some measure, it was her early enthusiasm that spurred White on to write *Stuart Little*. Moore had responded immediately to White's *Harper's* article about children's books, writing him impassioned letters throughout 1939 in which she praised his talent and expressed delight at the prospect of his writing a children's book.

All the more ironic, therefore, that when Moore actually read *Stuart Little* in galleys, White recalled, she found it "non-affirmative, inconclusive, unfit for children," and not only wrote to Harper & Brothers, but also sent a fourteen-page letter to Katharine White, urging her to dissuade White from publishing the book. Nor was her published review more encouraging (see Appendix E, page 246).

Moore's reservations obviously did not diminish *Stuart*'s reception. And not least of the happy consequences of the book was that its creation marked the beginning of White's long, harmonious, and productive association with Harper's distinguished children's editor Ursula Nordstrom (1910–1988).

Nordstrom had been head of the children's book department at Harper & Brothers since 1940. In the course of her career, she comforted, coaxed, cajoled, exhorted, and encouraged many of the greatest names in American children's books—Ruth Krauss, Maurice Sendak, Laura Ingalls Wilder, Tomi Ungerer, Shel Silverstein, as well as White's illustrator, Garth Williams.

Beginning with *Stuart Little* (1945), and continuing through *Charlotte's Web* (1952) and White's last children's book, *The Trumpet of the Swan* (1970), Nordstrom was ever available for White as friend and editor, to do what needed doing.

In the world of book publishing, what "needs" doing by an editor will vary greatly with different authors. In White's case, as he was writing *Charlotte*, what needed doing included answering queries such as whether she (Nordstrom) was aware of any other books in which spiders spin words,[17] discussing royalty arrangements—or just, simply, keeping in touch. But most helpfully, Nordstrom was there to keep smooth the path that ran between writer and illustrator.

It was Beatrix Potter who said once that "genius—like murder—will out—its bent being merely a matter of circumstance."[18] Genius

White certainly possessed; but what could have shaped its bent in the direction of a romantic, wandering mouse-boy and a writing spider? Of all the stories White *might* have written, what was it about himself that made the skeptical *New Yorker* essayist hit upon the idea of the saga of the plucky lilliputian adventurer Stuart? And what was it that made White meditate with such concentration on the glories of a barn, a farm, a spider, a rat, a repetitively gaggling goose goose goose?

Part of the answer is suggested in the plot of *Stuart Little*, in which the mouse-boy falls in love with Margalo, "a pretty little hen-bird, brown, with a streak of yellow on her breast."[19] The second half of the book consists of Stuart's pursuit of his dream—of Stuart heading north—since, as the telephone repairman had told him, "A person who is heading north is not making a mistake, in my opinion."[20]

The pursuit of the dream was central to White's conception of the story of Stuart. The author made this clear to inquiring readers when he explained that Stuart had been a searcher, and that "his journey symbolize[d] the continuing journey that everybody takes—in search of what is perfect and unattainable."[21] Simply put, Stuart's journey was a "quest."[22]

And what was the object of Stuart's quest; what grail was the mouse-boy in pursuit of? We get a hint when Stuart takes over a school class whose teacher is out sick with "rhinestones,"[23] and asks his pupils: "How many of you know what's important?"[24]

Not only are the students' answers telling; the question itself is significant, for it's a question White had been asking for many years, and one that had been particularly pressing during the years of *Stuart*'s incubation.*

And "what is important" for White lies very much at the heart of the story of *Charlotte's Web* as well. The earliest drafts of the manuscript give it away—a pig, a spider living in a doorway, a dung heap, or, as in one of the first versions of Chapter I, the rural temple itself, where little Fern attends in awe and wonderment in "the ~~best~~ & warmest & pleasantest part of Zuckerman's barn."[25]

Or, as White himself schematized "what was important" in one of those numerous, meticulous preparatory exercises in which he engaged before writing his novels:

> The happiness of Charlotte and Wilbur when reunited. The gratitude of Wilbur. "Oh Charlotte."

---

*Some of the schoolroom discussion deals with government—including world government, a subject of repeated interest to White. In 1945, *TNY* sent White to cover the San Francisco conference from which emerged the United Nations. For more discussion of White's global political concerns at this time, see E, pp. 24–49. See also *ACW*, page 90.

The depth of their friendship & what it means. The feeling of peace & safety, knowing that Wilbur will not be killed.

The Ferris Wheel.

"There's nothing finer than to be high above the earth with the person you like best."[26]

Or, again, "what is important" is clearly stated at the outset of any of the book's early chapters—Chapter IV, "Loneliness," the description of interminable rain; in Chapter VI, "Summer Days"—those days that White calls "the happiest and fairest days of the year."[27] Or, for that matter, the chapter titles themselves suggest thematic centers for White's book and emotional triggers for the author.

Summer days, rural life, animals, a barn—these were the cardinal points of White's compass. First chance he had, White in 1957 fled the metropolis that had been good to him, escaped what Charlotte called men's "rush, rush, rush,"[28] and hied himself permanently to rural Maine, and to his pigs, geese, chickens, and to a lovely barn of his own. But the getting there was circuitous.

Throughout White's life, especially in the 1930s and 1940s, there runs a continuing note of anxiety that may be perceived in the *Letters* and has been noted by both his and Katharine's biographers. One senses that White felt that somewhere, somehow, he ought to be writing something longer or more serious or less ephemeral—something described by a phrase that crops up in his writing periodically—an *opus*, a *magnum opus*, as he put it with that defensively self-mocking irony that forestalls the critic.*

To do this, to think and to write removed from the incessant pressures of weekly deadlines, to "improve the nick of time," as White quoted Thoreau in a letter to his brother,[29] perhaps to undertake that *magnum opus*, White, like Stuart, journeyed "north" both literally and metaphorically virtually all his life.

And that "quest" for the "north," that "journey [that] symbolizes the continuing journey that everybody takes—in search of what is perfect and unattainable,"[30] is what eventually brought White to that arable land, that farm, that barn in Maine.

Already as a child, White had been taken on Maine vacations by his parents. As a young man, he worked at a summer camp in Ontario, Canada. Katharine and he summered in Maine

*The Annotated *Charlotte's Web* is not the occasion to pursue the subject of White's anxieties. The matter is discussed in E, pp. 250–252 and 267–271, and especially in Epstein (see *ACW*, pages 249–50). White's collected letters tell their own story. Almost needless to say, given what White called his own "sketchy health," the joy and affirmation of his life's work is nothing less than a triumph. Regarding the phrase *"magnum opus"* see *ACW*, p. 144.

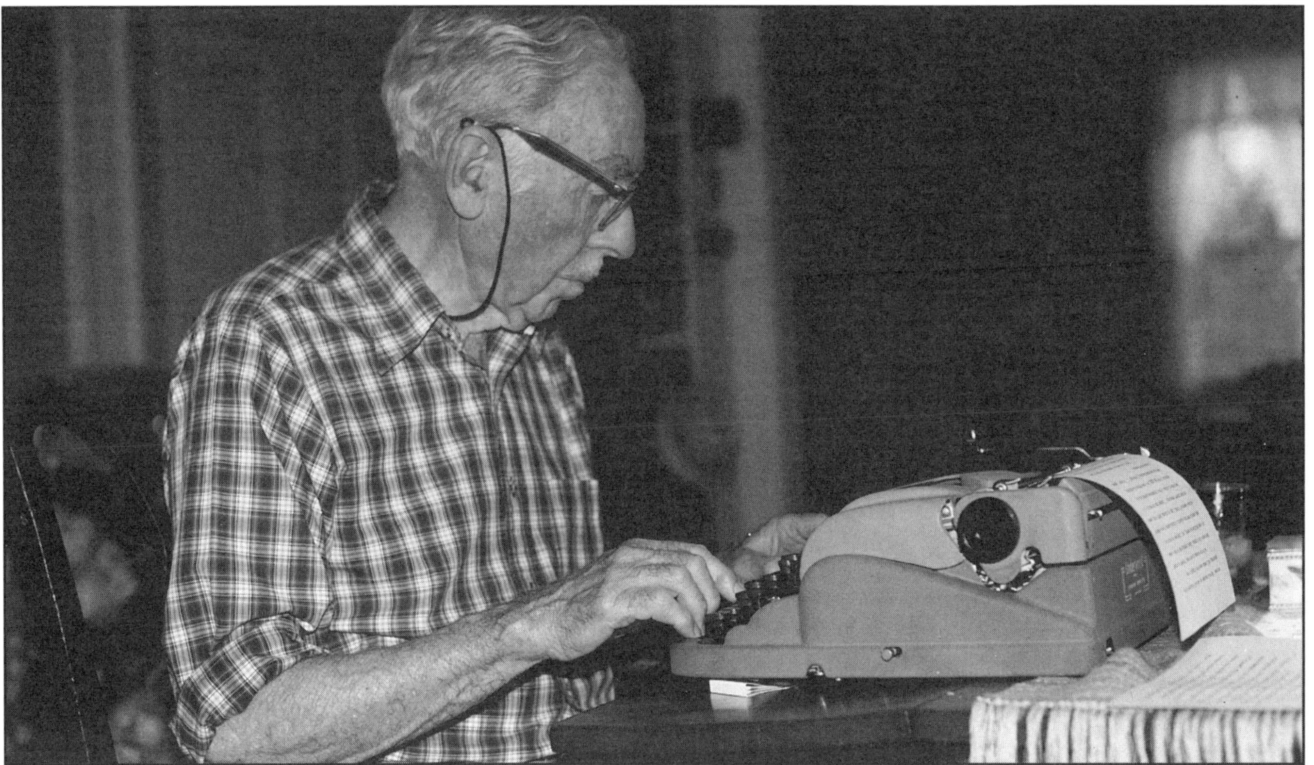

E. B. White at his typewriter.

from 1931 on, and in 1933, they bought the farm. In 1937, White retreated to Maine for what he termed a "sabbatical," and the next year he actually did persuade Katharine to move too. For the next five years the Whites stayed in Maine—along with 15 grade sheep, 112 New Hampshire Red pullets, 36 White Plymouth Rock pullets, "three Toulouse geese . . . a dog, a tomcat, a pig, and a captive mouse."[31] And although the *magnum opus* never came to be, the rural sojourn must be counted a success, having left White productive and happy. As, later, White reported to Elledge, he later thought of those Maine years as the best period in his life.[32]

The Whites again returned to New York, commuting between there and Maine until 1957, when they moved to the farm permanently. But it was that first long stay, beginning in 1937, that provided fertile soil from which would spring the whole crowded, fruitful, cyclical world of farm and barn and seasons that comprise the universe of *Charlotte's Web.*

White, himself, wrote several accounts of the first stirrings of the idea for Charlotte. One immediate moment of inspiration White related explicitly:

> The idea [for the writing of *Charlotte's Web*] came to me one day when I was on my way down through the orchard carrying a pail of slops to my pig. I had made up my mind to write a children's book about animals, and I needed a way to save a pig's life, and I had been watching a large spider in the backhouse, and what with one thing and another, the idea came to me.[33]

Another experience that White himself never actually cited as a direct source was pointed out to him in a letter from Judy Zuckerman, then a young student in Alison Lurie's children's literature class at Cornell and now a children's librarian in New York. This was an incident White memorialized in one of his most accomplished essays, which he had contributed for the ninetieth-anniversary issue of *Atlantic Monthly*. Kindly, but perhaps disingenuously, White's reply to Judy Zuckerman suggests he'd never thought of the connection himself.[34]

The essay in question, "Death of a Pig," is one of White's finest. It is the story of White's bedside attendance on an ailing pig.

> I spent several days and nights in mid-September with an ailing pig and I feel driven to account for this stretch of time, more particularly since the pig died at last, and I lived, and things might easily have gone the other way round and none left to do the accounting. . . .
>
> The scheme of buying a spring pig in blossomtime, feeding it through summer and fall, and butchering it when the solid cold weather arrives, is a familiar scheme to me and follows an antique pattern.[35]

And from there White continues to relate, in one of the most carefully chiseled essays he ever wrote, the agony of the sick watch, the arrival of the veterinarian, the burial attended by him and by his dachshund, Fred. The solemn, melancholy last sentence of the panegyric evokes melodies of John Donne and echoes of Thoreau:

> . . . The grave in the woods is unmarked, but Fred can direct the mourner to it unerringly and with immense good will, and I know he and I shall often revisit it, singly and together, in seasons of reflection and despair, on flagless memorial days of our own choosing.[36]

The essay demonstrates that, whatever the pressures of *Harper's* deadlines, or of work for *The New Yorker*, or whatever the status of what White called his "sketchy" health, Maine proved fertile soil for White's creative powers. He missed nothing as he observed the little miracles surrounding him—such as the "pink, corrugated area" of the pig's gullet down which he poured the castor oil.

Asked about the meaning of his writing once, White replied, "[A]ll that I hope to say in books, all that I ever hope to say, is that I love the world," and, as Elledge has noted, "[M]ost of what White loved in the world is rendered in *Charlotte's Web*."[37]

A list of all that White loved in this world would be a long one. First, of course, White's world and that of the book is a rural world, a farm, fertile and productive, a fact underlined even by Fern's family name—Arable, meaning plowable, potentially fecund (see page 1). The "Plowables," then, own a farm, a hog house, and the extra-large newborn litter of pigs.

And spiders White loved—not only loved, but took seriously, so that for years he resisted both the threat of a cinematic caricature of *Aranea cavatica* and the illustrator's inclination to personify her excessively with long, batting eyelashes.[38] As White wrote to one entrepreneur hoping to film the barnyard saga, "I saw a spider spin the egg sac described in the story, and I wouldn't trade the sight for all the animated chimpmunks in filmland."[39]

And pigs, obviously. And rats. Rats White loved to hate! Templeton the rat is truly the incarnation of physical and moral putridness. Mice White felt differently about. He had a pet mouse, and at the age of nine, he had written a prize-winning poem about one,[40] but rats he would shoot and exterminate. As he wrote from his farm in 1940, "I was spreading some poison in the barn the other day for mine enemies the rats. . . ."[41]

And geese, and especially eggs. To a class of fifth graders in Los Angeles, White sent "what I think is one of the most beautiful and miraculous things in the world—an egg." And, of course, he loved the hens and the geese that laid the eggs. As White told those fifth graders, "I have a goose named Felicity and she lays about forty eggs every spring." Each egg, said White, "is a perfect thing."[42]

And of all places, White loved barns most especially. As a boy, he had loved playing in neighborhood barns and stables and, like Fern, had spent long, quiet hours sitting, watching. And so, in our book, the third chapter begins with a hymn of praise to that wonderful place: "The barn was very large. It was very old. It smelled of hay and it smelled of manure."[43] In fact, when he began writing *Charlotte's Web*, White had intended that chapter in praise of the barn to open the book.

And the manure—well, that White loved too, and he wrote about it often, calling it "dressing" occasionally, as Down-Easters are wont to do, and combining his own and Charlotte's interest in vocabulary when he writes: "Manure is always dressing, never manure. I think, although I'm not sure, that manure is considered a nasty word, not fit for polite company."[44]

A list of the objects of White's attention will suggest the themes that infuse our book: fertility, seasons, cycles, life, death, birth, and resurrection.

Thus—for starters—if you ponder long on the subject of manure, your mind may well drift to thoughts of growth and fertility. You realize that the table scraps for Wilbur's trough go into pig Wilbur. And some of what goes into pig Wilbur will fertilize the tomatoes and the cabbages. And what does not fertilize the tomatoes and cabbages would normally become bacon or ham for you, for the Zuckermans and the Arables. Or, as White wrote of the man contemplating the trough: "[T]he stuff that goes into the trough and is received with such enthusiasm is an earnest of some later feast of his own."[45]

And fecundity suggests the cycle of the seasons, the lyric interludes in *Charlotte's Web* in which White sings his hymn to the eternal rhythm. A "paean to life," White called the book (and, in the same letter, "an acceptance of dung"),[46] and Chapter VI begins:

> The early summer days on a farm are the happiest and fairest days of the year. Lilacs bloom and make the air sweet, and then fade. Apple blossoms come with the lilacs, and the bees visit around among the apple trees. The days grow warm and soft. School ends, and children have time to play and to fish for trouts in the brook. . . .[47]

And the year grows older, the days shorter:

> The crickets sang in the grasses. They sang the song of summer's ending, a sad, monotonous song. "Summer is over and gone," they sang. "Over and gone, over and gone. Summer is dying, dying."[48]

"Over and gone," "dying, dying." The words sound a melancholy note: The year has gone its round; the young girl, Fern, has grown away from childish delights—and lost something very precious in the bargain; doubtless, some of the barnyard animals have been less fortunate than Wilbur; and our heroine, Charlotte, the bright, elegant teacher, friend, writer, has died, in a passage that brought tears even to the author's eyes.

But, of course, the phoenix rises from the ashes: The new year will come, the spring flowers will burst, new life burgeoning everywhere. And autumn, and winter, while you wait, while Wilbur waits ("Life is always a rich and steady time when you are waiting for something to happen or to hatch"[49]). And although Charlotte is dead, the eggs hatch, Charlotte's progeny are here at last ballooning up, away, on the warm updraft—their "moment for setting forth" having arrived.[50] (See page 179.)

Ursula Nordstrom clearly recognized the note of triumph. She perceived that even in death, in tragedy, as White had written it, there is both an exaltation and a release. And so it was Ursula Nordstrom who suggested to White that "The Death of Charlotte," White's original title for the penultimate chapter (see page 163), was not really to the point—that actually, the point was the new lives out of the old, the setting forth on "A Warm Wind"—the name White then settled on for the concluding chapter.[51]

Nordstrom's perception that the book is, essentially, an ode to joy, an exultation in the cycles and the seasons, of birth out of death, a story of resurrection, is fully in keeping with E. B. White's own understanding of the book. "'Charlotte,' White summed up twenty years after he wrote the book, "'Charlotte' was a story of friendship, life, death, salvation."[52]

—Peter F. Neumeyer, 1994

TITLE, COVER, ENDPAPERS, FRONTISPIECE

TITLE: CHARLOTTE'S WEB

After he has labored as hard on a book as White did on *Charlotte's Web*, an author is not going to select the title lightly. White chose to name his work not for any one character, but for the "miraculous" web itself.

Shortly before writing *Charlotte's Web*, White worked on the introduction to Don Marquis's wry, sad comic verse novel *archy & mehitabel.* On that occasion, he said that "to interpret humor is as futile as explaining a spider's web in terms of geometry."[1] The subject of spiderwebs was on White's mind, obviously.

The centrality of the Miracle evidently did not impress itself on translators into other languages. The French title is *Les aventures de Narcisse* (*The Adventures of Narcissa*—the French publisher renamed *Charlotte*!); the Norwegian, *Fantastiske Valdemar* (*Fantastic Valdemar*—now it is Wilbur who is renamed); the Spanish, *Las aventuras de Wilbur y Carlota* (*The Adventures of Wilbur and Charlotte*); the Swedish, *Fantastiska Wilbur* (*Fantastic Wilbur*); and the German, *Schweinchen Wilbur und seine Freunde* (*Piglet Wilbur and his Friends*). White's all-important web made as little impression on the translators as it did on Mrs. Arable.

COVER

E. B. White approved of the cover illustration, although he had some suggestions about an early sketch for it. He wrote his editor, Ursula Nordstrom, "I like everything. . . . My only complaint is that the goose looks, for some reason, a bit snakelike."[2]

When he saw the proofs two months later, he again wrote Nordstrom (13 July [1952]), "The proof of the jacket is very gay and I think all five of the characters are beguiling."[3]

ENDPAPERS

Endpapers—the often decorative pages glued inside the front and back covers of a book—may add greatly not only to the beauty but also to the substance of a book. Some children's books, like *Winnie-the-Pooh*, have maps, for example, that orient the reader to the world of the story.

The endpapers originally proposed for *CW* did not have the spiderweb on blue design that we find in the hardcover edition today.

There is not much evidence that White participated in many general book-design decisions, although he took a deep interest in Garth Williams's illustrations. He did, however, respond to Ursula Nordstrom's point about the endpapers:

> I agree with you that the endpaper is too bright. But on the other hand, I'm not sure that anybody thinks about endpaper except publishers, and probably not more than 1800 people in the United States have ever heard the word "endpaper," and they are all Stevenson people.*[4]

FRONTISPIECE

The frontispiece is the illustration found opposite a title page. *Charlotte's Web* does not have a frontispiece. However, there was discussion of one. Garth Williams probably submitted a picture of Templeton, the rat, either the one on page 141 or the one on page 147, for on June 23, 1952, White wrote Nordstrom regarding illustrations that had been submitted to him:

*Adlai Stevenson, former governor of Illinois, ran for president of the United States in 1952 and 1956. The mention of "Stevenson people" is a reference to the fact that Stevenson was a literate man who employed a distinguished vocabulary and an elegant and elevated rhetorical form in his speeches and public writing.

> No. . . . Unsuitable for use opposite title page, I think, because it might suggest that this book is a sequel to Stuart. I like the drawing itself, and would like to see it used in the body of the text but not opposite title page. If you want something for that location, I think it should be a web drawing—perhaps Charlotte thinking. . . . I feel that it would be dishonest to put the rat in the lead-off position—give people the wrong idea.[5]

White's letters to Ursula Nordstrom were often retyped at Harper & Brothers and circulated as necessary. In this instance, Nordstrom wrote "O.K.—very right," in the margin. Sometimes she would write, "Send to Garth."

It's amusing to note that in this letter, which begins "I have a few suggestions which may be helpful," Nordstrom circled part of the following sentence: "And I am quite willing to be overruled on any or all," writing in the margin, "omit this line." It's reasonable to think that the retyped letter, minus that line, which would needlessly reveal White's hand, went to Williams.

Charlotte's Web

Chapter 1

Before Breakfast

"WHERE'S Papa going with that ax?"[1] said Fern to her mother as they were setting the table for breakfast.

"Out to the hoghouse," replied Mrs. Arable.[2] "Some pigs were born last night."[3]

"I don't see why he needs an ax," continued Fern, who was only eight.

"Well," said her mother, "one of the pigs is a runt. It's very small and weak, and it will never amount to anything. So your father has decided to do away with it."

"Do *away* with it?" shrieked Fern. "You mean *kill* it?[4] Just because it's smaller than the others?"[5]

Mrs. Arable put a pitcher of cream on the table. "Don't yell, Fern!" she said. "Your father is right. The pig would probably die anyway."

Fern pushed a chair out of the way and ran outdoors. The grass was wet and the earth smelled of springtime. Fern's sneakers were sopping by the time she caught up with her father.

Page 1

1. This is actually not the way White originally began the story. In the Cornell University Library, Division of Rare & Manuscript Collections, there are eight successive drafts for the book. (All references to earlier versions of *CW* are to those manuscripts.) White wrote me, "From the evidence, I had as much trouble getting off the ground as did the Wright Brothers."[1]

2. Many novelists, from Henry Fielding to Ken Kesey, have given their characters names indicative of their nature. White, too, demonstrates the significance of the names of main characters. *Arable* means "plowable," thus potentially fruitful. White's farm family, called the Arables, is thus the "plowables," and their daughter is appropriately called Fern, the fern being, botanically and paleontologically speaking, almost as prime, as basic, as fundamental a plant as there is, dating to the Carboniferous Age, which began 260 million years ago. Thematically, the family name suggests both the rural and the fecund and affirming theme that interweaves the text.

In 1944, White wrote a poem that was published in *The New Yorker* and was used in abridged form on his Christmas cards. It contains the line "Home is the part of our life that's arable."[2]

Some years after publication of *CW*, White became owner of a twenty-foot sloop, a double ender, built for him in Denmark from a design by Aage Nielsen. White named the boat *Fern*.[3]

3. White had personal experience with the birth of pigs.

In an essay titled "The Shape of Television,"

Continued on page 2

Page 1 (continued)

White tells of a televised farm program he watched one morning to see a sow during farrowing "in a white-walled hospital room, under anesthesia," as a "farmer, dressed for surgery and sterile up to his elbows, was removing her uterus and its interesting load, in order that the pigs might come into the world without being exposed to disease germs." White recalls "certain delicious nights when [he] had sat up with a sow, receiving each tiny pig as it came slithering into the lantern gleam."[4]

4. Fern calls it as White sees it. With childlike directness and lack of hypocrisy, Fern expresses her exasperation at her mother's genteelism, "do *away* with," when she means, simply, "kill." See also page 158.

In "Death of a Pig," White wrote about his ailing pig, "I had assumed that there could be nothing much wrong with a pig during the months it was being groomed for murder . . ."[5] (see page 232).

In another essay, "I find it hard to live in the country without slipping into the role of murderer."[6]

In 1959, E. B. White published *The Elements of Style*, his handbook for good, clear, precise writing, based largely on a booklet prepared by White's Cornell University professor of composition, William Strunk, Jr. In this succinct book, White, following his own advice to "[p]ut statements in positive form," exhorts us to "[u]se definite, specific, concrete language."[7]

5. Since we have committed ourselves to the world of this pig, "smaller than the others," we should know that in the sixteenth century, the smallest pig of the litter was referred to as a "tantony pig," deriving that name from Saint Anthony, the patron saint of swineherds.

"Please don't kill it!" she sobbed. "It's unfair."

Mr. Arable stopped walking.

"Fern," he said gently, "you will have to learn to control yourself."

"Control myself?" yelled Fern. "This is a matter of life and death, and you talk about *controlling* myself."

Tears ran down her cheeks and she took hold of the ax and tried to pull it out of her father's hand.

"Fern," said Mr. Arable, "I know more about raising a litter of pigs than you do. A weakling makes trouble. Now run along!"

"But it's unfair," cried Fern. "The pig couldn't help being born small, could it? If *I* had been very small at birth, would you have killed *me*?"

Mr. Arable smiled. "Certainly not," he said, looking down at his daughter with love. "But this is different. A little girl is one thing, a little runty pig is another."

"I see no difference," replied Fern, still hanging on to the ax. "This is the most terrible case of injustice I ever heard of."

A queer look came over John Arable's face. He seemed almost ready to cry himself.

"All right," he said. "You go back to the house and I will bring the runt when I come in. I'll let you start it on a bottle, like a baby. Then you'll see what trouble a pig can be."

When Mr. Arable returned to the house half an hour later, he carried a carton under his arm. Fern was upstairs changing her sneakers. The kitchen table was set for breakfast, and the room smelled of coffee, bacon, damp plaster, and wood smoke from the stove.[6]

"Put it on her chair!" said Mrs. Arable. Mr. Arable set the carton down at Fern's place. Then he walked

Page 3

6. In early drafts of his novels, White would often set the scene at some length at the beginning of the chapter. Here the description is incorporated succinctly into the text (though, still, in the book's very first sentence, we are informed that the table was being set).

Note, too, that *bacon* (i.e., pig) is being served!

Page 4

7. In one early draft, White began the story by introducing Wilbur, telling us that he was "a white pig, ~~unless he was dirty in which case if you~~ but his living conditions were such that he did not always *seem* to be a white pig."

8. White liked to attribute to fathers such a slightly preposterous grandiloquence. In his last novel, *The Trumpet of the Swan*, the father swan (the cob) sounds like Polonius in *Hamlet* as he, too, talks with ponderous gravity:

> "Look out!" [baby swan Louis's father] trumpeted. "Look out for the fox, who is creeping toward you even as I speak, his eyes bright, his bushy tail out straight, his mind lusting for blood, his belly almost touching the ground! You are in grave danger, and we must act immediately."[8]

9. White employs an ironical double vision—both of child and of adult.

Since an air rifle and a wooden dagger do not amount to heavy armaments, White has assumed an adult voice that articulates ten-year-old Avery's perception—which, however, the ten-year-old could not have articulated.

Thus, by way of a complex narrative strategy, White is actually commenting wryly on events.

Page 5

10. Mice and rats are often on White's mind. In 1909, at the age of nine, White won a prize from *Woman's Home Companion* for a poem about a mouse.[9] As early as 1935, White had written some episodes for *Stuart Little*.

Also relevant to *CW* are the lines below, which White wrote in 1944 and used on a family Christmas card (see page 1 for an additional line of this poem):

to the sink and washed his hands and dried them on the roller towel.

Fern came slowly down the stairs. Her eyes were red from crying. As she approached her chair, the carton wobbled, and there was a scratching noise. Fern looked at her father. Then she lifted the lid of the carton. There, inside, looking up at her, was the newborn pig. It was a white one.[7] The morning light shone through its ears, turning them pink.

"He's yours," said Mr. Arable. "Saved from an untimely death. And may the good Lord forgive me for this foolishness."[8]

Fern couldn't take her eyes off the tiny pig. "Oh," she whispered. "Oh, *look* at him! He's absolutely perfect."

She closed the carton carefully. First she kissed her father, then she kissed her mother. Then she opened the lid again, lifted the pig out, and held it against her cheek. At this moment her brother Avery came into the room. Avery was ten. He was heavily armed —an air rifle in one hand, a wooden dagger in the other.[9]

"What's that?" he demanded. "What's Fern got?"

"She's got a guest for breakfast," said Mrs. Arable. "Wash your hands and face, Avery!"

"Let's see it!" said Avery, setting his gun down. "You call that miserable thing a pig? That's a *fine*

specimen of a pig—it's no bigger than a white rat."[10]

"Wash up and eat your breakfast, Avery!" said his mother. "The school bus will be along in half an hour."

"Can I have a pig, too, Pop?" asked Avery.

"No, I only distribute pigs to early risers." said Mr. Arable. "Fern was up at daylight, trying to rid the world of injustice.[11] As a result, she now has a pig. A small one, to be sure, but nevertheless a pig. It just shows what can happen if a person gets out of bed promptly. Let's eat!"

But Fern couldn't eat until her pig had had a drink of milk. Mrs. Arable found a baby's nursing bottle and a rubber nipple. She poured warm milk into the bottle,[12]

Ever at home are the mice in hiding
Our dust and trash, and the truth abiding,
Dark is the secret of home's hall closet—
Home's disorderly safe deposit.[10]

11. Mr. Arable sounds like one of the voices White frequently assumed in his essays. His words acquire their humor from a device White may have learned from reading Mark Twain—from whom, said Hemingway, all modern American literature derives anyway.*

One may "distribute" candy, but hardly pigs, in a context such as this. The word is humorously inappropriate. Thus, suddenly and ever so slightly, White has skewed the diction in his text, making Mr. Arable sound more like White, or like a narrator who winks at the reader over the heads of the characters.

Such "winking" is a device that was much used in the nineteenth century by writers such as William Thackeray, who employed it in his fairy tale *The Rose and the Ring*.

Although White now merely suggests his own bemusement through the voices of his characters, later he will break the surface of his story by using an intrusive narrator—an "I" voice—who actually steps right into the story to comment on the proceedings.

The same Twain-like dislocation of the diction is seen in a letter White wrote to the vice president of the Consolidated Edison Company when he was informed that his refrigerator might be discharging poisonous gas and that he should leave his window open. Note the amusing incongruity of the word *unpopular*.

Continued on page 6

*"All modern American literature comes from one book by Mark Twain called *Huckleberry Finn*." Hemingway, p. 22.

Page 5 (continued)

> Dear Mr. Aiken:
>
> I am a stockholder in the Consolidated Edison Company. . . . So I have a double interest in your letter of December 19. It seems to me a very odd letter indeed.
>
> You say that my refrigerator, even if it seems to be operating properly, may be producing poison gas, and you suggest that I open a window. I do not want to open a window. It would be a very *unpopular* move with the cook. [Italics added][11]

Twain had written his gas company in a remarkably similar tone:

> Dear Sirs:
>
> Some day you will move me almost to the verge of irritation by your chuckle-headed Goddamned fashion of shutting your Goddamned gas off without giving any notice to your Goddamned parishioners.[12]

The use of *parishioners*, just like that of *distribute*, is not expected and is sufficiently aslant to skew the tone of the passage.

12. In draft E, White has Fern phone the veterinarian, Dr. Speck. *Speck*, in German, means bacon. Dr. Bacon will check the runty porker. (For identification of the drafts, see Appendix B, pages 205–6.)

Page 6

13. In the screenplay manuscript in Box 2, White wrote a scene in which Mrs. Arable speaks of the temperature of the milk.

> MRS. ARABLE: [*It's just right.*] He's just a baby.
>
> AVERY: And Fern is his mamma. Ha! My sister is a pig's mamma. My sister is a pig's . . .
>
> MR. ARABLE: Avery! Cut!

13

fitted the nipple over the top, and handed it to Fern. "Give him his breakfast!" she said.

A minute later, Fern was seated on the floor in the corner of the kitchen with her infant between her

knees, teaching it to suck from the bottle. The pig, although tiny, had a good appetite and caught on quickly.

The school bus honked from the road.

"Run!" commanded Mrs. Arable, taking the pig from Fern and slipping a doughnut into her hand. Avery grabbed his gun and another doughnut.

The children ran out to the road and climbed into the bus. Fern took no notice of the others in the bus. She just sat and stared out of the window, thinking what a blissful world it was and how lucky she was to have entire charge of a pig.[14] By the time the bus reached school, Fern had named her pet, selecting the most beautiful name she could think of.

"Its name is Wilbur," she whispered to herself.

She was still thinking about the pig when the teacher said: "Fern, what is the capital of Pennsylvania?"

"Wilbur," replied Fern, dreamily. The pupils giggled. Fern blushed.

Page 7

14. Compare the conclusion of White's last novel for children, *The Trumpet of the Swan* (1970):

> . . . As Louis relaxed and prepared for sleep, all his thoughts were of how lucky he was to inhabit such a beautiful earth, how lucky he had been to solve his problems with music, and how pleasant it was to look forward to another night of sleep. . . .[13]

Both in his essays and in his novels, White frequently stressed the theme that ours is a precious world, not to be polluted and defaced.

White wrote to a reader of *CW*: "All that I hope to say in books, all that I ever hope to say, is that I love the world."[14] Evidence of the truth of that claim is pervasive, and any reader of White will cite his or her own favorites. The novelist and critic Eleanor Cameron likes to point to the essay "Twins," in which White tells of a miserable morning when he went to the Bronx Zoo "to see the moose calf" and serendipitously came upon a red deer and her newborn spotted fawn, "small and perfect as a trinket seen through a reducing glass."[15]

The White farm in North Brooklin, Maine

Page 8

1. White was fond of the notion of little girls mothering, playing with dolls, giving bottles. In one draft, White ended the previous chapter with a schoolroom scene in which Fern's teacher asks the children in the class an arithmetic question: "And now, here is a problem for one of the girls in the room. If you are feeding a baby from a bottle, and you give the baby eight ounces of milk in one feeding, how many ounces of milk would the baby drink in *two* feedings?" Fern raises her hand and answers the question. White did not use this page in *CW*, but eighteen years later transferred one version, as written for Fern, to *The Trumpet of the Swan* and let Linda Staples answer the question.[1]

2. Although Wilbur is not yet personified, this is the first instance in which human emotions are imputed to the pig.

3. *Charlotte's Web* is a book that celebrates the seasons. Chapters VI, IX, and XV contain lyrical passages in the pastoral mode. The pastoral tradition, extolling country life, is an old one in literature, traceable at least as far back as the Greek Hesiod's poem *Works and Days* (eighth century B.C.), and the Roman Virgil's *Eclogues* (first century B.C.), a work not only celebrating rural life, but full of practical advice concerning the arts of husbandry. Typically, the pastoral genre looks at the past through a golden haze and imputes to it an innocence and a simplicity that historical evidence might not fully support. Fern inhabits such an innocent world of yesteryear. Mid book, things will change for Fern—or, rather, Fern will change. And that change, and perhaps lost innocence, can be regarded with mixed feelings. Rueful retrospection is not foreign to the pastoral mode.

One critic has astutely observed that in contrast to Kenneth Grahame's *The Wind in the Willows*, in which the characters themselves articulate the

Chapter II

Wilbur

FERN loved Wilbur more than anything. She loved to stroke him, to feed him, to put him to bed. Every morning, as soon as she got up, she warmed his milk, tied his bib on, and held the bottle for him. Every afternoon, when the school bus stopped in front of her house, she jumped out and ran to the kitchen to fix another bottle for him.[1] She fed him again at suppertime, and again just before going to bed. Mrs. Arable gave him a feeding around noontime each day, when Fern was away in school. Wilbur loved his milk, and he was never happier than when Fern was warming up a bottle for him. He would stand and gaze up at her with adoring eyes.[2]

For the first few days of his life, Wilbur was allowed to live in a box near the stove in the kitchen. Then, when Mrs. Arable complained, he was moved to a bigger box in the woodshed. At two weeks of age, he was moved outdoors. It was apple-blossom time,[3] and the days were getting warmer. Mr. Arable fixed a small yard specially for Wilbur under an apple tree, and

gave him a large wooden box full of straw, with a doorway cut in it so he could walk in and out as he pleased.

"Won't he be cold at night?" asked Fern.

"No," said her father. "You watch and see what he does."

Carrying a bottle of milk, Fern sat down under the

4

apple tree inside the yard. Wilbur ran to her and she held the bottle for him while he sucked. When he had finished the last drop, he grunted and walked sleepily into the box. Fern peered through the door. Wilbur was poking the straw with his snout. In a short time he had dug a tunnel in the straw. He crawled into the tunnel and disappeared from sight, completely covered with straw. Fern was enchanted. It relieved her mind to know that her baby would sleep covered up, and would stay warm.

pastoral perspective, *Charlotte's Web* is a pastoral because of the voice of the storyteller. It is *his* awareness, his judgments, on which we rely.[2]

For more observation about E. B. White and the pastoral, please wait until we meet Dr. Dorian.

Page 9

4. Time passes in illustrations too. Fern had pigtails in the first illustration, loose hair in the second, and now again, pigtails. White was sensitive to the length of Fern's hair and commented on it in letters.

Page 10

5. "Pigs can make affectionate pets, easily house-broken, walking on leashes, coming when they are called, and even riding skate boards."[3]

6. I know of no other instance in White's voluminous writings in which he uses this word. In the case of *cute*, then, White has slipped into the mind of Fern herself, using an expression a little girl might use.

Every morning after breakfast, Wilbur walked out to the road with Fern and waited with her till the bus came. She would wave good-bye to him, and he would stand and watch the bus until it vanished around a turn. While Fern was in school, Wilbur was shut up inside his yard. But as soon as she got home in the afternoon, she would take him out and he would follow her around the place.[5] If she went into the house, Wilbur went, too. If she went upstairs, Wilbur would wait at the bottom step until she came down again. If she took her doll for a walk in the doll carriage, Wilbur followed along. Sometimes, on these journeys, Wilbur would get tired, and Fern would pick him up and put him in the carriage alongside the doll. He liked this. And if he was *very* tired, he would close his eyes and go to sleep under the doll's blanket. He looked cute[6] when his eyes were closed, because his lashes were so long. The doll would close her eyes, too, and Fern would wheel the carriage very slowly and smoothly so as not to wake her infants.

One warm afternoon, Fern and Avery put on bathing suits and went down to the brook for a swim. Wilbur tagged along at Fern's heels. When she waded into the brook, Wilbur waded in with her. He found the water quite cold—too cold for his liking. So while the children swam and played and splashed water at each other, Wilbur amused himself in the mud along

the edge of the brook, where it was warm and moist and delightfully sticky and oozy.

Every day was a happy day, and every night was peaceful.

Wilbur was what farmers call a spring pig, which simply means that he was born in springtime.[7] When he

Page 11

7. This was the third sentence of the third draft of the book.

> Chapter I. Escape
>
> I shall speak first of Wilbur. Wilbur was a beautifully small, nicely-behaved pig living in a manure symmetric pile in the cellar of a barn. He was what farmers call a spring pig—which . . .[4]

White revised constantly, and advised revision for other writers as well:

> Revising is part of writing. Few writers are so expert that they can produce what they are after on the first try. Quite often the writer will discover, on examining the completed work, that there are serious flaws in the arrangement of the material, calling for transpositions. When this is the case, he can save himself much labor and time by using scissors on his manuscript, cutting it to pieces and fitting the pieces together in a better order. . . . Remember, it is no sign of weakness or defeat that your manuscript ends up in need of major surgery. This is a common occurrence in all writing, and among the best writers.[5]

8. Fern's uncle's name is a bit odd for a New England farmer—and what the Greek and, possibly, Jewish amalgam signifies remains a mystery. The reference to Homer, however, evoking the Greek epic poet, is not mysterious. We discuss the subject when we consider Dr. Dorian in Chapter XIV.

9. The protagonists of all three of White's novels are aberrant: Wilbur is a runt. Stuart Little is a boy, two inches tall, who looks like a mouse. And Louis, the Trumpeter Swan, is born mute. Not everything in White's bucolic universe comes up roses. For further rumination on that point, see Epstein (Appendix F, pages 249–50).

10. White had great respect for barn cellars. To Gene Deitch, who proposed to film *CW*, White wrote, "When you enter the barn cellar, remove your hat."[6]

The first two chapters viewed events entirely from the human perspective. From Chapter III on, events take place in both the human world and the "fabulous and pure world"[1] of the animals.

was five weeks old, Mr. Arable said he was now big enough to sell, and would have to be sold. Fern broke down and wept. But her father was firm about it. Wilbur's appetite had increased; he was beginning to eat scraps of food in addition to milk. Mr. Arable was not willing to provide for him any longer. He had already sold Wilbur's ten brothers and sisters.

"He's got to go, Fern," he said. "You have had your fun raising a baby pig, but Wilbur is not a baby any longer and he has got to be sold."

"Call up the Zuckermans," suggested Mrs. Arable to Fern. "Your Uncle Homer[8] sometimes raises a pig. And if Wilbur goes there to live, you can walk down the road and visit him as often as you like."

"How much money should I ask for him?" Fern wanted to know.

"Well," said her father, "he's a runt.[9] Tell your Uncle Homer you've got a pig you'll sell for six dollars, and see what he says."

It was soon arranged. Fern phoned and got her Aunt Edith, and her Aunt Edith hollered for Uncle Homer, and Uncle Homer came in from the barn and talked to Fern. When he heard that the price was only six dollars, he said he would buy the pig. Next day Wilbur was taken from his home under the apple tree and went to live in a manure pile in the cellar of Zuckerman's barn.[10]

Chapter III

Escape

THE BARN was very large. It was very old. It smelled of hay and it smelled of manure. It smelled of the perspiration of tired horses and the wonderful sweet breath of patient cows. It often had a sort of peaceful smell—as though nothing bad could happen ever again in the world.[1] It smelled of grain and of harness dressing and of axle grease and of rubber boots and of new rope. And whenever the cat was given a fish-head to eat, the barn would smell of fish. But mostly it smelled of hay, for there was always hay in the great loft up overhead. And there was always hay being pitched down to the cows and the horses and the sheep.

The barn was pleasantly warm in winter when the animals spent most of their time indoors, and it was pleasantly cool in summer when the big doors stood wide open to the breeze. The barn had stalls on the main floor for the work horses, tie-ups on the main floor for the cows, a sheepfold down below for the sheep, a pigpen down below for Wilbur, and it was

Page 13

1. See plate 1, page 185.

Obviously, the glories of the barn were very much on White's mind when he began this novel. In Draft B, White began the novel with a description of the barn, and this passage is the seventh line in that draft (see page 208).

Elledge notes that the smell of manure and other organic matter was always reassuring to White, who wrote that "life can be cyclic and chemically perfect and aromatic and continuous."[2]

In the letter to Gene Deitch cited on p. 12, White made his crucial and memorable comment that the film of *CW* should be "a paean to life, a hymn to the barn, an acceptance of dung."[3]

Elledge calls the world of the barn "a kind of paradise regained."[4]

Indeed, the richness of White's barn epitomizes the medieval concept of plenitude, the notion that God created the world full and complete. Such a notion is wholly compatible with the pastoral tradition that underlies a great number of children's books. The presence of death in White's idealized and bucolic paradise also is in keeping with the literary and artistic tradition of the pastoral.[5]

Page 14

2. White employs lists, catalogues such as this, to good effect, but he rations himself in the use of them. Another of several such lists is in *CW*, page 139, describing the leftover picnic Templeton, the rat, finds in the dump.

Lists also are specific, and specificity is one of White's primary criteria for good writing.

> If those who have studied the art of writing are in accord on any one point, it is on this: the surest way to arouse and hold the attention of the reader is by being specific, definite, and concrete. The great writers—Homer, Dante, Shakespeare—are effective largely because they deal in particulars and report the details that matter. Their words call up pictures.[6]

White cites an example from Herbert Spencer's *Philosophy of Style*, demonstrating how

> the vague and general can be turned into the vivid and particular:

In proportion as the manners, customs, and amusements of a nation are cruel and barbarous, the regulations of its penal code will be severe.	In proportion as men delight in battles, bullfights, and combats of gladiators, will they punish by hanging, burning, and the rack.[7]

An inside view of the barn

full of all sorts of things that you find in barns:[2] ladders, grindstones, pitch forks, monkey wrenches, scythes, lawn mowers, snow shovels, ax handles, milk pails, water buckets, empty grain sacks, and rusty rat traps.[3] It was the kind of barn that swallows like to build their nests in. It was the kind of barn that children like to play in. And the whole thing was owned by Fern's uncle, Mr. Homer L. Zuckerman.

Wilbur's new home was in the lower part of the barn, directly underneath the cows. Mr. Zuckerman knew that a manure pile is a good place to keep a young pig. Pigs need warmth, and it was warm and comfortable down there in the barn cellar on the south side.

Fern came almost every day to visit him. She found

an old milking stool that had been discarded, and she placed the stool in the sheepfold next to Wilbur's pen. Here she sat quietly during the long afternoons, thinking and listening and watching Wilbur.[4] The

5

sheep soon got to know her and trust her. So did the geese, who lived with the sheep. All the animals trusted her, she was so quiet and friendly. Mr. Zuckerman did not allow her to take Wilbur out, and he did not allow

3. Judging by the care with which White attended every aspect of his composition, he would have been aware that the comma before the terminal item in a series violated frequent journalistic practice (although most books do use it), and followed the "Rule" he would later articulate in *ES* ("In a series of three or more terms with a single conjunction, use a comma after each term except the last. Thus write, [']red, white, and blue.[']"[8]). During the writing of *TS*, White kept a handwritten chart of just such punctuation niceties close at hand.

See plate 2, page 186.

Page 15

4. Of himself as a boy, White wrote, "The total number of hours he spent just standing watching animals, or refilling their water pans, would be impossible to estimate. . . ."[11] Nor did his quiet pleasure in observing other creatures leave him as an adult, as evidenced in his moving and precisely observed account of a doe and a fawn in the Bronx Zoo.[12] White's longest poem in *ST* is titled "Zoo Revisited."

5. As work commenced on the illustrations, White wrote Ursula Nordstorm, "Tell Garth [Williams] I love the way he has done Fern and Charlotte and that I think he has perfectly caught the mood and spirit of my barn cellar."[9]

In an early sketch, Williams had probably given Fern pigtails in this picture, but White preferred the ponytail from page 11. To Ursula Nordstrom, he wrote, "I wish . . . that Garth would give Fern the horsetail hairdo again, instead of the pigtails. Her hair seems so incredibly abundant—she just couldn't have grown that amount of hair since Picture No. 6b. . . . But otherwise I love the scene."[10]

6. Although the author has attributed human sentiments to Wilbur before, this is the first time Wilbur speaks in English.

Talking-animal stories are a hazardous undertaking for children's authors in the twentieth century, and more than one children's-book editor has warned against the form. Given the acknowledged success of *Charlotte's Web*, it is worth close attention to notice how White almost surreptitiously wins our acceptance by the gradual manner in which he eases us into the world of talking animals. Note: "That's where you're wrong, my friend"—the voice of the goose, at the bottom of the page. She understands what Wilbur said.

Observe carefully who can talk to whom, and who understands whom.

her to get into the pigpen. But he told Fern that she could sit on the stool and watch Wilbur as long as she wanted to. It made her happy just to be near the pig, and it made Wilbur happy to know that she was sitting there, right outside his pen. But he never had any fun—no walks, no rides, no swims.

One afternoon in June, when Wilbur was almost two months old, he wandered out into his small yard outside the barn. Fern had not arrived for her usual visit. Wilbur stood in the sun feeling lonely and bored.

"There's never anything to do around here," he thought. He walked slowly to his food trough and sniffed to see if anything had been overlooked at lunch. He found a small strip of potato skin and ate it. His back itched, so he leaned against the fence and rubbed against the boards. When he tired of this, he walked indoors, climbed to the top of the manure pile, and sat down. He didn't feel like going to sleep, he didn't feel like digging, he was tired of standing still, tired of lying down. "I'm less than two months old and I'm tired of living,"[6] he said. He walked out to the yard again.

"When I'm out here," he said, "there's no place to go but in. When I'm indoors, there's no place to go but out in the yard."

"That's where you're wrong, my friend, my friend," said a voice.

Escape

Wilbur looked through the fence and saw the goose standing there.

"You don't have to stay in that dirty-little dirty-little dirty-little yard,"[7] said the goose, who talked rather fast. "One of the boards is loose. Push on it, push-push-push on it, and come on out!"

"What?" said Wilbur. "Say it slower!"

"At-at-at, at the risk of repeating myself," said the goose.[8] "I suggest that you come on out. It's wonderful out here."

"Did you say a board was loose?"

"That I did, that I did," said the goose.

Wilbur walked up to the fence and saw that the goose was right—one board was loose. He put his head down, shut his eyes, and pushed. The board gave way. In a minute he had squeezed through the fence and was standing in the long grass outside his yard. The goose chuckled.

"How does it feel to be free?" she asked.[9]

"I like it," said Wilbur. "That is, I *guess* I like it." Actually, Wilbur felt queer to be outside his fence, with nothing between him and the big world.

"Where do you think I'd better go?"

"Anywhere you like, anywhere you like," said the goose. "Go down through the orchard, root up the sod! Go down through the garden, dig up the radishes! Root up everything! Eat grass! Look for corn! Look

Page 17

7. A good novelist distinguishes characters not only by *what* they do and say, but also by the manner in which they say it. Different characters have distinctive "voices." We'll hear the voices of Charlotte and Templeton when they come onstage.

8. "And probably the best line in the book is when the goose says, 'At-at-at, at the risk of repeating myself . . .'" said E. B. White.[13] For more on repetitive words, see page 86.

Of humor, White wrote that "it won't stand much blowing up, and it won't stand much poking. It has a certain fragility, an evasiveness, which one had best respect."[14] Thus he lets the characters' words speak for themselves.

9. This is an old and a serious philosophical question treated in literature by Sophocles, Milton, Camus, and countless other authors. In the world of children's books, Beatrix Potter perhaps unwittingly raises the question in *The Tale of Peter Rabbit*, both in the reckless nature of the hero of the tale and in the illustrations of rabbits, fettered and unfettered by human clothing. For Potter, "divestment" (in both senses) is equated with freedom. White underscores the theme and the issue in all three of his children's books.

10. Sentiments that an author believes deeply need not necessarily be attributed to major or even to perceptive characters.

White frequently stated that the world is a wonderful place—especially if you are young. For other expressions of the sentiment, see the essay "Once More to the Lake,"[15] or the classroom scenes in which, when Stuart Little asks his fifth graders what "is important," the answers range from "a shaft of sunlight at the end of a dark afternoon" to "the way the back of a baby's neck smells if its mother keeps it tidy."[16] That chapter may be one of the more self-revealing passages White wrote.

11. Lurvy, the hired man, was called Larry in Chapter II ("Loneliness") in Folder B. White, we might guess, was in search of a homey, rustic name. Whether the name of pig tender Lurvy ought to raise associations with a pig's "sLURPing" is up to the reader.

Generally, my editorial assumption is: There are no accidents in White's prose.

for oats! Run all over! Skip and dance, jump and prance! Go down through the orchard and stroll in the woods! The world is a wonderful place when you're young." **10**

"I can see that," replied Wilbur. He gave a jump in the air, twirled, ran a few steps, stopped, looked all around, sniffed the smells of afternoon, and then set off walking down through the orchard. Pausing in the shade of an apple tree, he put his strong snout into the ground and began pushing, digging, and rooting. He felt very happy. He had plowed up quite a piece of ground before anyone noticed him. Mrs. Zuckerman was the first to see him. She saw him from the kitchen window, and she immediately shouted for the men.

"Ho-*mer*!" she cried. "Pig's out! Lurvy! **11** Pig's out! Homer! Lurvy! Pig's out. He's down there under that apple tree."

"Now the trouble starts," thought Wilbur. "Now I'll catch it."

The goose heard the racket and she, too, started hollering. "Run-run-run downhill, make for the woods, the woods!" she shouted to Wilbur. "They'll never-never-never catch you in the woods."

The cocker spaniel heard the commotion and he ran out from the barn to join the chase. Mr. Zuckerman heard, and he came out of the machine shed where he was mending a tool. Lurvy, the hired man, heard the

noise and came up from the asparagus patch where he was pulling weeds. Everybody walked toward Wilbur and Wilbur didn't know what to do. The woods seemed a long way off, and anyway, he had never been down there in the woods and wasn't sure he would like it.

"Get around behind him, Lurvy," said Mr. Zuckerman, "and drive him toward the barn! And take it easy—don't rush him! I'll go and get a bucket of slops."

The news of Wilbur's escape spread rapidly among the animals on the place. Whenever any creature broke loose on Zuckerman's farm, the event was of great interest to the others. The goose shouted to the nearest cow that Wilbur was free, and soon all the cows knew.[12] Then one of the cows told one of the sheep, and soon all the sheep knew. The lambs learned about it from their mothers. The horses, in their stalls in the barn, pricked up their ears when they heard the goose hollering; and soon the horses had caught on to what was happening. "Wilbur's out," they said. Every animal stirred and lifted its head and became excited to know that one of his friends had got free and was no longer penned up or tied fast.

Wilbur didn't know what to do or which way to run. It seemed as though everybody was after him. "If this is what it's like to be free," he thought, "I believe I'd rather be penned up in my own yard."[13]

The cocker spaniel was sneaking up on him from one

Page 19

12. The incremental quality of one telling another, telling another, telling another, mimics a traditional folktale device.

13. Since freedom also implies responsibility, the rejection of freedom makes an important point about Wilbur. It's also a thought-provoking statement in the context of White's own life. After his brief youthful peregrinations, White seems not to have thrived away from his farm. He was skilled at turning down invitations and honors when they involved travel.

Page 20

14. In an early draft (Draft A), the cocker spaniel played a role in assisting Charlotte at a critical moment (see page 97.)

side, Lurvy the hired man was sneaking up on him from the other side. Mrs. Zuckerman stood ready to head him off if he started for the garden, and now Mr. Zuckerman was coming down toward him carrying a pail. "This is really awful," thought Wilbur. "Why doesn't Fern come?" He began to cry.

The goose took command and began to give orders.

"Don't just stand there, Wilbur! Dodge about, dodge about!" cried the goose. "Skip around, run toward me, slip in and out, in and out, in and out! Make for the woods! Twist and turn!"

The cocker spaniel sprang for Wilbur's hind leg.[14] Wilbur jumped and ran. Lurvy reached out and grabbed. Mrs. Zuckerman screamed at Lurvy. The goose cheered for Wilbur. Wilbur dodged between

Lurvy's legs. Lurvy missed Wilbur and grabbed the spaniel instead. "Nicely done, nicely done!" cried the goose. "Try it again, try it again!"

"Run downhill!" suggested the cows.

"Run toward me!" yelled the gander.

"Run uphill!" cried the sheep.

"Turn and twist!" honked the goose.

"Jump and dance!" said the rooster.[15]

16

Page 21

15. This slapstick chase is a good one to read aloud to children. It is one of the exceptions to Nodelman's contention that "*Charlotte's Web* is a surprisingly inactive novel."[17]

16. Williams's illustration captures the chaos and shows a good portion of the barnyard population in a four-inch square.

Page 22

17. The animals know the names of the people. Therefore, they not only speak English, but understand human beings as well.

There are no extant worksheets giving evidence of White's having pondered who understands whom, but the novel is consistent and flawless in this respect.

18. Pigs don't cry, and the fact that Wilbur does considerably anthropomorphizes him. However, on most occasions, White expressed concern that the animals not be made to appear overly human. To the filmmaker Gene Deitch, White wrote that he "should never lose sight of the fact that [Charlotte's miraculous web] was a web spun by a true arachnid, not by a *de facto* person."[18]

19. White likes the idea of recycling food. It occurs several times in the book. The food from the human beings' table goes into the pig, and the pig, in turn, returns to the human beings' table. The Arables have bacon for breakfast on page 3. See also page 231.

Shakespeare plays with the same idea. Hamlet has just killed the meddling old Polonius, and his stepfather, the king, asks him where Polonius is:

> HAMLET: At supper.
>
> KING: At supper! where?
>
> HAMLET: Not where he eats, but where he is eaten: a certain convocation of politic worms are e'en at him. Your worm is your only emperor for diet: we fat all creatures else to fat us, and we fat ourselves for maggots: your fat king and your lean beggar is but variable service,—two dishes, but to one table: that's the end.
>
> KING: Alas, alas!
>
> HAMLET: A man may fish with the worm that

"Look out for Lurvy!" called the cows.[17]

"Look out for Zuckerman!" yelled the gander.

"Watch out for the dog!" cried the sheep.

"Listen to me, listen to me!" screamed the goose.

Poor Wilbur was dazed and frightened by this hullabaloo. He didn't like being the center of all this fuss. He tried to follow the instructions his friends were giving him, but he couldn't run downhill and uphill at the same time, and he couldn't turn and twist when he was jumping and dancing, and he was crying so hard he could barely see anything that was happening.[18] After all, Wilbur was a very young pig—not much more than a baby, really. He wished Fern were there to take him in her arms and comfort him. When he looked up and saw Mr. Zuckerman standing quite close to him, holding a pail of warm slops, he felt relieved. He lifted his nose and sniffed. The smell was delicious—warm milk, potato skins, wheat middlings, Kellogg's Corn Flakes, and a popover left from the Zuckermans' breakfast.[19]

"Come, pig!" said Mr. Zuckerman, tapping the pail. "Come pig!"

Wilbur took a step toward the pail.

"No-no-no!" said the goose. "It's the old pail trick, Wilbur. Don't fall for it, don't fall for it! He's trying to lure you back into captivity-ivity. He's appealing to your stomach."

Wilbur didn't care. The food smelled appetizing. He took another step toward the pail.

"Pig, pig!" said Mr. Zuckerman in a kind voice, and began walking slowly toward the barnyard, looking all about him innocently, as if he didn't know that a little white pig was following along behind him.

"You'll be sorry-sorry-sorry," called the goose.

Wilbur didn't care. He kept walking toward the pail of slops.

"You'll miss your freedom," honked the goose. "An hour of freedom is worth a barrel of slops."

Wilbur didn't care.

When Mr. Zuckerman reached the pigpen, he climbed over the fence and poured the slops into the trough. Then he pulled the loose board away from the fence, so that there was a wide hole for Wilbur to walk through.

"Reconsider, reconsider!" cried the goose.[20]

Wilbur paid no attention. He stepped through the fence into his yard. He walked to the trough and took a long drink of slops, sucking in the milk hungrily and chewing the popover. It was good to be home again.[21]

While Wilbur ate, Lurvy fetched a hammer and some 8-penny nails and nailed the board in place. Then he and Mr. Zuckerman leaned lazily on the fence and Mr. Zuckerman scratched Wilbur's back with a stick.

"He's quite a pig," said Lurvy.[22]

hath eat of a king, and eat of the fish that hath fed of that worm.

KING: What dost thou mean by this?

HAMLET: Nothing but to show you how a king may go a progress through the guts of a beggar. [19]

Page 23

20. If you read this page aloud, you'll see how White composed, almost in the musical sense of the word. The whole page has its rhythm—the triple warnings, staccato "Wilbur didn't care" or "paid no attention" response, each followed by a short, expository paragraph.

21. Wilbur is immature and totally self-absorbed early in the book. Only near the end does he begin to perceive beyond himself. As long as he is childishly blind to all but his own needs, he finds being cared for far more gratifying than having the responsibilities that go with freedom.

22. Foreshadows comments made about Wilbur after the "miracle." The characterization of Lurvy by his speech is fun too. No blabbermouth, this Down-Easter.

Page 24

23. Mr. Zuckerman surely has in mind that Wilbur will "make a good pig" when it comes to market time, if Wilbur keeps eating heartily. Wilbur hears the "words of praise" and interprets them in his own (childishly self-centered) way.

This doubleness or disjunction in understanding constitutes irony, a rather serious irony for a "mere" children's book.

24. A most sensuous paragraph, a good one on which to end an evening's reading.

Charlotte will actually be the only animal in no way beholden to human beings.

"Yes, he'll make a good pig," said Mr. Zuckerman.[23]

Wilbur heard the words of praise. He felt the warm milk inside his stomach. He felt the pleasant rubbing of the stick along his itchy back. He felt peaceful and happy and sleepy. This had been a tiring afternoon. It was still only about four o'clock but Wilbur was ready for bed.[24]

"I'm really too young to go out into the world alone," he thought as he lay down.

Chapter IV

Loneliness

THE NEXT day was rainy and dark. Rain fell on the roof of the barn and dripped steadily from the eaves. Rain fell in the barnyard and ran in crooked courses down into the lane where thistles and pigweed grew. Rain spattered against Mrs. Zuckerman's kitchen windows and came gushing out of the downspouts. Rain fell on the backs of the sheep as they grazed in the meadow.[1] When the sheep tired of standing in the rain, they walked slowly up the lane and into the fold.

Rain upset Wilbur's plans. Wilbur had planned to go out, this day, and dig a new hole in his yard. He had other plans, too. His plans for the day went something like this:

Breakfast at six-thirty. Skim milk, crusts, middlings, bits of doughnuts, wheat cakes with drops of maple syrup sticking to them, potato skins, leftover custard pudding with raisins, and bits of Shredded Wheat.[2]

Breakfast would be finished at seven.

From seven to eight, Wilbur planned to have a talk

Page 25

1. Artfully, White makes us feel the seemingly interminable rain as he begins four successive sentences identically—"Rain fell . . ."—and then resolves the paragraph with a lovely, loose, sinuous sentence that winds its way as do the tired sheep. White thought highly of the paragraph as a writerly device, stating his position explicitly: "Make the paragraph the unit of composition."[1]

2. One of those lists that are White's specialty, heightened here by the repetition of *s* and *k* sounds: skim, crusts, cakes, skins, custards. (See note for page 14.)

As noted earlier, White had written, "[T]he stuff that goes into the trough and is received with such enthusiasm is an earnest of some later feast of [a human being's] own."[2]

3. This is the first mention of the scamp, the rascal. The letter *t* is often associated with him—*Templeton, rat, trough*.

As for his name, the poet and critic David McCord has suggested that White was thinking of the telephone exchange of that name in Manhattan.[3]

4. White is actually rendering the precise sequence in which Wilbur's mind works.

Another writer who loved lists of food was Kenneth Grahame, the author of *The Wind in the Willows*. Halfway through the first chapter of that book, in a state of orgiastic ecstasy, Ratty cites the contents of a picnic basket—"There's cold chicken . . . coldtonguecoldhamcoldbeefpickledgherkinssalad-frenchrollscresssandwidgespottedmeatgingerbeer-lemonadesodawater—."[4]

with Templeton, the rat that lived under his trough.[3] Talking with Templeton was not the most interesting occupation in the world but it was better than nothing.

From eight to nine, Wilbur planned to take a nap outdoors in the sun.

From nine to eleven he planned to dig a hole, or trench, and possibly find something good to eat buried in the dirt.

From eleven to twelve he planned to stand still and watch flies on the boards, watch bees in the clover, and watch swallows in the air.

Twelve o'clock—lunchtime. Middlings, warm water, apple parings, meat gravy, carrot scrapings, meat scraps, stale hominy, and the wrapper off a package of cheese. Lunch would be over at one.

From one to two, Wilbur planned to sleep.

From two to three, he planned to scratch itchy places by rubbing against the fence.

From three to four, he planned to stand perfectly still and think of what it was like to be alive, and to wait for Fern.

At four would come supper.[4] Skim milk, provender, leftover sandwich from Lurvy's lunch box, prune skins, a morsel of this, a bit of that, fried potatoes, marmalade drippings, a little more of this, a little more of that, a piece of baked apple, a scrap of upsidedown cake.

Wilbur had gone to sleep thinking about these plans.

Loneliness

He awoke at six and saw the rain, and it seemed as though he couldn't bear it.

"I get everything all beautifully planned out and it has to go and rain," he said.

For a while he stood gloomily indoors. Then he walked to the door and looked out. Drops of rain struck his face. His yard was cold and wet. His trough had an inch of rainwater in it. Templeton was nowhere to be seen.

"Are you out there, Templeton?" called Wilbur. There was no answer. Suddenly Wilbur felt lonely and friendless.[5]

"One day just like another," he groaned. "I'm very young, I have no real friend here in the barn, it's going to rain all morning and all afternoon, and Fern won't come in such bad weather. Oh, *honestly*!" And Wilbur was crying again, for the second time in two days.

At six-thirty Wilbur heard the banging of a pail. Lurvy was standing outside in the rain, stirring up breakfast.

"C'mon, pig!" said Lurvy.

Wilbur did not budge. Lurvy dumped the slops, scraped the pail, and walked away.[6] He noticed that something was wrong with the pig.

Wilbur didn't want food, he wanted love. He wanted a friend—someone who would play with him. He mentioned this to the goose, who was sit-

Page 27

5. Loneliness is a significant subtheme that may be a necessary precondition for White's main theme of *friendship*, to which he again refers in the last paragraph on this page.

6. Of slops and scrapings, White has created a line of poetry. You can hear it if you read the sentence aloud—the music of the repetition of initial consonants, the rhythm of the two staccato phrases, and the mellow soft conclusion, "walked away." White did feel a writer had to have a good "ear."

Page 28

7. Pretty witty for Wilbur. White couldn't resist.

8. The paradoxical phrase "less than nothing" had been bobbing about in White's mind for at least twenty-five years, for the very first item listed in the exhaustive bibliographical catalogue of his manuscripts at Cornell is *Less than Nothing—or The Life and Times of Sterling Finny* (1927), a collection of ten parodic ads White wrote to promote the circulation of *The New Yorker.*

See plate 3, page 187.

In addition, "Wilbur's response shows something of his creator's concern for verbal behavior," says the British literary critic D. J. Enright.[5]

ting quietly in a corner of the sheepfold.

"Will you come over and play with me?" he asked.

"Sorry, sonny, sorry," said the goose. "I'm sitting-sitting on my eggs. Eight of them. Got to keep them toasty-oasty-oasty warm. I have to stay right here, I'm no flibberty-ibberty-gibbet. I do not play when there are eggs to hatch. I'm expecting goslings."

"Well, I didn't think you were expecting woodpeckers," said Wilbur, bitterly.[7]

Wilbur next tried one of the lambs.

"Will you please play with me?" he asked.

"Certainly not," said the lamb. "In the first place, I cannot get into your pen, as I am not old enough to jump over the fence. In the second place, I am not interested in pigs. Pigs mean less than nothing to me."[8]

"What do you mean, *less* than nothing?" replied Wilbur. "I don't think there is any such thing as *less* than nothing. Nothing is absolutely the limit of nothingness. It's the lowest you can go. It's the end of the line. How can something be less than nothing? If there were something that was less than nothing, then nothing would not be nothing, it would be something—even though it's just a very little bit of something. But if nothing is *nothing*, then nothing has nothing that is less than *it* is."

"Oh, be quiet!" said the lamb. "Go play by yourself! I don't play with pigs."

Loneliness

Sadly, Wilbur lay down and listened to the rain. Soon he saw the rat climbing down a slanting board that he used as a stairway.

"Will you play with me, Templeton?" asked Wilbur.

"Play?" said Templeton, twirling his whiskers. "Play? I hardly know the meaning of the word."[9]

"Well," said Wilbur, "it means to have fun, to frolic, to run and skip and make merry."

"I never do those things if I can avoid them," replied the rat, sourly. "I prefer to spend my time eating, gnawing, spying, and hiding.[10] I am a glutton but not a merry-

Page 29

9. As Templeton sounds a note of sardonic worldliness among these rustic farmyard animals, we again have characterization by way of speech—just as we did for the garrulous goose.

And as we saw in the Introduction and on pages 4–5, White's relationship to rodents was complex and meaningful.

In 1944, after having undergone what he called "a nervous crack-up" and suffering general psychological malaise, White wrote a poem titled "Vermin":

The mouse of Thought infests my head,
He knows my cupboard and the crumb.
Vermin! I despise vermin.
I have no trap, no skill with traps,
No bait, no hope, no cheese, no bread—
I fumble with the task to no avail.
I've seen him several times lately.
He is too quick for me,
I only see his tail.[6]

10. In Draft B, White became quite carried away by the thought of Templeton's gormandizing. In that version, Templeton says, "Mostly I gnaw, chew, bite, and grind. I also sniff, smell, sift, and test; and sometimes I spy, squint, gaze, look, watch and descry; but I rarely if ever carouse, skip, twirl, gambol, dance, frolic, cavort, or play. . . ."

Page 30

11. White here characterizes Templeton not only by the words he uses to describe him but by their very sounds. *Dug, door, trough*, blunt, plow-nosed words. Not clean, easy words with pure, open vowels and crisp consonants, but "ough" words of off sound, *trough* being deceptive even in the way in which it is spelled.

Page 31

12. The Agricultural Extension Service at the University of California, San Diego, was unfamiliar with this particular pick-me-up, but White's daughter-in-law, Allene White, assures us that "[s]ulfur and molasses is [a] Yankee remedy, usually given early in the spring. Spring tonics are probably not necessary in CALIFORNIA but it wouldn't hurt."[7]

13. Although White has Wilbur sobbing, and this illustration shows tears running down his jowls, White was vehemently opposed to the artist's anthropomorphizing Charlotte, and wrote Cass Canfield, Sr. (who had become White's general editor at Harper & Bros. when Eugene Saxton died in 1942), that he preferred "attitudes and postures, rather than facial expression."[8]

Originally, in this illustration, Williams must have shown Wilbur's right front hoof too, for White wrote Ursula Nordstrom, "The right hoof still bothers me—not because there is anything wrong about the way it is drawn but merely because of an optical accident which causes the foot to appear to be the snout on first glance. I think this is unfortunate, but not serious. It could easily be corrected by amputating the foot."[9]

maker. Right now I am on my way to your trough to eat your breakfast, since you haven't got sense enough to eat it yourself." And Templeton, the rat, crept stealthily along the wall and disappeared into a private tunnel that he had dug between the door and the trough in Wilbur's yard.[11] Templeton was a crafty rat, and he had things pretty much his own way. The tunnel was an example of his skill and cunning. The tunnel enabled him to get from the barn to his hiding place under the pig trough without coming out into the open. He had tunnels and runways all over Mr. Zuckerman's farm and could get from one place to another without being seen. Usually he slept during the daytime and was abroad only after dark.

Wilbur watched him disappear into his tunnel. In a moment he saw the rat's sharp nose poke out from underneath the wooden trough. Cautiously Templeton pulled himself up over the edge of the trough. This was almost more than Wilbur could stand: on this dreary, rainy day to see his breakfast being eaten by somebody else. He knew Templeton was getting soaked, out there in the pouring rain, but even that didn't comfort him. Friendless, dejected, and hungry, he threw himself down in the manure and sobbed.

Late that afternoon, Lurvy went to Mr. Zuckerman. "I think there's something wrong with that pig of yours. He hasn't touched his food."

Loneliness

"Give him two spoonfuls of sulphur and a little molasses," said Mr. Zuckerman.[12]

Wilbur couldn't believe what was happening to him when Lurvy caught him and forced the medicine down his throat. This was certainly the worst day of his life. He didn't know whether he could endure the awful loneliness any more.

13

Darkness settled over everything.[14] Soon there were only shadows and the noises of the sheep chewing their cuds, and occasionally the rattle of a cow-chain up overhead. You can imagine Wilbur's surprise when, out of the darkness, came a small voice he had never heard before. It sounded rather thin, but pleasant. "Do you want a friend, Wilbur?" it said. "I'll be a friend to you. I've watched you all day and I like you."[15]

"But I can't see you," said Wilbur, jumping to his feet. "Where are you? And *who* are you?"

"I'm right up here," said the voice. "Go to sleep. You'll see me in the morning."

14. At this point, White steps back from what was a closeup of Wilbur taking his medicine. He now views the rural scene from a distance, putting his protagonists within the context of the world at evening. Whenever he assumes such distance, White expands the relevance and enlarges the meaning of his book.

15. This is the title character's entrance!

As any dramatist knows, the first words of any important character can be extremely significant. In his troubled sleep later that night (*CW*, page 33), Wilbur hears the same voice and the same offer of friendship. The major theme and epigrammatic last description of Charlotte ("a true friend and a good writer," *CW*, page 184) is here foreshadowed.

Notice, too, how thin the words *thin* and *pleasant* sound, compared to the tough, blunt words associated with Templeton.

Chapter V

Charlotte

THE NIGHT seemed long. Wilbur's stomach was empty and his mind was full. And when your stomach is empty and your mind is full, it's always hard to sleep.

A dozen times during the night Wilbur woke and stared into the blackness, listening to the sounds and trying to figure out what time it was. A barn is never perfectly quiet. Even at midnight there is usually something stirring.

The first time he woke, he heard Templeton gnawing a hole in the grain bin. Templeton's teeth scraped loudly against the wood and made quite a racket. "That crazy rat!" thought Wilbur. "Why does he have to stay up all night, grinding his clashers and destroying people's property? Why can't he go to sleep, like any decent animal?"

The second time Wilbur woke, he heard the goose turning on her nest and chuckling to herself.

"What time is it?" whispered Wilbur to the goose.

"Probably-obably-obably about half-past eleven," said the goose. "Why aren't you asleep, Wilbur?"

"Too many things on my mind," said Wilbur.

"Well," said the goose, "that's not *my* trouble.[1] I have nothing at all on my mind, but I've too many things under my behind. Have you ever tried to sleep while sitting on eight eggs?"

"No," replied Wilbur. "I suppose it *is* uncomfortable. How long does it take a goose egg to hatch?"

"Approximately-oximately thirty days, all told," answered the goose. "But I cheat a little. On warm afternoons, I just pull a little straw over the eggs and go out for a walk."

Wilbur yawned and went back to sleep. In his dreams he heard again the voice saying, "I'll be a friend to you. Go to sleep—you'll see me in the morning."

[2]About half an hour before dawn, Wilbur woke and listened. The barn was still dark. The sheep lay motionless. Even the goose was quiet. Overhead, on the main floor, nothing stirred: the cows were resting, the horses dozed. Templeton had quit work and gone off somewhere on an errand. The only sound was a slight scraping noise from the rooftop, where the weather-vane swung back and forth. Wilbur loved the barn when it was like this—calm and quiet, waiting for light.

"Day is almost here," he thought.

Through a small window, a faint gleam appeared.

Page 33

1. The goose is not very sympathetic about Wilbur's insomnia. As White explained, "[I]t would be quite untrue to suggest that barnyard creatures are dependent on each other. The barn is a community of rugged individualists. . . ."[1]

2. The whole paragraph is like a short musical composition—the succession of short sentences that resolve into one winding, languorous one, and the whole paragraph ending with the summary conclusion, "—calm and quiet, waiting for light."

Page 34

3. Lovable as he may be, Wilbur is neither bright nor subtle. The official and officious-sounding command, with its bureaucratic "the party," instead of "the person," and "himself or herself," is ("at this point in time," as Wilbur might have added) as distinctly the tone of the unsophisticated Wilbur as repetition is the mark of the garrulous goose. ("Lawyerese," the critic Sonia Landes calls the language.[2])

One by one the stars went out. Wilbur could see the goose a few feet away. She sat with head tucked under a wing. Then he could see the sheep and the lambs. The sky lightened.

"Oh, beautiful day, it is here at last! Today I shall find my friend."

Wilbur looked everywhere. He searched his pen thoroughly. He examined the window ledge, stared up at the ceiling. But he saw nothing new. Finally he decided he would have to speak up. He hated to break the lovely stillness of dawn by using his voice, but he couldn't think of any other way to locate the mysterious new friend who was nowhere to be seen. So Wilbur cleared his throat.

"Attention, please!" he said in a loud, firm voice. "Will the party who addressed me at bedtime last night kindly make himself or herself known by giving an appropriate sign or signal!" [3]

Wilbur paused and listened. All the other animals lifted their heads and stared at him. Wilbur blushed. But he was determined to get in touch with his unknown friend.

"Attention, please!" he said. "I will repeat the message. Will the party who addressed me at bedtime last night kindly speak up. Please tell me where you are, if you are my friend!"

The sheep looked at each other in disgust.

Charlotte

"Stop your nonsense, Wilbur!" said the oldest sheep. "If you have a new friend here, you are probably disturbing his rest; and the quickest way to spoil a friendship is to wake somebody up in the morning before he is ready.[4] How can you be sure your friend is an early riser?"

"I beg everyone's pardon," whispered Wilbur. "I didn't mean to be objectionable."[5]

He lay down meekly in the manure, facing the door. He did not know it, but his friend was very near. And the old sheep was right—the friend was still asleep.

Soon Lurvy appeared with slops for breakfast. Wilbur rushed out, ate everything in a hurry, and licked the trough. The sheep moved off down the lane, the gander waddled along behind them, pulling grass. And then, just as Wilbur was settling down for his morning nap, he heard again the thin voice that had addressed him the night before.

"Salutations!" said the voice.

Wilbur jumped to his feet. "Salu-*what*?" he cried.

"Salutations!" repeated the voice.

"What are *they*, and where are *you*?" screamed Wilbur. "Please, *please*, tell me where you are. And what are salutations?"

"Salutations are greetings," said the voice.[6] "When I say 'salutations,' it's just my fancy way of saying hello or good morning. Actually, it's a silly expression, and

Page 35

4. The pattern of this sentence resembles one White employed in his essays. Often White illustrated a general principle by way of a homely instance.

5. Generally, conversation among the barnyard animals is informal and easy. Wilbur, however, is just "entering society," and he does not yet really know the language. In his effort to talk appropriately, he strains comically.

6. Charlotte uses Latinate vocabulary—befitting her own name and Latin classification in *CW*, page 37. Throughout the book, she acts intermittently as mother, savior, and teacher—explaining to Wilbur the difficult words he is so eager to learn. Nonetheless, White's advice, at least for human beings, was to "[a]void fancy words."[3]

Page 36

7. "There is no misanthropy in *Charlotte's Web*, but the heroic spider is both more noble and more adorable than any other creature in the story. . . ."[4]

8. In an early draft, White wrote that Charlotte lived "in a beautiful web." He crossed that out and wrote more accurately, "in a doorway." Garth Williams got the spiderweb just right—as he does in the illustration in *CW*, page 59, where Charlotte also hangs head down.

I am surprised that I used it at all. As for my whereabouts, that's easy. Look up here in the corner of the doorway! Here I am. Look, I'm waving!"

At last Wilbur saw the creature[7] that had spoken to him in such a kindly way. Stretched across the upper part of the doorway was a big spiderweb, and hanging

8

from the top of the web, head down, was a large grey spider. She was about the size of a gumdrop. She had eight legs,[9] and she was waving one of them at Wilbur in friendly greeting. "See me now?" she asked.

"Oh, yes indeed," said Wilbur. "Yes indeed! How are you? Good morning! Salutations! Very pleased to meet you. What is your name, please? May I have your name?"

"My name," said the spider, "is Charlotte."

"Charlotte what?" asked Wilbur, eagerly.

"Charlotte A. Cavatica.[10] But just call me Charlotte."

"I think you're beautiful," said Wilbur.

"Well, I *am* pretty," replied Charlotte. "There's no denying that. Almost all spiders are rather nice-looking. I'm not as flashy as some, but I'll do. I wish I could see you, Wilbur, as clearly as you can see me."

"Why can't you?" asked the pig. "I'm right here."

"Yes, but I'm near-sighted," replied Charlotte. "I've always been dreadfully near-sighted. It's good in some ways, not so good in others. Watch me wrap up this fly."

A fly that had been crawling along Wilbur's trough had flown up and blundered into the lower part of Charlotte's web and was tangled in the sticky threads. The fly was beating its wings furiously, trying to break loose and free itself.

"First," said Charlotte, "I dive at him." She plunged

Page 37

9. One critic has referred to Charlotte as an "insect."[5] In contrast to insects, however, which have three pairs of legs, and wings, the spiders—class Arachnida—have four pairs of legs. They never have wings, and they are relatives to scorpions and mites.[6]

10. E. B. White did an enormous amount of research on spiders, studying their habits for about a year before he even started writing.[7]

White first called his spider Charlotte Epeira, thinking she was a Grey Cross spider, called *Epeira sclopetaria* in old books.[8] In Folder A, he wrote, "Charlotte's last name is Epeira. . . . She is a sedentary spider."

In point of fact, the current scientific name of the spider is *Araneus cavaticus*. The species name has been changed to agree in gender with *Araneus*.[9] (See page 182.)

Page 38

11. EBW noted in Folder A: "Spider does not kill prey with sting, merely stuns it. Easier to suck blood, probably, when prey is still alive." He had read Gertsch:

> All spiders are predacious, subsist on the body juices of living animals, and only rarely can be duped to accept dead food. The bulk of their food is made up of insects, which are subdued by their venom.[10]

Page 39

12. From both Comstock and Gertsch, White obtained information about the food of spiders. He would also have read that some eat not only snakes and lizards, but even birds.[11]

13. White was not sentimental about life in the barnyard. "It just comes natural to me to keep animals pure and not distort them or take advantage of them," he wrote filmmaker Gene Deitch (see page 224).[12]

14. True friend and good writer though she may be, Charlotte's bloodthirstiness is as much a part of her nature as are her competence, her sophistication, and her loving kindness.

Instead of stating the expected—that Charlotte's voice became cruel or frightening—White says that it became "thinner and more pleasant." The effect is strangely chilling, just because of its indirection.

15. Some arachnid ancestors of spiders "were among the first animals to crawl out upon the land and adjust themselves to terrestrial existence."[13] Shortly before *Charlotte's Web*, White had been writing an introduction to Don Marquis's *archy & mehitabel*, a book he had admired for years. Marquis's hero, archy, is a cockroach—a species that, like the spiders, has inhabited the planet since time immemorial. And as White wrote in *The Wild Flag*, "archy himself is

headfirst toward the fly. As she dropped, a tiny silken thread unwound from her rear end.

"Next, I wrap him up." She grabbed the fly, threw a few jets of silk around it, and rolled it over and over, wrapping it so that it couldn't move. Wilbur watched

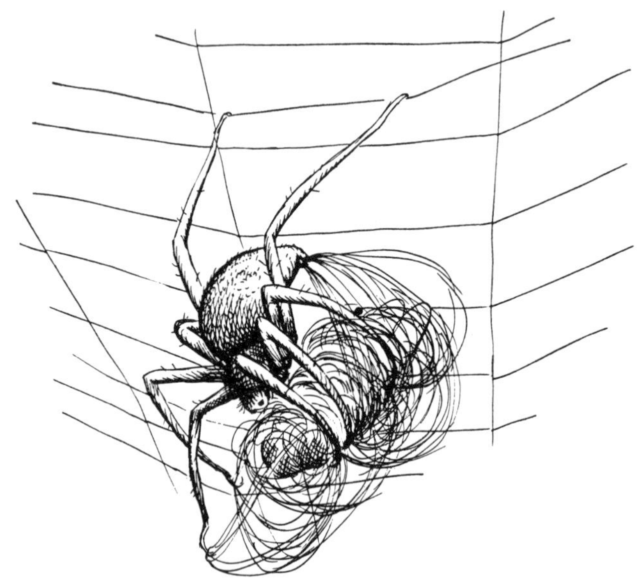

in horror. He could hardly believe what he was seeing, and although he detested flies, he was sorry for this one.

"There!" said Charlotte. "Now I knock him out, so he'll be more comfortable.[11]" She bit the fly. "He can't feel a thing now," she remarked. "He'll make a perfect breakfast for me."

Charlotte

"You mean you *eat* flies?" gasped Wilbur.

"Certainly. Flies, bugs, grasshoppers, choice beetles, moths, butterflies, tasty cockroaches, gnats, midges, daddy longlegs, centipedes, mosquitoes, crickets[12]—anything that is careless enough to get caught in my web. I have to live, don't I?"[13]

"Why, yes, of course," said Wilbur. "Do they taste good?"

"Delicious. Of course, I don't really eat them. I drink them—drink their blood. I love blood,"[14] said Charlotte, and her pleasant, thin voice grew even thinner and more pleasant.

"Don't say that!" groaned Wilbur. "Please don't say things like that!"

"Why not? It's true, and I have to say what is true. I am not entirely happy about my diet of flies and bugs, but it's the way I'm made. A spider has to pick up a living somehow or other, and I happen to be a trapper. I just naturally build a web and trap flies and other insects. My mother was a trapper before me. Her mother was a trapper before her. All our family have been trappers. Way back for thousands and thousands of years we spiders have been laying for flies and bugs."[15]

"It's a miserable inheritance,[16]" said Wilbur, gloomily. He was sad because his new friend was so bloodthirsty.

"Yes, it is," agreed Charlotte. "But I can't help it. I don't know how the first spider in the early days of the

probably good for another hundred million years."[14]

16. The author raises a serious philosophical issue—the puzzlingly cannibalistic, carnivorous, amoral nature of that very universe in praise of which the book is written. White merely suggests the problem, however, making it issue from the snout of the least philosophical of his characters. Still, he felt sufficiently strongly about the matter to break the surface of the narrative in order to evoke this theme.

To Gene Deitch, White wrote of the book:

> It is, I think, an *appreciative* story. . . . It celebrates life, the seasons, the goodness of the barn, the beauty of the world, the glory of everything. But it is essentially amoral, because animals are essentially amoral, and I respect them, and I think this respect is implicit in the tale. I discovered . . . that there was no need to tamper in any way with the habits and characteristics of spiders, pigs, geese, and rats.[15]

Page 40

17. White may have had in mind Gertsch, Chapter 11, "Economic and Medical Importance" of spiders. Gertsch cites the control of bedbugs in Greek refugee camps in Athens and, perhaps more to the point, agricultural pest control.[16]

18. White uses Wilbur's naïveté to good advantage, allowing Charlotte to explain to him and to us the place spiders hold in the larger scheme of the world.

19. The goose knows the ways of man. She's not one for sentimentalizing.

Life expectancy for a pig is about ten years. At six to ten months, hogs are deemed ready for slaughter.

world happened to think up this fancy idea of spinning a web, but she did, and it was clever of her, too. And since then, all of us spiders have had to work the same trick. It's not a bad pitch, on the whole."

"It's cruel," replied Wilbur, who did not intend to be argued out of his position.

"Well, *you* can't talk," said Charlotte. "*You* have your meals brought to you in a pail. Nobody feeds me. I have to get my own living. I live by my wits. I have to be sharp and clever, lest I go hungry. I have to think things out, catch what I can, take what comes. And it just so happens, my friend, that what comes is flies and insects and bugs. And *further*more," said Charlotte, shaking one of her legs, "do you realize that if I didn't catch bugs and eat them, bugs would increase and multiply and get so numerous that they'd destroy the earth, wipe out everything?"[17]

"Really?" said Wilbur.[18] "I wouldn't want *that* to happen. Perhaps your web is a good thing after all."

The goose had been listening to this conversation and chuckling to herself. "There are a lot of things Wilbur doesn't know about life," she thought. "He's really a very innocent little pig. He doesn't even know what's going to happen to him around Christmastime;[19] he has no idea that Mr. Zuckerman and Lurvy are plotting to kill him." And the goose raised herself a bit and poked her eggs a little further under her so that they would

receive the full heat from her warm body and soft feathers.

Charlotte stood quietly over the fly, preparing to eat it. Wilbur lay down and closed his eyes. He was tired from his wakeful night and from the excitement of meeting someone for the first time. A breeze brought him the smell of clover[20]—the sweet-smelling world beyond his fence. "Well," he thought, "I've got a new friend, all right. But what a gamble friendship is![21] Charlotte is fierce, brutal, scheming, bloodthirsty—everything I don't like. How can I learn to like her, even though she is pretty and, of course, clever?"

Wilbur was merely suffering the doubts and fears that often go with finding a new friend.[22] In good time he was to discover that he was mistaken about Charlotte. Underneath her rather bold and cruel exterior, she had a kind heart, and she was to prove loyal and true to the very end.

Page 41

20. On White's appreciation of the olfactory pleasures of the barn, see page 13.

21. Through Wilbur, White again states the major theme of friendship, which weaves its way in and out of the fabric of the book.

22. As a matter of novelistic technique, this is one of the most interesting passages in the book. White here firmly establishes himself as an omniscient author—an author who knows the whole story, who knows more than any one character, and who, in fact, knows *how the story is going to turn out even before it has been told.*

Was White defusing the suspense by intruding his omniscience? The distinguished critic Roger Sale has no doubt: "White . . . drops a stitch, as it were, and ends this chapter with a needless reassuring note about Charlotte's true kind heart. . . . Beatrix Potter never makes such mistakes, and White, fortunately, makes very few."[17]

Actually, White had trouble with this passage, as the facsimile draft page shows.

See plate 4, page 188.

Page 42

1. The beginning of this chapter is a hymn of praise to Nature, to the season—one of the several lyrical passages that White has interspersed throughout his novel. It is not, however, merely adjectival indulgence, for the celebration of Nature and of the seasons *is* one of the major themes of the book, as White himself noted when he wrote in 1961 to filmmaker Louis de Rochemont about the book:

> It has a thread of fantasy, but essentially it is a hymn to the barn. It is pastoral, seasonal. . . .[1]

White repeated the point ten years later in a letter to Gene Deitch.[2]

For more on *Charlotte's Web* as a pastoral, please see page 8, note 3, and page 105, note 1.

White expressed the joy he felt in nature in a poem written for Katharine White in 1928. Part of the poem reads:

Keep most carefully alive in me
Something of the expectancy
That is somehow likeliest to be
In a child waking,
In a day breaking,
A robin singing,
Or a telephone ringing.

Give me again the strange thrill
Of a boy climbing a Maine hill, topping the rise,
Coming on the farmer's band of sheep:
Give me the terrible surprise
Of their raised heads, their startled eyes. . . .[3]

The ringing telephone seems jarring. Perhaps White had actually been looking forward to calls from Katharine; perhaps he was searching for a word to rhyme with *singing*.

2. This is a subtle shift from our conventional perspective. It's a view represented later by Dr. Dorian.

Chapter VI

Summer Days

THE EARLY summer days on a farm are the happiest and fairest days of the year. Lilacs bloom and make the air sweet, and then fade. Apple blossoms come with the lilacs, and the bees visit around among the apple trees. The days grow warm and soft. School ends, and children have time to play and to fish for trouts in the brook. Avery often brought a trout home in his pocket, warm and stiff and ready to be fried for supper.[1]

Now that school was over, Fern visited the barn almost every day, to sit quietly on her stool. The animals treated her as an equal.[2] The sheep lay calmly at her feet.

Around the first of July, the work horses were hitched to the mowing machine, and Mr. Zuckerman climbed into the seat and drove into the field. All morning you could hear the rattle of the machine as it went round and round, while the tall grass fell down behind the cutter bar in long green swathes. Next day, if there was no thunder shower, all hands would help rake and pitch and load, and the hay would be hauled to the

barn in the high hay wagon, with Fern and Avery riding at the top of the load. Then the hay would be hoisted, sweet and warm, into the big loft, until the whole barn seemed like a wonderful bed of timothy and clover. It was fine to jump in, and perfect to hide in. And sometimes Avery would find a little grass snake in the hay, and would add it to the other things in his pocket.

Early summer days are a jubilee time for birds. In the fields, around the house, in the barn, in the woods, in the swamp—everywhere love and songs and nests and eggs. From the edge of the woods, the white-throated sparrow (which must come all the way from Boston) calls, "Oh, Peabody, Peabody, Peabody!"[3] On an apple bough, the phoebe teeters[4] and wags its tail and says, "Phoebe, phoe-bee!" The song sparrow, who knows how brief and lovely life is,[5] says, "Sweet, sweet, sweet interlude; sweet, sweet, sweet interlude." If you enter the barn, the swallows swoop down from their nests and scold. "Cheeky, cheeky!" they say.

In early summer there are plenty of things for a child to eat and drink and suck and chew. Dandelion stems are full of milk,[6] clover heads are loaded with nectar, the Frigidaire is full of ice-cold drinks. Everywhere you look is life; even the little ball of spit on the weed stalk, if you poke it apart, has a green worm inside it. And on

Page 43

3. In his essays, White assumed the persona of a Down East countryman, and so we have come to associate him with New England. However, in *Charlotte's Web*, this sparrow from Boston is the only internal clue that this is a New England story.

4. The alliterative sound play should be appreciated.

5. The bird does not say that; it is the author's intrusion—so this idea of the brevity of life is what today would be called a "subtext" for the book. It is a part of the pastoral, or Arcadian (ancient, idealized Greek), myth, which is taken up again on page 113.

White is not the first to have injected the sobering note in a book for children. In Kenneth Grahame's river-and-woodland idyll *The Wind in the Willows*, the same theme is sounded in Chapter IV, where Badger speaks of his network of underground corridors:

> ". . . [V]ery long ago, on the spot where the Wild Wood waves now, before ever it had planted itself and grown up to what it now is, there was a city—a city of people. . . ."
>
> "But what has become of them all?" asked the Mole.
>
> "Who can tell?" said the Badger. *"People come—they stay for a while, they flourish, they build—and they go. It is their way. But we remain. . . ."* [Italics added][4]

The important point is that White was writing in a great literary tradition. The current buzzword *intertextuality*, meaning one literary work's referring, overtly or elliptically, to other concepts or works, is a useful one.

Continued on page 44

Page 43 (continued)

6. White's convincing evocation of what it *feels like* to be a child must be one of the qualities that make *CW* the superlative children's book that it is.

Page 44

7. White kept geese at his own farm, and of course he had ample opportunity to observe just what Fern is watching.

8. Charlotte's manner of speaking here—as well as her general deportment—are again reminiscent of Don Marquis's cat mehitabel, of whom White had written recently. White used Marquis's description of mehitabel—*toujours gai*, ever gay—for Charlotte: "I would hate to see Charlotte turned into a 'dedicated' spider: she is, if anything, more the Mehitabel type—toujours gai."[5]

E. B. White with geese on his farm

the under side of the leaf of the potato vine are the bright orange eggs of the potato bug.

It was on a day in early summer that the goose eggs hatched.[7] This was an important event in the barn cellar. Fern was there, sitting on her stool, when it happened.

Except for the goose herself, Charlotte was the first to know that the goslings had at last arrived. The goose knew a day in advance that they were coming—she could hear their weak voices calling from inside the egg. She knew that they were in a desperately cramped position inside the shell and were most anxious to break through and get out. So she sat quite still, and talked less than usual.

When the first gosling poked its grey-green head through the goose's feathers and looked around, Charlotte spied it and made the announcement.

"I am sure," she said, "that every one of us here will be gratified to learn that after four weeks of unremitting effort and patience on the part of our friend the goose, she now has something to show for it.[8] The goslings have arrived. May I offer my sincere congratulations!"

"Thank you, thank you, thank you!" said the goose, nodding and bowing shamelessly.

"Thank you," said the gander.

"Congratulations!" shouted Wilbur. "How many goslings are there? I can only see one."

"There are seven," said the goose.

"Fine!" said Charlotte. "Seven is a lucky number."

"Luck had nothing to do with this," said the goose.[9] "It was good management and hard work."

At this point, Templeton showed his nose from his hiding place under Wilbur's trough.[10] He glanced at Fern, then crept cautiously toward the goose, keeping close to the wall. Everyone watched him, for he was not well liked, not trusted.

"Look," he began in his sharp voice, "you say you have seven goslings. There were eight eggs. What happened to the other egg? Why didn't it hatch?"

"It's a dud, I guess," said the goose.

"What are you going to do with it?" continued Templeton, his little round beady eyes fixed on the goose.

"You can have it," replied the goose. "Roll it away and add it to that nasty collection of yours."[11] (Templeton had a habit of picking up unusual objects around the farm and storing them in his home. He saved everything.)

"Certainly-ertainly-ertainly," said the gander. "You may have the egg. But I'll tell you one thing, Templeton, if I ever catch you poking-oking-oking your ugly nose around our goslings, I'll give you the worst pounding a rat ever took."[12] And the gander opened his strong wings and beat the air with them to show his power. He was strong and brave, but the truth is, both the

Page 45

9. The goose is not sentimental. It's not luck—it's staying put on top of eight eggs for a long time.

10. In his essay titled "Sanitation," White wrote, "I was spreading some poison in the barn the other day for mine enemies the rats, when . . ."[6]

The character of Templeton is skillfully developed by White, partly by the words used to describe him, partly by the scene, and partly by the brief colloquy showing Templeton's scavenging avarice.

Templeton creeps, and he has a sharp voice. Jonathan Swift used the same word, *creep*, in *Gulliver's Travels* to describe his petty and scheming Lilliputians' small-minded competitiveness—"leaping and creeping" to attain their little prizes.

In addition to the words White as narrator uses, we have the report of witnesses to the barnyard scene who, in their conversation, give us reliable firsthand information that the rat is a collector of all things putrid.

11. "A collection, whether of birds' eggs or of funny pieces, is likely to reveal more about the collector than about the subject."[7]

White held similar views about "style" in expression, maintaining that the *manner* in which one said something indicated as much about one's person as *what* one said. "Style," he said, "takes its final shape . . . from attitudes of mind."[8]

12. Indeed, geese are strong and can do considerable damage.

Page 46

13. Henceforth, Fern will take a backseat with the illustrator, not only because of her changing role in the story, but also, perhaps, because White wrote Nordstrom that she should not be pictured too often because that would make the animals appear too small in the pictures.[13]

14. White no more trims the sails of his lexicon than does Beatrix Potter when she says that the "sparrows implored [Peter Rabbit] to exert himself."[9]

White's personal view of rats was even less friendly than that expressed in the book. In *SL*, one of the "laws for the world" the fifth graders devise is "Never poison anything but rats."[10] And in the confessional vein, White wrote,

> I shot twelve or thirteen rats last winter and poisoned as many more. . . . The rat has only one thing to be said for him: he supplies you with a tangible enemy on whom to vent your hate. I can take out a good deal on rats.[11]

Of Templeton, specifically, White wrote Gene Deitch:

> As for Templeton, he's an old acquaintance and I know him well. He starts as a rat and he ends as a rat—the perfect opportunist and a great gourmand.[12]

15. Even were there nothing on the page but this, we'd be amply rewarded.

13

goose and the gander were worried about Templeton. And with good reason. The rat had no morals, no conscience, no scruples,[14] no consideration, no decency, no milk of rodent kindness,[15] no compunctions, no higher feeling, no friendliness, no anything. He would kill a gosling if he could get away with it—the goose knew that. Everybody knew it.

With her broad bill the goose pushed the unhatched egg out of the nest, and the entire company watched in disgust while the rat rolled it away. Even Wilbur, who could eat almost anything, was appalled. "Imagine wanting a junky old rotten egg!" he muttered.

"A rat is a rat," said Charlotte. She laughed a tinkling little laugh. "But, my friends, if that ancient egg ever breaks, this barn will be untenable."

"What's that mean?" asked Wilbur.[16]

"It means nobody will be able to live here on account of the smell. A rotten egg is a regular stink bomb."

"I won't break it," snarled Templeton. "I know what I'm doing. I handle stuff like this all the time."[17]

He disappeared into his tunnel, pushing the goose egg in front of him. He pushed and nudged till he succeeded in rolling it to his lair under the trough.

That afternoon, when the wind had died down and the barnyard was quiet and warm, the grey goose led her seven goslings off the nest and out into the world. Mr. Zuckerman spied them when he came with Wilbur's supper.

"Well, hello there!" he said, smiling all over. "Let's see . . . one, two, three, four, five, six, seven. Seven baby geese. Now isn't that lovely!"

Page 47

16. Again Charlotte as teacher, as Wilbur asks her the meaning of the word.

17. Each creature is characterized by his or her diction—the language used. Templeton uses the lingo of a garbage man—or, to be more up-to-date, the manager of a toxic waste dump.

Page 48

1. This is another of the passages modulated syntactically in a manner White is fond of and employs frequently: several brief, staccato sentences followed by a longer, melodious one. Contemplate the pace, the alternation of the liquid and the hard sounds of the two concluding phrases: "complaining about them, and putting up screens"—the slow whine of "complaining about," and the rat-tat-tat of "putting up screens."

For discussions of White's syntax, see Fuller (1959) and Neumeyer (1987).

2. Spiders don't normally eat dead prey; they do, actually, literally stun or put their victims to sleep. At the same time, White, surely consciously, continues his campaign for straight talk, not genteelisms like "put to sleep" when you mean "murder."

"Put to sleep" may be the cliché through which Wilbur, just learning the language and uttering pomposities like "the person or persons," *would* perceive the occasion.

On the next page, however, the sheep, who has been around, doesn't mince words, saying, straight out, "murder" and "kill."

As we did in the case of Templeton (see page 17), we can again infer character from someone's mode of expression. Of Charlotte, we are told that she has a sweet, musical voice. But with that voice, she says words that are really quite sinister—in her sophisticated and disarming way: "I always give them [her victims] an anesthetic so they won't feel pain. It's a little service I throw in." *"Toujours gai"* indeed!

Chapter VII

Bad News

WILBUR liked Charlotte better and better each day. Her campaign against insects seemed sensible and useful. Hardly anybody around the farm had a good word to say for a fly. Flies spent their time pestering others. The cows hated them. The horses detested them. The sheep loathed them. Mr. and Mrs. Zuckerman were always complaining about them, and putting up screens.[1]

Wilbur admired the way Charlotte managed. He was particularly glad that she always put her victim to sleep before eating it.[2]

"It's real thoughtful of you to do that, Charlotte," he said.

"Yes," she replied in her sweet, musical voice, "I always give them an anaesthetic so they won't feel pain. It's a little service I throw in."

As the days went by, Wilbur grew and grew. He ate three big meals a day. He spent long hours lying on his side, half asleep, dreaming pleasant dreams. He enjoyed

good health and he gained a lot of weight. One afternoon, when Fern was sitting on her stool, the oldest sheep walked into the barn, and stopped to pay a call on Wilbur.

"Hello!" she said. "Seems to me you're putting on weight."

"Yes, I guess I am," replied Wilbur. "At my age it's a good idea to keep gaining."

"Just the same, I don't envy you," said the old sheep. "You know why they're fattening you up, don't you?"

"No," said Wilbur.

"Well, I don't like to spread bad news," said the sheep, "but they're fattening you up because they're going to kill you, that's why."

"They're going to *what*?" screamed Wilbur. Fern grew rigid on her stool.[3]

"Kill you. Turn you into smoked bacon and ham,"[4] continued the old sheep. "Almost all young pigs get murdered by the farmer as soon as the real cold weather sets in.[5] There's a regular conspiracy around here to kill you at Christmastime. Everybody is in the plot—Lurvy, Zuckerman, even John Arable."

"Mr. Arable?" sobbed Wilbur. "Fern's father?"

"Certainly. When a pig is to be butchered, everybody helps. I'm an old sheep and I see the same thing, same old business, year after year. Arable arrives with his .22, shoots the . . ."[6]

3. There is, of course, no question but that the barnyard animals understand each other. Still, this is the first really strong suggestion that Fern understands what the animals say. Since there's a slight chance that Fern grew rigid simply because Wilbur screamed, we will have to wait for conclusive evidence that she truly does understand the animals.

4. Another player characterized by mode of expression. The sheep is socially obtuse, and Wilbur's innocence is further accentuated in this passage as well.

5. If we still need evidence that this book is concerned with the use of language, and that White was being not only scientifically accurate but ironic as well when he used the phrase "put to sleep," the evidence is here. Although Charlotte, in Wilbur's way of thinking, "puts her victims to sleep," the farmer, in the sheep's gauche but accurate manner of speaking, "murders" pigs.

It has been argued that we perceive and reflect our universe by the words we use. Here, then, we learn how Mr. Arable, Wilbur, and the sheep view their worlds.

6. The sheep's gaucheness defies description. Still, in Draft F the passage was even worse: "shoots ~~the pig behind the ear, then Lurvy takes a sharp knife and . . .~~"

Page 50

7. White etches deeper the picture of Wilbur as a creature of mercurial emotions, mood swings, hysteria. For the young reader, it is important to make clear distinctions between the two protagonists—cool Charlotte and emotional Wilbur.

In addition, White is laying groundwork, for by book's end, Wilbur will have grown beyond this egocentrism and will have acted selflessly. Early speeches such as this one permit the development of his character. They allow the author to show, and the reader to perceive, Wilbur's growth.

8. If we didn't know it before, we know now: Charlotte is masterful.

9. The word *awful* is a judgment by the objective narrator.

"Stop!" screamed Wilbur. "I don't want to die! Save me, somebody! Save me!"[7] Fern was just about to jump up when a voice was heard.

"Be quiet, Wilbur!" said Charlotte,[8] who had been listening to this awful[9] conversation.

"I can't be quiet," screamed Wilbur, racing up and down. "I don't want to be killed. I don't want to die. Is it true what the old sheep says, Charlotte? Is it true they are going to kill me when the cold weather comes?"

"Well," said the spider, plucking thoughtfully at her

web, "the old sheep has been around this barn a long time. She has seen many a spring pig come and go. If she says they plan to kill you, I'm sure it's true. It's also the dirtiest trick I ever heard of. What people don't think of!"

Wilbur burst into tears. "I don't *want* to die," he moaned. "I want to stay alive, right here in my comfortable manure pile with all my friends. I want to breathe the beautiful air and lie in the beautiful sun."

"You're certainly making a beautiful noise," snapped the old sheep.

"I don't want to die!" screamed Wilbur, throwing himself to the ground.

"You shall not die," said Charlotte, briskly.

"What? Really?" cried Wilbur. "Who's going to save me?"

"I am," said Charlotte.

"How?" asked Wilbur.

"That remains to be seen. But I am going to save you, and I want you to quiet down immediately. You're carrying on in a childish way. Stop your crying! I can't stand hysterics."[10]

Page 51

10. At the end of the chapter, Charlotte's talent for control is stressed.

This chapter has provided a welcome change of pace. In contrast to the somewhat static lyricism and description ("weather," Mark Twain called it) of Chapter VI, fast-paced conversation furthers the narrative in Chapter VII.

Like a musical composition, a longer work of fiction may have varying tempi. White succeeded in this art of changing pace even though this was only his second experience at writing a novel. It's not a strategy particularly noticeable in *Stuart Little*.

Page 52

1. The novel's stereotype of little boys persists. Or: Avery continues to fulfill a societal stereotype. Or: Boys and slingshots do have a natural affinity.

2. Important, for here is proof positive that Fern truly can understand what the animals say to each other. We have it on the authority of the omniscient author that the goose did tell Templeton what Fern here says he said, and we have it from the reliable narrator as well that the rat's name is Templeton. These, both, are facts in the universe of the novel. There is no way Fern could know them if she did not understand what the animals were saying to each other.

We have no evidence or reason to believe that Fern can talk *to* animals, however.

After composing several false starts without a central human character, White realized he needed one in the story; and once he had inserted a whole "realistic" human family, he needed a device to make the barnyard conversations plausible.

It's one of the bittersweet melodies in the book that, in time, Fern loses her power to understand.

3. Significantly, Fern still thinks of the barnyard animals and herself as "us." This, of course, will change soon.

Chapter VIII

A Talk At Home

ON SUNDAY morning Mr. and Mrs. Arable and Fern were sitting at breakfast in the kitchen. Avery had finished and was upstairs looking for his slingshot.[1]

"Did you know that Uncle Homer's goslings had hatched?" asked Fern.

"How many?" asked Mr. Arable.

"Seven," replied Fern. "There were eight eggs but one egg didn't hatch and the goose told Templeton she didn't want it any more, so he took it away."[2]

"The goose did what?" asked Mrs. Arable, gazing at her daughter with a queer, worried look.

"Told Templeton she didn't want the egg any more," repeated Fern.

"Who is Templeton?" asked Mrs. Arable.

"He's the rat," replied Fern. "None of us like him much."[3]

"Who's 'us'?" asked Mr. Arable.

"Oh, everybody in the barn cellar. Wilbur and the

sheep and the lambs and the goose and the gander and the goslings and Charlotte and me."

"Charlotte?" said Mrs. Arable. "Who's Charlotte?"

"She's Wilbur's best friend. She's terribly clever."[4]

"What does she look like?" asked Mrs. Arable.

"Well-l," said Fern, thoughtfully, "she has eight legs. All spiders do, I guess."

"Charlotte is a spider?" asked Fern's mother.

Fern nodded. "A big grey one. She has a web across the top of Wilbur's doorway. She catches flies and sucks their blood. Wilbur adores her."

"Does he really?" said Mrs. Arable, rather vaguely. She was staring at Fern with a worried expression on her face.

"Oh, yes, Wilbur adores Charlotte," said Fern. "Do you know what Charlotte said when the goslings hatched?"

"I haven't the faintest idea," said Mr. Arable. "Tell us."

"Well, when the first gosling stuck its little head out from under the goose, I was sitting on my stool in the corner and Charlotte was on her web. She made a speech. She said: 'I am sure that every one of us here in the barn cellar will be gratified to learn that after four weeks of unremitting effort[5] and patience on the part of the goose, she now has something to show for

Page 53

4. Testimony of a credible witness. As evidence, this technique for developing character lies somewhere between "showing" and "telling."

5. Since the absolutely reliable narrator quotes what Charlotte actually said (see page 44), we have irrefutable evidence that Fern heard and understood the animals' talk. "Gratified" and "unremitting" would not be in Fern's vocabulary. (By contrast, in Maurice Sendak's *Where the Wild Things Are*, Max's monsters speak to the little boy in just the language Max would use—and which he had undoubtedly heard from his mother.)

Page 54

6. The portrait of the worried, and then abstracted, Mrs. Arable is amusing. On the previous page, Fern for the first time told Mrs. Arable about a spider named Charlotte, whom Wilbur adores. Mrs. Arable asked, "Does he really ?" and looked a bit concerned about her daughter. Now she says, in effect, "That's right, dear," and then dismisses the conversation with the day's humdrum business—as though she meant, "Yes, you go right ahead and have your little imaginative game, but now let's get going on *real* things." Of course, in reality she hasn't dismissed the matter from her mind at all. Two paragraphs later, she expresses her concern to her husband when she says, "I worry about Fern."

Mr. Arable's "Maybe they do talk. . . . I've sometimes wondered" sounds like the E. B. White of the skeptical and bemused essays.

7. Again, Mr. Arable at times speaks for White. His views are quite like those of Dr. Dorian later.

it.' Don't you think that was a pleasant thing for her to say?"

"Yes, I do," said Mrs. Arable.[6] "And now, Fern, it's time to get ready for Sunday School. And tell Avery to get ready. And this afternoon you can tell me more about what goes on in Uncle Homer's barn. Aren't you spending quite a lot of time there? You go there almost every afternoon, don't you?"

"I like it there," replied Fern. She wiped her mouth and ran upstairs. After she had left the room, Mrs. Arable spoke in a low voice to her husband.

"I worry about Fern," she said. "Did you hear the way she rambled on about the animals, pretending that they talked?"

Mr. Arable chuckled. "Maybe they do talk," he said. "I've sometimes wondered. At any rate, don't worry about Fern—she's just got a lively imagination. Kids think they hear all sorts of things."

"Just the same, I *do* worry about her," replied Mrs. Arable. "I think I shall ask Dr. Dorian about her the next time I see him. He loves Fern almost as much as we do, and I want him to know how queerly she is acting about that pig and everything. I don't think it's normal. You know perfectly well animals don't talk."

Mr. Arable grinned. "Maybe our ears aren't as sharp as Fern's," he said.[7]

Chapter IX

Wilbur's Boast

A SPIDER'S web is stronger than it looks. Although it is made of thin, delicate strands, the web is not easily broken. However, a web gets torn every day by the insects that kick around in it, and a spider must rebuild it when it gets full of holes. Charlotte liked to do her weaving during the late afternoon,[1] and Fern liked to sit nearby and watch. One afternoon she heard a most interesting conversation and witnessed a strange event.

"You have awfully hairy legs, Charlotte," said Wilbur, as the spider busily worked at her task.

"My legs are hairy for a good reason," replied Charlotte. "Furthermore, each leg of mine has seven sections—the coxa, the trochanter, the femur, the patella, the tibia, the metatarsus, and the tarsus."[2]

Wilbur sat bolt upright. "You're kidding," he said.

"No, I'm not, either."

"Say those names again, I didn't catch them the first time."

Page 55

1. We actually know a little more about the weaving ritual now than White could have known. Dr. Donald Edmonds and Dr. Friz Vollrath, Oxford University, have found that a number of spiders who cannot wander looking for moisture, but must remain near their webs to take their prey, have a real problem retaining enough moisture. In the early-morning hours, dewdrops form on the webs, and the spiders, who seem actually to be devouring their webs every morning, are, in fact, drinking in the moisture from the web and from the insects caught in it, therewith restoring about 10 percent of the daily respiratory loss of water.

Not only that, but the water taken up by the web during the day helps make the web itself stickier, thus more efficient as a trap for the insects.[1]

2. On White's worksheets, one may observe how carefully he studied the anatomy of spiders.

See plate 5, page 189.

Page 56

3. White does not often exploit his privileged position as an omniscient narrator in order to tell us what a character is feeling.

On the draft sheet for this page, we may see the extent of White's deletions. Clarity, brevity, and positive assertion were the main stylistic heritage White obtained from William Strunk, Jr. White cut his own text ruthlessly. One can get a sense of this simply from the change of "'I might be able to spin a web'" to "'I could spin a web.'"

See plate 6, page 190.

"Coxa, trochanter, femur, patella, tibia, metatarsus, and tarsus."

"Goodness!" said Wilbur, looking down at his own chubby legs. "I don't think *my* legs have seven sections."

"Well," said Charlotte, "you and I lead different lives. You don't have to spin a web. That takes real leg work."

"I could spin a web if I tried," said Wilbur, boasting. "I've just never tried."

"Let's see you do it," said Charlotte. Fern chuckled softly, and her eyes grew wide with love for the pig.[3]

"O.K.," replied Wilbur. "You coach me and I'll spin one. It must be a lot of fun to spin a web. How do I start?"

"Take a deep breath!" said Charlotte, smiling. Wilbur breathed deeply. "Now climb to the highest place you can get to, like this." Charlotte raced up to the top of the doorway. Wilbur scrambled to the top of the manure pile.

"Very good!" said Charlotte. "Now make an attachment with your spinnerets, hurl yourself into space, and let out a dragline as you go down!"

Wilbur hesitated a moment, then jumped out into the air. He glanced hastily behind to see if a piece of rope was following him to check his fall, but nothing seemed to be happening in his rear, and the next thing

he knew he landed with a thump. "Ooomp!" he grunted.

Charlotte laughed so hard her web began to sway.

"What did I do wrong?" asked the pig, when he recovered from his bump.

"Nothing," said Charlotte. "It was a nice try."

"I think I'll try again," said Wilbur, cheerfully. "I believe what I need is a little piece of string to hold me."

The pig walked out to his yard. "You there, Templeton?" he called. The rat poked his head out from under the trough.

"Got a little piece of string I could borrow?" asked Wilbur. "I need it to spin a web."

"Yes, indeed," replied Templeton, who saved string. "No trouble at all. Anything to oblige." He crept down into his hole, pushed the goose egg out of the way, and returned with an old piece of dirty white string. Wilbur examined it.

"That's just the thing," he said. "Tie one end to my tail, will you, Templeton?"

Wilbur crouched low, with his thin, curly tail toward the rat. Templeton seized the string, passed it around the end of the pig's tail, and tied two half hitches. Charlotte watched in delight. Like Fern, she was truly fond of Wilbur, whose smelly pen and stale food attracted the flies that she needed,[4] and she was proud to see that

Page 57

4. Again, in the most important letter pertaining to *Charlotte's Web*, White wrote that "it would be quite untrue to suggest that barnyard creatures are dependent on each other."[2] But certainly precisely such an interdependency was his frequent theme—not only for the barnyard, but for world affairs (see, e.g., *SL*, Chapter 12).

Pages 58, 59

5. The illustrations of Templeton on these two pages make one think that Garth Williams must have had a special affection for him. If we note the accurately small rodent eyes and compare them to other Williams rodents, we can conclude that the artist almost heeded White's request not to give animals human faces.

Note again that the illustrator is attracted to moments of action in a book filled with rumination.

5

he was not a quitter and was willing to try again to spin a web.

While the rat and the spider and the little girl watched, Wilbur climbed again to the top of the manure pile, full of energy and hope.

"Everybody watch!" he cried. And summoning all his strength, he threw himself into the air, headfirst. The string trailed behind him. But as he had neglected to fasten the other end to anything, it didn't really do any good, and Wilbur landed with a thud, crushed and hurt. Tears came to his eyes. Templeton grinned. Charlotte just sat quietly. After a bit she spoke.

"You can't spin a web, Wilbur, and I advise you to put the idea out of your mind. You lack two things needed for spinning a web."

"What are they?" asked Wilbur, sadly.

"You lack a set of spinnerets, and you lack know-

6. This is a verbal joke—a very little one, but a nice one nonetheless. One catches things *in* a web. Charlotte has explained the Queensborough Bridge as though it were a web. Wilbur does not know that things are *on* the bridge, not *in* it—and he applies the same preposition, *in*, that is appropriate for the web, to the bridge.

White moved the word *bugs* to follow *Bridge*, rather than placing it after "asked Wilbur." Probably this was for euphony and precision: "Keep related words together."[3] Even though this instance is not identical to White's bad examples in his style manual, his reason is undoubtedly the same, as always—clarity.

See plate 7, page 191.

7. That's what White felt when he lived in New York. It's why he moved to Maine in 1938.

how. But cheer up, you don't need a web. Zuckerman supplies you with three big meals a day. Why should you worry about trapping food?"

Wilbur sighed. "You're ever so much cleverer and brighter than I am, Charlotte. I guess I was just trying to show off. Serves me right."

Templeton untied his string and took it back to his home. Charlotte returned to her weaving.

"You needn't feel too badly, Wilbur," she said. "Not many creatures can spin webs. Even men aren't as good at it as spiders, although they *think* they're pretty good, and they'll *try* anything. Did you ever hear of the Queensborough Bridge?"

Wilbur shook his head. "Is it a web?"

"Sort of," replied Charlotte. "But do you know how long it took men to build it? Eight whole years. My goodness, I would have starved to death waiting that long. I can make a web in a single evening."

"What do people catch in the Queensborough Bridge—bugs?" asked Wilbur.[6]

"No," said Charlotte. "They don't catch anything. They just keep trotting back and forth across the bridge thinking there is something better on the other side. If they'd hang head-down at the top of the thing and wait quietly, maybe something good would come along. But no—with men it's rush, rush, rush, every minute.[7] I'm glad I'm a sedentary spider."

Wilbur's Boast

"What does sedentary mean?" asked Wilbur.[8]

"Means I sit still a good part of the time and don't go wandering all over creation.[9] I know a good thing when I see it, and my web is a good thing. I stay put and wait for what comes. Gives me a chance to think."

"Well, I'm sort of sedentary myself, I guess," said the pig. "I have to hang around here whether I want to or not. You know where I'd really like to be this evening?"

"Where?"

"In a forest looking for beechnuts and truffles and delectable roots, pushing leaves aside with my wonderful strong nose, searching and sniffing along the ground, smelling, smelling, smelling . . ."

"You smell just the way you are,"[10] remarked a lamb who had just walked in. "I can smell you from here. You're the smelliest creature in the place."

Wilbur hung his head. His eyes grew wet with tears. Charlotte noticed his embarrassment and she spoke sharply to the lamb.

"Let Wilbur alone!"[11] she said. "He has a perfect right to smell, considering his surroundings. You're no bundle of sweet peas yourself. Furthermore, you are interrupting a very pleasant conversation. What were we talking about, Wilbur, when we were so rudely interrupted?"

"Oh, I don't remember," said Wilbur. "It doesn't

Page 61

8. How often Charlotte teaches Wilbur new words!

9. In Folder A, White had written, "Means I sit still a good part of the time and don't go

promenading prancing wandering gallivanting	all over."

10. Among other things, *Charlotte's Web* is very much a book about words—so this double entendre is irresistible for White.

11. Charlotte as mother.

Page 62

12. This is one of the lyrical passages with which White modulates his story and changes his pace. White places the celebrations of the beauty of nature, the passing of time, the progress of the seasons, between longer passages of fast action and dialogue.

13. E. B. White's sentiments exactly (see also page 7).

make any difference. Let's not talk any more for a while, Charlotte. I'm getting sleepy. You go ahead and finish fixing your web and I'll just lie here and watch you. It's a lovely evening." Wilbur stretched out on his side.

Twilight settled over Zuckerman's barn, and a feeling of peace. Fern knew it was almost suppertime but she couldn't bear to leave. Swallows passed on silent wings,[12] in and out of the doorways, bringing food to their young ones. From across the road a bird sang "Whippoorwill, whippoorwill!" Lurvy sat down under an apple tree and lit his pipe; the animals sniffed the familiar smell of strong tobacco. Wilbur heard the trill of the tree toad and the occasional slamming of the kitchen door. All these sounds made him feel comfortable and happy, for he loved life and loved to be a part of the world on a summer evening.[13] But as he lay there he remembered what the old sheep had told him. The thought of death came to him and he began to tremble with fear.

"Charlotte?" he said, softly.

"Yes, Wilbur?"

"I don't want to die."

"Of course you don't," said Charlotte in a comforting voice.

"I just love it here in the barn," said Wilbur. "I love everything about this place."

"Of course you do," said Charlotte. "We all do."

The goose appeared, followed by her seven goslings. They thrust their little necks out and kept up a musical whistling, like a tiny troupe of pipers. Wilbur listened to the sound with love in his heart.

"Charlotte?" he said.

"Yes?" said the spider.

"Were you serious when you promised you would keep them from killing me?"

"I was never more serious in my life. I am not going to let you die, Wilbur."

"How are you going to save me?" asked Wilbur, whose curiosity was very strong on this point.[14]

"Well," said Charlotte, vaguely, "I don't really know. But I'm working on a plan."

"That's wonderful," said Wilbur. "How is the plan coming, Charlotte? Have you got very far with it? Is it coming along pretty well?" Wilbur was trembling again, but Charlotte was cool and collected.

"Oh, it's coming all right," she said, lightly. "The plan is still in its early stages and hasn't completely shaped up yet, but I'm working on it."

"When do you work on it?" begged Wilbur.

"When I'm hanging head-down at the top of my web. That's when I do my thinking, because then all the blood is in my head."[15]

"I'd be only too glad to help in any way I can."

Page 63

14. Since obviously Wilbur is curious how his life will be saved, this ironic understatement is another instance of the narrator's stance of tolerant bemusement.

15. Yes, spiders do have blood.[4]

16. This sounds very much like advice White occasionally gave to himself in the face of writing to deadlines—in fact, in the face of life itself. The same may be said for the advice "Never hurry and never worry!" We don't know whether White hurried, but worry he certainly did.

> As a child, I was frightened but not unhappy. . . . I lacked for nothing except confidence. I suffered nothing except the routine terrors of childhood: fear of the dark, fear of the future, fear of the return to school after a summer on a lake in Maine, fear of the lavatory in the school basement where the slate urinals cascaded, fear that I was unknowing about things I should know about.[5]

17. Again, Charlotte as mother.

"Oh, I'll work it out alone," said Charlotte. "I can think better if I think alone."

"All right," said Wilbur. "But don't fail to let me know if there's anything I can do to help, no matter how slight."

"Well," replied Charlotte, "you must try to build yourself up. I want you to get plenty of sleep, and stop worrying. Never hurry and never worry! Chew your food thoroughly and eat every bit of it, except you must leave just enough for Templeton. Gain weight and stay well—that's the way you can help. Keep fit, and don't lose your nerve.[16] Do you think you understand?"

"Yes, I understand," said Wilbur.

"Go along to bed, then," said Charlotte. "Sleep is important."

Wilbur trotted over to the darkest corner of his pen and threw himself down. He closed his eyes. In another minute he spoke.

"Charlotte?" he said.

"Yes, Wilbur?"

"May I go out to my trough and see if I left any of my supper? I think I left just a tiny bit of mashed potato."

"Very well," said Charlotte. "But I want you in bed again without delay."[17]

Wilbur started to race out to his yard.

Wilbur's Boast

"Slowly, slowly!" said Charlotte. "Never hurry and never worry!"

Wilbur checked himself and crept slowly to his trough. He found a bit of potato, chewed it carefully, swallowed it, and walked back to bed. He closed his eyes and was silent for a while.

"Charlotte?" he said, in a whisper.

"Yes?"

"May I get a drink of milk? I think there are a few drops of milk left in my trough."

"No, the trough is dry, and I want you to go to sleep. No more talking! Close your eyes and go to sleep!"

Wilbur shut his eyes. Fern got up from her stool[18] and started for home, her mind full of everything she had seen and heard.

"Good night, Charlotte!" said Wilbur.

"Good night, Wilbur!"[19]

There was a pause.

"Good night, Charlotte!"

"Good night, Wilbur!"

"Good night!"

"Good night!"[20]

Page 65

18. We have been so taken up in the barnyard conversation that we probably forgot that Fern has been silently sitting here through the whole chapter.

19. "It is seldom advisable to tell all. Be sparing, for instance, in the use of adverbs after 'he said,' 'she replied,' and the like. . . . Let the conversation itself disclose the speaker's manner or condition."[6]

20. This chapter concludes like a musical composition. Lyrically it dwindles into night, into sleep. White sometimes wrote prose that is indistinguishable from poetry.

Page 66

1. Notwithstanding all White's objections to all attempts to make the animals appear human, not only does he personify Charlotte, but as an omniscient narrator, he knows what she's thinking. It would be difficult to imagine this novel if he did not employ these devices.

2. This is the illustration about which Garth Williams wrote me, "[White] put two dots on the edge of her face looking down and put 3 strokes to suggest hair on the top of her head" (Appendix A, page 199).

See plate 8, page 192.

Chapter X

An Explosion

DAY AFTER day the spider waited, head-down, for an idea to come to her. Hour by hour she sat motionless, deep in thought. Having promised Wilbur that she would save his life, she was determined to keep her promise.[1]

Charlotte was naturally patient. She knew from ex-

2

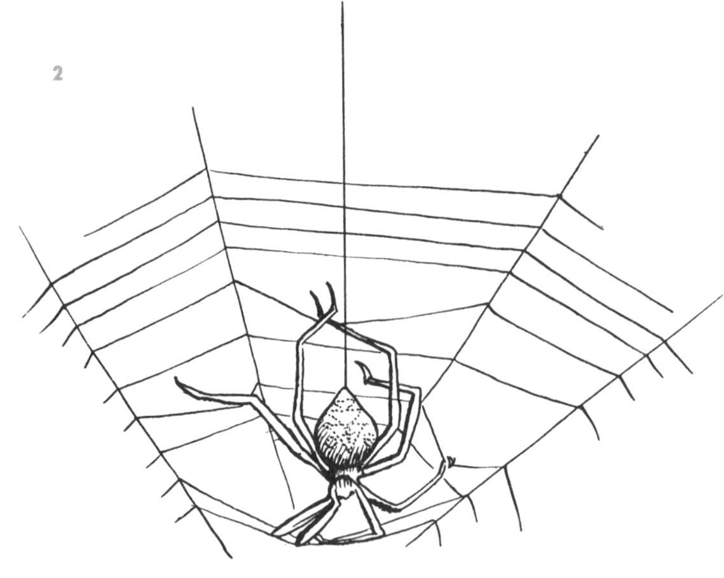

perience that if she waited long enough a fly would come to her web; and she felt sure that if she thought long enough about Wilbur's problem, an idea would come to her mind.

Finally, one morning toward the middle of July,[3] the idea came. "Why, how perfectly simple!" she said to herself. "The way to save Wilbur's life is to play a trick on Zuckerman. If I can fool a bug," thought Charlotte, "I can surely fool a man. People are not as smart as bugs."[4]

Wilbur walked into his yard just at that moment.

"What are you thinking about, Charlotte?" he asked.

"I was just thinking," said the spider, "that people are very gullible."

"What does 'gullible' mean?"

"Easy to fool," said Charlotte.

"That's a mercy," replied Wilbur, and he lay down in the shade of his fence and went fast asleep. The spider, however, stayed wide awake, gazing affectionately at him and making plans for his future. Summer was half gone. She knew she didn't have much time.[5]

That morning, just as Wilbur fell asleep, Avery Arable wandered into the Zuckerman's front yard, followed by Fern. Avery carried a live frog in his hand.

Page 67

3. Remember, Wilbur was a "spring pig" (see page 11). So he is less than six months old.

4. On the matter of the intelligence of animals, White is in good company, for even John Milton, in *Paradise Lost*, stated of animals that they "reason not contemptibly."[1]

5. Observe the manner in which White moves to stark statement of the inexorable course of nature.

6. This scene with the frog jumping into the dishpan and onto the blueberry pie is the sort of slapstick that signals Avery's presence throughout. See also pages 126–28.

Fern had a crown of daisies in her hair. The children ran for the kitchen.

"Just in time for a piece of blueberry pie," said Mrs. Zuckerman.

"Look at my frog!" said Avery, placing the frog on the drainboard and holding out his hand for pie.

"Take that thing out of here!" said Mrs. Zuckerman.

"He's hot," said Fern. "He's almost dead, that frog."

"He is not," said Avery. "He lets me scratch him between the eyes." The frog jumped and landed in Mrs. Zuckerman's dishpan full of soapy water.

"You're getting your pie on you," said Fern. "Can I look for eggs in the henhouse, Aunt Edith?"

"Run outdoors, both of you! And don't bother the hens!"

"It's getting all over everything," shouted Fern. "His pie is all over his front."

"Come on, frog!" cried Avery. He scooped up his frog. The frog kicked, splashing soapy water onto the blueberry pie.[6]

"Another crisis!" groaned Fern.

"Let's swing in the swing!" said Avery.

The children ran to the barn.

Mr. Zuckerman had the best swing in the county. It was a single long piece of heavy rope tied to the beam over the north doorway. At the bottom end of the rope was a fat knot to sit on. It was arranged so that you

could swing without being pushed. You climbed a ladder to the hayloft.[7] Then, holding the rope, you stood at the edge and looked down, and were scared and dizzy. Then you straddled the knot, so that it acted as a seat. Then you got up all your nerve, took a deep breath, and jumped. For a second you seemed to be falling to the barn floor far below, but then suddenly the rope would begin to catch you, and you would sail through the barn door going a mile a minute, with the wind whistling in your eyes and ears and hair. Then you would zoom upward into the sky, and look up at the clouds, and the rope would twist and you would twist and turn with the rope. Then you would drop down, down, down out of the sky and come sailing back into the barn almost into the hayloft, then sail out again (not quite so far this time), then in again (not quite so high), then out again, then in again, then out, then in; and then you'd jump off and fall down and let somebody else try it.

Mothers for miles around worried about Zuckerman's swing. They feared some child would fall off. But no child ever did. Children almost always hang onto things tighter than their parents think they will.

Avery put the frog in his pocket and climbed to the hayloft. "The last time I swang[8] in this swing, I almost crashed into a barn swallow," he yelled.

"Take that frog out!" ordered Fern.

Page 69

7. Observe the manner in which this paragraph—especially the last half—actually simulates the action of riding such a rope swing: first, the short, factual sentences as you stand there gathering your nerve. Then the sentence beginning "For a second you seemed to be falling," and winding on and on as the sentence itself replicates the long swoop down until the new sentence, starting "Then you would zoom upward," takes you up again. And, finally, as the arcs of the rope swing diminish, the short sentences, ending with the full stop of "let somebody else try it."

8. "Only the writer whose ear is reliable is in a position to use bad grammar deliberately."[2] White's ear is very reliable.

9. This is the most striking instance of the syntactic structure of the sentence mimicking the action described. In the beginning, Avery sails up on the rope, reaches the apex of his trajectory with the words "frog and all," and descends with the words following.

10. This paragraph is worth reading aloud a couple of times. The frog sentence is typical of the manner in which White brings us down to earth just as we are in danger of becoming sentimental. (Some have suggested that White kept a defensive distance in the face of emotional situations. I believe that theory—believe it, in fact, to be the motivation of many humorists. White believed likewise, as we can read in the preface to the *Subtreasury*.)

> . . . [Y]ou certainly don't have to be a humorist to taste the sadness of situation and mood. But, as everyone knows, there is often a rather fine line between laughing and crying, and if a humorous piece of writing brings a person to the point where his emotional responses are untrustworthy and seem likely to break over into the opposite realm, it is because humorous writing, like poetical writing, has an extra content. It plays, like an active child, close to the big hot fire which is Truth. And sometimes the reader feels the heat.[3]

Avery straddled the rope and jumped. He sailed out through the door, frog and all, and into the sky, frog and all.[9] Then he sailed back into the barn.

"Your tongue is purple!" screamed Fern.

"So is yours!" cried Avery, sailing out again with the frog.

"I have hay inside my dress! It itches!" called Fern.

"Scratch it!" yelled Avery, as he sailed back.

"It's my turn," said Fern. "Jump off!"

"Fern's got the itch!" sang Avery.

When he jumped off, he threw the swing up to his sister. She shut her eyes tight and jumped. She felt the dizzy drop, then the supporting lift of the swing. When she opened her eyes she was looking up into the blue sky and was about to fly back through the door.

They took turns for an hour.

When the children grew tired of swinging, they went down toward the pasture and picked wild raspberries and ate them. Their tongues turned from purple to red. Fern bit into a raspberry that had a bad-tasting bug inside it, and got discouraged. Avery found an empty candy box and put his frog in it. The frog seemed tired after his morning in the swing. The children walked slowly up toward the barn. They, too, were tired and hardly had energy enough to walk.[10]

"Let's build a tree house," suggested Avery. "I want to live in a tree, with my frog."

"I'm going to visit Wilbur," Fern announced.

They climbed the fence into the lane and walked lazily toward the pigpen. Wilbur heard them coming and got up.

Avery noticed the spider web, and, coming closer, he saw Charlotte.

Page 71

11. Elledge relates that when White lived, as a boy, on Summit Avenue, Mount Vernon, not only did he spend happy hours in his father's stable, but later he ventured to a neighbor's barn, "where the coachman allowed the boys to swing down from the loft on a rope."[4]

12. Thus Templeton, in his gluttony, has unwittingly been the instrument of salvation for Charlotte in the first instance, but ultimately for Wilbur too. (In an early draft, White actually had Wilbur save Charlotte by grabbing the stick away from Avery.)

White laid the groundwork for this passage in *CW*, page 47, where Templeton pushed the rotten goose egg in front of him.

The sequence of action in the sentences describing Avery's fall is scrupulous.

"Hey, look at that big spider!" he said. "It's tremenjus."

"Leave it alone!" commanded Fern. "You've got a frog—isn't that enough?"

"That's a fine spider and I'm going to capture it," said Avery. He took the cover off the candy box. Then he picked up a stick. "I'm going to knock that ol' spider into this box," he said.

Wilbur's heart almost stopped when he saw what was going on. This might be the end of Charlotte if the boy succeeded in catching her.

"You stop it, Avery!" cried Fern.

Avery put one leg over the fence of the pigpen. He was just about to raise his stick to hit Charlotte when he lost his balance. He swayed and toppled and landed on the edge of Wilbur's trough. The trough tipped up and then came down with a slap. The goose egg was right underneath. There was a dull explosion as the egg broke, and then a horrible smell.[12]

Fern screamed. Avery jumped to his feet. The air was filled with the terrible gases and smells from the rotten egg. Templeton, who had been resting in his home, scuttled away into the barn.

"Good *night*!" screamed Avery. "Good *night*! What a stink! Let's get out of here!"

Fern was crying. She held her nose and ran toward the house. Avery ran after her, holding his nose.

An Explosion

Charlotte felt greatly relieved to see him go. It had been a narrow escape.

Later on that morning, the animals came up from the pasture—the sheep, the lambs, the gander, the goose, and the seven goslings. There were many complaints

about the awful smell, and Wilbur had to tell the story over and over again, of how the Arable boy had tried to capture Charlotte, and how the smell of the broken egg drove him away just in time. "It was that rotten goose egg that saved Charlotte's life," said Wilbur.[13]

The goose was proud of her share in the adventure.

Page 73

13. Wilbur's understanding reflects my comment for the previous page.

As for the importance of eggs in White's scheme of things, consider White's views while World War II was raging:

> Countries are ransacked, valleys drenched with blood. Though it seems untimely I still publish my belief in the egg, the contents of the egg, the warm coal, and the necessity for pursuing whatever fire delights and sustains you.[5]

Both in real life as a poultry farmer and in two of his novels (*CW*, *TS*), eggs played a significant and symbolic role for E. B. White.

14. Lurvy speaks for White, again.

15. Not Lurvy's word, surely, but rather White's ironic commentary in the form of an elevated word in an unelevated context. This paragraph, too, deserves to be read aloud. The cumulative effect of "drooling," "slops," "sucked," "gulped," "swishing," and "swooshing" is as hilarious as it is poetical. Or hilarious *because* it is poetical.

"I'm delighted that the egg never hatched," she gabbled.

Templeton, of course, was miserable over the loss of his beloved egg. But he couldn't resist boasting. "It pays to save things," he said in his surly voice. "A rat never knows when something is going to come in handy. I never throw anything away."

"Well," said one of the lambs, "this whole business is all well and good for Charlotte, but what about the rest of us? The smell is unbearable. Who wants to live in a barn that is perfumed with rotten egg?"

"Don't worry, you'll get used to it," said Templeton. He sat up and pulled wisely at his long whiskers, then crept away to pay a visit to the dump.

When Lurvy showed up at lunchtime carrying a pail of food for Wilbur, he stopped short a few paces from the pigpen. He sniffed the air and made a face.

"What in thunder?" he said. Setting the pail down, he picked up the stick that Avery had dropped and pried the trough up. "Rats!" he said. "Fhew! I might a' known a rat would make a nest under this trough. How I hate a rat!"[14]

And Lurvy dragged Wilbur's trough across the yard and kicked some dirt into the rat's nest, burying the broken egg and all Templeton's other possessions.[15] Then he picked up the pail. Wilbur stood in the trough, drooling with hunger. Lurvy poured. The slops ran creamily down around the pig's eyes and ears. Wilbur grunted. He gulped and sucked, and sucked and gulped, making swishing and swooshing noises, anxious to get everything at once.[16] It was a delicious meal—skim milk, wheat middlings, leftover pancakes, half a doughnut, the rind of a summer squash, two pieces of stale toast, a third of a gingersnap, a fish tail, one orange peel, several noodles from a noodle soup, the scum off a cup of cocoa, an ancient jelly roll, a strip of paper from the lining of the garbage pail, and a spoonful of raspberry jello.

Wilbur ate heartily. He planned to leave half a noodle and a few drops of milk for Templeton. Then he remembered that the rat had been useful in saving Charlotte's life, and that Charlotte was trying to save *his* life. So he left a whole noodle, instead of a half.

Now that the broken egg was buried, the air cleared and the barn smelled good again. The afternoon passed, and evening came. Shadows lengthened. The cool and kindly breath of evening entered through doors and windows. Astride her web, Charlotte sat moodily eating a horsefly and thinking about the future.[17] After a while she bestirred herself.

She descended to the center of the web and there she began to cut some of her lines. She worked slowly but steadily while the other creatures drowsed. None of the others, not even the goose, noticed that she was

Page 75

16. Here is one of White's magnificent lists, even enumerating the precise quantities of stale toast, gingersnap, doughnut. Compare it to a somewhat similar list in *Stuart Little*, where Stuart, who has just been dumped onto a garbage scow on the East River, complains of egg on his pants, butter on his cap, gravy on his shirt, and orange pulp in his ear.[6]

17. One of White's artful sentences in which he uses a rhetorical device very typical of him—the juxtaposition of the homely and the grand, in this instance "a horsefly" and "the future."

at work. Deep in his soft bed, Wilbur snoozed. Over in their favorite corner, the goslings whistled a night song.

Charlotte tore quite a section out of her web, leaving an open space in the middle. Then she started weaving something to take the place of the threads she had removed.[18] When Templeton got back from the dump, around midnight, the spider was still at work.[19]

Page 76

18. What Charlotte is doing deviates from arachnid possibility. A spider "can build another orb with the pattern and peculiarities of its clan, but cannot repeat an earlier step out of its turn."[7]

19. White employs the device of the serialized story, ending the chapter with a suspenseful moment. And since the next chapter begins with something quite different, we remain on tenterhooks.

Chapter XI

The Miracle[1]

THE NEXT day was foggy. Everything on the farm was dripping wet. The grass looked like a magic carpet. The asparagus patch looked like a silver forest.

On foggy mornings, Charlotte's web was truly a thing of beauty. This morning each thin strand was decorated with dozens of tiny beads of water. The web glistened in the light and made a pattern of loveliness and mystery, like a delicate veil. Even Lurvy, who wasn't particularly interested in beauty, noticed the web when he came with the pig's breakfast. He noted how clearly it showed up and he noted how big and carefully built it was. And then he took another look and he saw something that made him set his pail down. There, in the center of the web, neatly woven in block letters, was a message. It said:

SOME PIG!

Lurvy felt weak. He brushed his hand across his eyes and stared harder at Charlotte's web.

Page 77

1. "Some Pig," written in the web, will obviously seem a miracle to our human characters. To E. B. White, however, the very web itself is amply miraculous. The lovely second paragraph on this page is evidence, but so is a great deal of White's other nature writing.

Specifically, White had in mind that, entirely by instinct, a "baby orb weaver spins a perfect orb web soon after it leaves the egg sac."[1]

As to White's explicit commentary on miracles, in the margin of the film version (see pages 208–9), he wrote, "and when you are dealing in miracles, the place to begin is at the beginning."

Page 78

2. In this dramatic moment, White does not interject his own voice. The characters' words speak for themselves.

"To air one's views gratuitously . . . is to imply that the demand for them is brisk, which may not be the case. . . ."[2]

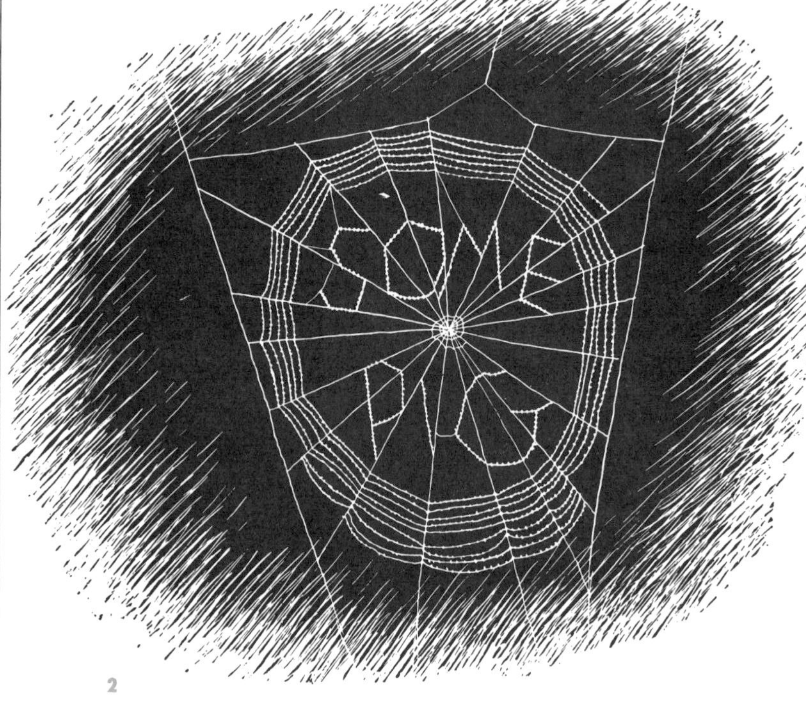

2

"I'm seeing things," he whispered. He dropped to his knees and uttered a short prayer. Then, forgetting all about Wilbur's breakfast, he walked back to the house and called Mr. Zuckerman.

"I think you'd better come down to the pigpen," he said.

"What's the trouble?" asked Mr. Zuckerman. "Anything wrong with the pig?"

"N-not exactly," said Lurvy. "Come and see for yourself."

The Miracle

The two men walked silently down to Wilbur's yard. Lurvy pointed to the spider's web. "Do you see what I see?" he asked.

Zuckerman stared at the writing on the web. Then he murmured the words "Some Pig." Then he looked at Lurvy. Then they both began to tremble. Charlotte, sleepy after her night's exertions, smiled as she watched. Wilbur came and stood directly under the web.

"Some pig!" muttered Lurvy in a low voice.

"Some pig!" whispered Mr. Zuckerman. They stared and stared for a long time at Wilbur. Then they stared at Charlotte.

"You don't suppose that that spider . . ." began Mr. Zuckerman—but he shook his head and didn't finish the sentence. Instead, he walked solemnly back up to the house and spoke to his wife. "Edith, something has happened," he said, in a weak voice. He went into the living room and sat down, and Mrs. Zuckerman followed.

"I've got something to tell you, Edith," he said. "You better sit down."

Mrs. Zuckerman sank into a chair. She looked pale and frightened.

"Edith," he said, trying to keep his voice steady,[3] "I think you had best be told that we have a very unusual pig."

Page 79

3. White occasionally gives his characters a melodramatic tone—a voice reminiscent perhaps of the old radio drama. We find the same device in the language of the father swan, the cob, in *TS*.

Zuckerman thinks it's the pig who's unusual, not the web. This misperception foreshadows the general public misperceptions that follow.

Page 80

4. This simple, cumulative ("... and ... and ...") sentence pattern is unusual for White. It seems parodistic of biblical style and quite appropriate for a miracle.

Pages 80–81

5. Mr. Zuckerman is a little dense. He represents the view that if something is in writing, it must be so. He persists in this delusion four paragraphs later: "You see, Edith? It's just a common grey spider."

A look of complete bewilderment came over Mrs. Zuckerman's face. "Homer Zuckerman, what in the world are you talking about?" she said.

"This is a very serious thing, Edith," he replied. "Our pig is completely out of the ordinary."

"What's unusual about the pig?" asked Mrs. Zuckerman, who was beginning to recover from her scare.

"Well, I don't really know yet," said Mr. Zuckerman. "But we have received a sign, Edith—a mysterious sign. A miracle has happened on this farm. There is a large spider's web in the doorway of the barn cellar, right over the pigpen, and when Lurvy went to feed the pig this morning, he noticed the web because it was foggy, and you know how a spider's web looks very distinct in a fog. And right spang in the middle of the web there were the words 'Some Pig.' The words were woven right into the web. They were actually part of the web, Edith. I know, because I have been down there and seen them. It says, 'Some Pig,' just as clear as clear can be. There can be no mistake about it. A miracle has happened and a sign has occurred here on earth, right on our farm, and we have no ordinary pig."[4]

"Well," said Mrs. Zuckerman, "it seems to me you're a little off. It seems to me we have no ordinary *spider*."[5]

"Oh, no," said Zuckerman. "It's the pig that's unusual. It says so, right there in the middle of the web."

"Maybe so," said Mrs. Zuckerman. "Just the same, I intend to have a look at that spider."

"It's just a common grey spider," said Zuckerman.

They got up, and together they walked down to Wilbur's yard. "You see, Edith? It's just a common grey spider."

Wilbur was pleased to receive so much attention. Lurvy was still standing there, and Mr. and Mrs. Zuckerman, all three, stood for about an hour, reading the words on the web over and over, and watching Wilbur.

Charlotte was delighted with the way her trick was working. She sat without moving a muscle,[6] and listened to the conversation of the people. When a small fly blundered into the web,[7] just beyond the word "pig," Charlotte dropped quickly down, rolled the fly up, and carried it out of the way.

After a while the fog lifted. The web dried off and the words didn't show up so plainly. The Zuckermans and Lurvy walked back to the house. Just before they left the pigpen, Mr. Zuckerman took one last look at Wilbur.

"You know," he said, in an important voice, "I've thought all along that that pig of ours was an extra good one. He's a solid pig. That pig is as solid as they come.

Page 81

6. Yes, spiders do have muscles.

7. Nature takes its course in the barn. The delicate balance between fantasy and Darwinian reality was a concern for White, especially in connection with the illustrator's and the filmmakers' inclination to humanize and prettify (or trivialize) the characters. Nor did White ever make concessions to those who objected to Charlotte's own death at the end of the work.

Page 82

8. This is a rendering of two people trying to make conversation and at a loss for words. It is worth reading aloud.

9. It's amusing, the manner in which these good, skilled farm people pick up catch phrases that are in the air—in this case, very literally a catch phrase in the air.

You notice how solid he is around the shoulders, Lurvy?"[8]

"Sure. Sure I do," said Lurvy. "I've always noticed that pig. He's quite a pig."

"He's long, and he's smooth," said Zuckerman.

"That's right," agreed Lurvy. "He's as smooth as they come. He's some pig."[9]

When Mr. Zuckerman got back to the house, he took off his work clothes and put on his best suit. Then he got into his car and drove to the minister's house. He stayed for an hour and explained to the minister that a miracle had happened on the farm.

"So far," said Zuckerman, "only four people on earth know about this miracle—myself, my wife Edith, my hired man Lurvy, and you."

"Don't tell anybody else," said the minister. "We don't know what it means yet, but perhaps if I give thought to it, I can explain it in my sermon next Sunday. There can be no doubt that you have a most unusual pig. I intend to speak about it in my sermon and point out the fact that this community has been visited with a wondrous animal. By the way, does the pig have a name?"

"Why, yes," said Mr. Zuckerman. "My little niece calls him Wilbur. She's a rather queer child—full of

notions. She raised the pig on a bottle and I bought him from her when he was a month old." 10

He shook hands with the minister, and left.

Secrets are hard to keep. Long before Sunday came, the news spread all over the county. Everybody knew

11

that a sign had appeared in a spider's web on the Zuckerman place. Everybody knew that the Zuckermans had a wondrous pig. People came from miles around to look at Wilbur and to read the words on Charlotte's web. The Zuckermans' driveway was full of cars and trucks from morning till night—Fords and Chevvies 12 and Buick roadmasters and GMC pickups and Plym-

Page 83

10. To be precise, Uncle Homer bought Wilbur when the pig was five weeks old (see *CW*, p. 12).

11. There was some discussion about the design of the barn. E. B. White wrote Ursula Nordstrom, "Garth has drawn a set of double barn doors on a track, but they are at least twelve feet off the ground. Anybody coming through those doors would fall and break his neck. They (the doors) ought to be on ground level—on the side of the barn, not the end of the barn."[3]

When Katharine White saw the film version of *Charlotte's Web*, she expressed her dismay at the transformation the filmmakers had wrought on the Whites' barn.[4]

The barn that was eventually drawn for this page is, in fact, White's North Brooklin barn.

12. Again, White's penchant for specificity. As one critic noted, "You could . . . choose your car from his traffic jam."[5]

Page 84

13. White once wrote an amusing, satirical essay about innovations from Detroit, underscoring the idiocy of larger fenders, smaller windows, larger hoods, lower seats, and increasingly reduced visibility for the driver.[6]

14. Since among the Arables all admiration for the "miracle" went to Wilbur, it's not quite clear why Mrs. Arable should be shocked by Avery's going after the "mere" spider. And since Avery hadn't known of the miracle when he tried to hit the spider, the punishment seems misplaced.

Pages 84–85

15. White is wonderfully deadpan. Certainly *any* doctor of divinity must be able to explain a miracle!

ouths and Studebakers and Packards and De Sotos with gyromatic transmissions[13] and Oldsmobiles with rocket engines and Jeep station wagons and Pontiacs. The news of the wonderful pig spread clear up into the hills, and farmers came rattling down in buggies and buckboards, to stand hour after hour at Wilbur's pen admiring the miraculous animal. All said they had never seen such a pig before in their lives.

When Fern told her mother that Avery had tried to hit the Zuckermans' spider with a stick, Mrs. Arable was so shocked that she sent Avery to bed without any supper, as punishment.[14]

In the days that followed, Mr. Zuckerman was so busy entertaining visitors that he neglected his farm work. He wore his good clothes all the time now—got right into them when he got up in the morning. Mrs. Zuckerman prepared special meals for Wilbur. Lurvy shaved and got a haircut; and his principal farm duty was to feed the pig while people looked on.

Mr. Zuckerman ordered Lurvy to increase Wilbur's feedings from three meals a day to four meals a day. The Zuckermans were so busy with visitors they forgot about other things on the farm. The blackberries got ripe, and Mrs. Zuckerman failed to put up any blackberry jam. The corn needed hoeing, and Lurvy didn't find time to hoe it.

On Sunday the church was full. The minister ex-

plained the miracle.[15] He said that the words on the spider's web proved that human beings must always be on the watch for the coming of wonders.

All in all, the Zuckermans' pigpen was the center of attraction. Fern was happy, for she felt that Charlotte's trick was working and that Wilbur's life would be saved. But she found that the barn was not nearly as pleasant—too many people. She liked it better when she could be all alone with her friends the animals.[16]

Page 85

16. We should remember Fern's fondness for the closed universe of the barn, for later she will have quite different preferences.

Page 86

1. The triple repetition could be a reference to White's writing mentor at Cornell. In the introduction to *ES*, White relates that William Strunk, Jr., was so intent on his first rule of writing—to omit needless words—that frequently, in class, he was "a man left with nothing more to say yet with time to fill. . . . Will Strunk got out of this predicament by a simple trick: he uttered every sentence three times . . . . [H]e leaned forward over his desk, grasped his coat lapels in his hands, and, in a husky, conspiratorial voice, said, 'Rule Seventeen. Omit needless words! Omit needless words! Omit needless words!' "[1]

2. Without Charlotte, there'd have been chaos. Geese can be addled; or, as White put it, "Geese, we have found, are alert and articulate and they practically never sleep, but they are also indiscriminating, gossipy, and as easily diverted as children."[2]

Chapter XII

A Meeting

ONE EVENING, a few days after the writing had appeared in Charlotte's web, the spider called a meeting of all the animals in the barn cellar.

"I shall begin by calling the roll. Wilbur?"

"Here!" said the pig.

"Gander?"

"Here, here, here!" said the gander.[1]

"You sound like three ganders," muttered Charlotte. "Why can't you just say 'here'? Why do you have to repeat everything?"

"It's my idio-idio-idiosyncrasy," replied the gander.

"Goose?" said Charlotte.

"Here, here, here!" said the goose. Charlotte glared at her.

"Goslings, one through seven?"

"Bee-bee-bee!" "Bee-bee-bee!" "Bee-bee-bee!" "Bee-bee-bee!" "Bee-bee-bee!" "Bee-bee-bee!" "Bee-bee-bee!" said the goslings.

"This is getting to be quite a meeting," said Charlotte.[2]

"Anybody would think we had three ganders, three geese, and twenty-one goslings. Sheep?"

"He-aa-aa!" answered the sheep all together.

"Lambs?"

"He-aa-aa!" answered the lambs all together.

"Templeton?"

No answer.

"Templeton?"

No answer.

"Well, we are all here except the rat," said Charlotte. "I guess we can proceed without him. Now, all of you must have noticed what's been going on around here the last few days.[3] The message I wrote in my web, praising Wilbur, has been received. The Zuckermans have fallen for it, and so has everybody else. Zuckerman thinks Wilbur is an unusual pig, and therefore he won't want to kill him and eat him. I dare say my trick will work and Wilbur's life can be saved."

"Hurray!" cried everybody.

"Thank you very much," said Charlotte. "Now I called this meeting in order to get suggestions. I need new ideas for the web. People are already getting sick of reading the words 'Some Pig'! If anybody can think of another message, or remark, I'll be glad to weave it into the web. Any suggestions for a new slogan?"

"How about 'Pig Supreme'?" asked one of the lambs.[4]

Page 87

3. Just like the rapid opening of the story, this recapitulation of past action and the present situation is a smart novelistic device.

4. White's draft sheet enumerates the possibilities for Charlotte's miraculous writing.

See plate 9, page 193.

Page 88

5. Since White nowhere states that Fern is present for this conversation, it's the illustrator who establishes the fact. This is a fine example of the manner in which a skilled illustrator can complement an author and add new information.

This strategy of augmenting, undermining, or playing a sort of duet with the text is a common one for the best illustrators. Beatrix Potter uses it in *Peter Rabbit* when Mr. McGregor "hung up [Peter Rabbit's] little jacket . . . for a scarecrow to frighten the blackbirds," and Potter's accompanying illustration subverts and comments on the text by showing birds all about, looking up in wonderment at the pretty blue jacket with the gold buttons.[3]

5

"No good," said Charlotte. "It sounds like a rich dessert."

"How about 'Terrific, terrific, terrific'?" asked the goose.

"Cut that down to one 'terrific' and it will do very

nicely," said Charlotte. "I think 'terrific' might impress Zuckerman."

"But Charlotte," said Wilbur, "I'm *not* terrific."

"That doesn't make a particle of difference," replied Charlotte. "Not a particle.[6] People believe almost anything they see in print.[7] Does anybody here know how to spell 'terrific'?"

"I think," said the gander, "it's tee double ee double rr double rr double eye double ff double eye double see see see see see."

"What kind of an acrobat do you think I am?" said Charlotte in disgust. "I would have to have St. Vitus's Dance to weave a word like that into my web."

"Sorry, sorry, sorry," said the gander.

Then the oldest sheep spoke up. "I agree that there should be something new written in the web if Wilbur's life is to be saved. And if Charlotte needs help in finding words, I think she can get it from our friend Templeton. The rat visits the dump regularly and has access to old magazines. He can tear out bits of advertisements and bring them up here to the barn cellar, so that Charlotte can have something to copy."

"Good idea," said Charlotte. "But I'm not sure Templeton will be willing to help. You know how he is—always looking out for himself, never thinking of the other fellow."

"I bet I can get him to help," said the old sheep.[8] "I'll

Page 89

6. Again, it is always instructive to see how a good novelist differentiates his characters by the diction or manner of speech he attributes to each. We can't imagine the goose, or even Mrs. Arable, speaking with such magisterial finality.

7. A true observation. See Mr. Zuckerman's comment, last sentence on page 79 in *CW*, and discussion page 80.

8. One of the rare instances of inventiveness on the part of any animal other than Charlotte. Usually in this book, sheep have the mental agility of—well—sheep.

9. White continues to associate the word *creeping* with Templeton.

10. This sentence sounds like White, who maintained that poets had no business joining clubs. At the memorial service for White at the Blue Hill Congregational Church, James Russell Wiggins noted that, if White had been alive, he likely would not have attended. (He did, however, participate in town meetings, that most basic form of democracy as practiced in Maine. On the large scale, the need for world government was a topic about which he wrote and felt strongly. See page xxv in the introduction.)

11. A typical Templeton phrase. If you like tough-talking gangster rats, you'll love Russell Hoban's (allegedly) children's book *The Mouse and His Child* (1967), with its unforgettable extortionary thug Manny Rat.

12. In 1945, *The New Yorker* sent White to San Francisco to report on the conference establishing the United Nations. He had always perceived the need for mutuality in international affairs and the increasing necessity for international cooperation. Even in *Stuart Little* (published that same year), White made the same point in the classroom scene, when Stuart asks the class for "good laws for the world."[4]

appeal to his baser instincts, of which he has plenty. Here he comes now. Everybody keep quiet while I put the matter up to him!"

The rat entered the barn the way he always did—creeping along close to the wall.[9]

"What's up?" he asked, seeing the animals assembled.

"We're holding a directors' meeting," replied the old sheep.

"Well, break it up!" said Templeton.[10] "Meetings bore me." And the rat began to climb a rope that hung against the wall.

"Look," said the old sheep, "next time you go to the dump, Templeton, bring back a clipping from a magazine. Charlotte needs new ideas so she can write messages in her web and save Wilbur's life."

"Let him die," said the rat. "I should worry."[11]

"You'll worry all right when next winter comes," said the sheep. "You'll worry all right on a zero morning next January when Wilbur is dead and nobody comes down here with a nice pail of warm slops to pour into the trough. Wilbur's leftover food is your chief source of supply, Templeton.[12] *You* know that. Wilbur's food is your food; therefore Wilbur's destiny and your destiny are closely linked. If Wilbur is killed and his trough stands empty day after day, you'll grow so thin we can look right through your stomach and see objects on the other side."

A Meeting

Templeton's whiskers quivered.

"Maybe you're right," he said gruffly. "I'm making a trip to the dump tomorrow afternoon. I'll bring back a magazine clipping if I can find one."

"Thanks," said Charlotte. "The meeting is now adjourned. I have a busy evening ahead of me. I've got to tear my web apart and write 'Terrific.' "

Wilbur blushed. "But I'm *not* terrific, Charlotte. I'm just about average for a pig."

"You're terrific as far as *I'm* concerned," replied Charlotte, sweetly, "and that's what counts. You're my best friend,[13] and *I* think you're sensational. Now stop arguing and go get some sleep!"

Page 91

13. "*Charlotte* was a story of friendship, life, death, salvation. . . ."[5]

Page 92

White wrote a little note to himself:

Willis J. Gertsch
American Spiders

There is no trace of condescension as White "translates" Gertsch for children.[1]

See plate 10, page 194.

Pages 92–93

"The seemingly tremendous task of completely replacing an orb web ordinarily requires less than an hour."[2]

Different glands produce different types of silk.[3]

Chapter XIII

Good Progress

FAR INTO the night, while the other creatures slept, Charlotte worked on her web. First she ripped out a few of the orb lines near the center. She left the radial lines alone, as they were needed for support. As she worked, her eight legs were a great help to her. So were her teeth. She loved to weave and she was an expert at it. When she was finished ripping things out, her web looked something like this:

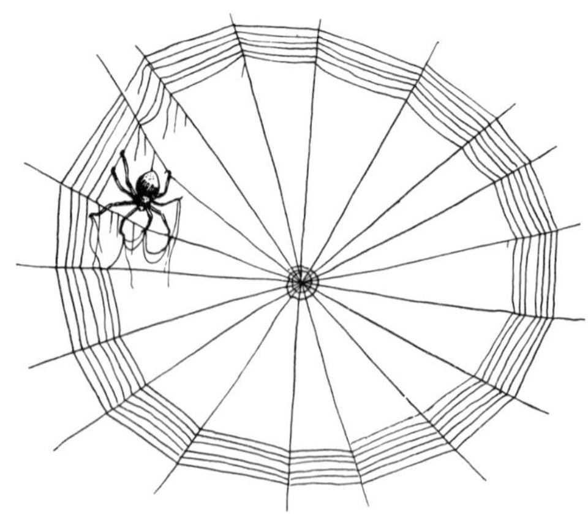

Good Progress

A spider can produce several kinds of thread. She uses a dry, tough thread for foundation lines, and she uses a sticky thread for snare lines—the ones that catch and hold insects. Charlotte decided to use her dry thread for writing the new message.

"If I write the word 'Terrific' with sticky thread," she thought, "every bug that comes along will get stuck in it and spoil the effect."

"Now let's see, the first letter is T."[1]

Charlotte climbed to a point at the top of the left hand side of the web. Swinging her spinnerets into position, she attached her thread and then dropped down. As she dropped, her spinning tubes went into action and she let out thread. At the bottom, she attached the thread. This formed the upright part of the letter T. Charlotte was not satisfied, however. She climbed up and made another attachment, right next to the first. Then she carried the line down, so that she had a double line instead of a single line. "It will show up better if I make the whole thing with double lines."

She climbed back up, moved over about an inch to the left, touched her spinnerets to the web, and then carried a line across to the right, forming the top of the T. She repeated this, making it double. Her eight legs were very busy helping.

"Now for the E!"

Charlotte got so interested in her work, she began to

Page 93

1. One might trace Charlotte's actions oneself with a thread to see just what's involved.

See plate 11, page 195.

Page 94

2. Landes here calls Charlotte "[t]he swinging square dance caller."[4]

3. This paragraph, again, is almost a parody of the cumulative folktale style (see *CW*, page 19).

talk to herself, as though to cheer herself on. If you had been sitting quietly in the barn cellar that evening, you would have heard something like this:

"Now for the R! Up we go! Attach! Descend! Pay out line! Whoa! Attach! Good! Up you go! Repeat! Attach! Descend![2] Pay out line. Whoa, girl! Steady now! Attach! Climb! Attach! Over to the right! Pay out line! Attach! Now right and down and swing that loop and around and around! Now in to the left! Attach! Climb! Repeat! O.K.! Easy, keep those lines together! Now, then, out and down for the leg of the R! Pay out line! Whoa! Attach! Ascend! Repeat! Good girl!"

And so, talking to herself, the spider worked at her difficult task. When it was completed, she felt hungry. She ate a small bug that she had been saving. Then she slept.

Next morning, Wilbur arose and stood beneath the web. He breathed the morning air into his lungs. Drops of dew, catching the sun, made the web stand out clearly. When Lurvy arrived with breakfast, there was the handsome pig, and over him, woven neatly in block letters, was the word TERRIFIC. Another miracle.

Lurvy rushed[3] and called Mr. Zuckerman. Mr. Zuckerman rushed and called Mrs. Zuckerman. Mrs. Zuckerman ran to the phone and called the Arables. The Arables climbed into their truck and hurried over.

Page 95

4. Since White doesn't describe the expression on Wilbur's face, this illustration is testimonial to Williams's own creative bent.

Page 96

5. Praise transforms. Just five pages earlier (*CW*, page 91), Wilbur had said that he wasn't terrific at all, but "just about average for a pig."

6. First, Wilbur is "Terrific!" because it's written in the web. Then the fact will be truly established by being printed—preferably with a photograph—in the *Weekly Chronicle*. Zuckerman's faith in the power of the written word is awe-inspiring.

7. On the second page of Draft H, White explained that Zuckerman "always took a shovel and pushed the cow manure through an opening in the floor, so that it dropped down into the cellar right in the middle of the pigpen." White went on to explain that this was not a dirty trick to play on Wilbur, but that Zuckerman knew "from experience that a convenient place to keep a young pig was in a manure pile. Pigs need warmth, and it was warm and comfortable down there in the cellar on the south side."

Everybody stood at the pigpen and stared at the web and read the word, over and over, while Wilbur, who really *felt* terrific,[5] stood quietly swelling out his chest and swinging his snout from side to side.

"Terrific!" breathed Zuckerman, in joyful admiration. "Edith, you better phone the reporter[6] on the *Weekly Chronicle* and tell him what has happened. He will want to know about this. He may want to bring a photographer. There isn't a pig in the whole state that is as terrific as our pig."

The news spread. People who had journeyed to see Wilbur when he was "some pig" came back again to see him now that he was "terrific."

That afternoon, when Mr. Zuckerman went to milk the cows and clean out the tie-ups, he was still thinking about what a wondrous pig he owned.

"Lurvy!" he called. "There is to be no more cow manure thrown down into that pigpen.[7] I have a terrific pig. I want that pig to have clean, bright straw every day for his bedding. Understand?"

"Yes, sir," said Lurvy.

"Furthermore," said Mr. Zuckerman, "I want you to start building a crate for Wilbur. I have decided to take the pig to the County Fair on September sixth. Make the crate large and paint it green with gold letters!"

"What will the letters say?" asked Lurvy.

"They should say *Zuckerman's Famous Pig*."

Good Progress

Lurvy picked up a pitchfork and walked away to get some clean straw. Having such an important pig was going to mean plenty of extra work, he could see that.

Below the apple orchard,[8] at the end of a path, was the dump where Mr. Zuckerman threw all sorts of trash and stuff that nobody wanted any more. Here, in a small clearing hidden by young alders and wild raspberry bushes, was an astonishing pile of old bottles and empty tin cans and dirty rags and bits of metal and broken bottles and broken hinges and broken springs and dead batteries and last month's magazines and old discarded dishmops and tattered overalls and rusty spikes and leaky pails and forgotten stoppers and useless junk of all kinds, including a wrong-size crank for a broken ice-cream freezer.

Templeton knew the dump and liked it. There were good hiding places there—excellent cover for a rat. And there was usually a tin can with food still clinging to the inside.

Templeton was down there now,[9] rummaging around. When he returned to the barn, he carried in his mouth an advertisement he had torn from a crumpled magazine.

"How's this?" he asked, showing the ad to Charlotte.

Page 97

8. Again, one of White's grand lists. One might say that an artist is sensitized to *see* what others would never even notice. That goes for painting, writing, photography.

9. White originally had other plans for how to get the words for the web. In Folder A, there is a note: "They get the cocker spaniel to bring Charlotte a spelling book from the boy's room." (We met the cocker spaniel on page 20.)

Page 98

10. White's earlier draft enumerates possibilities in Charlotte's web writing:

(argument about this)
(label of a shirt)

after the word "pre-shrunk."

See plate 9, page 193.

"It says 'Crunchy.' 'Crunchy' would be a good word to write in your web."

"Just the wrong idea," replied Charlotte. "Couldn't be worse. We don't want Zuckerman to think Wilbur is crunchy. He might start thinking about crisp,

crunchy bacon and tasty ham. That would put ideas into his head. We must advertise Wilbur's noble qualities, not his tastiness. Go get another word, please, Templeton!"

The rat looked disgusted. But he sneaked away to the dump and was back in a while with a strip of cotton cloth. "How's this?" he asked. "It's a label off an old shirt."

Charlotte examined the label. It said PRE-SHRUNK.[10]

Good Progress

"I'm sorry, Templeton," she said, "but 'Pre-shrunk' is out of the question. We want Zuckerman to think Wilbur is nicely filled out, not all shrunk up. I'll have to ask you to try again."

"What do you think I am, a messenger boy?" grumbled the rat. "I'm not going to spend all my time chasing down to the dump after advertising material."[11]

"Just once more—please!" said Charlotte.

"I'll tell you what I'll do," said Templeton. "I know where there's a package of soap flakes in the woodshed. It has writing on it. I'll bring you a piece of the package."

He climbed the rope that hung on the wall and disappeared through a hole in the ceiling. When he came back he had a strip of blue-and-white cardboard in his teeth.

"There!" he said, triumphantly. "How's that?"

Charlotte read the words: "With New Radiant Action."[12]

"What does it mean?" asked Charlotte, who had never used any soap flakes in her life.

"How should I know?" said Templeton. "You asked for words and I brought them. I suppose the next thing you'll want me to fetch is a dictionary."

Together they studied the soap ad. " 'With new radiant action,' " repeated Charlotte, slowly. "Wilbur!" she called.

Page 99

11. As noted on page xxi, White expressed his view of advertisers' hyperbole as far back as his first contribution to *The New Yorker*, in 1925.

New Beauty of Tone
in 1925 Song Sparrow

Into every one of this season's song sparrows has been built the famous VERNAL tone. Look for the distinguishing white mark on the breast.[5]

12. On his worksheet, White wrote right after this phrase, "they settle for just the word RADIANT."

See plate 9, page 193.

Page 100

13. Wilbur's looped tail echoes the loop of his exuberant back somersault.

Wilbur, who was asleep in the straw, jumped up.

"Run around!" commanded Charlotte. "I want to see you in action, to see if you are radiant."

Wilbur raced to the end of his yard.

"Now back again, faster!" said Charlotte.

Wilbur galloped back. His skin shone. His tail had a fine, tight curl in it.

"Jump into the air!" cried Charlotte.

Wilbur jumped as high as he could.

"Keep your knees straight and touch the ground with your ears!" called Charlotte.

13

Wilbur obeyed.

"Do a back flip with a half twist in it!" cried Charlotte.

Wilbur went over backwards, writhing and twisting as he went.

"O.K., Wilbur," said Charlotte. "You can go back to sleep. O.K., Templeton, the soap ad will do, I guess. I'm not sure Wilbur's action is exactly radiant, but it's interesting."

"Actually," said Wilbur, "I *feel* radiant."

"Do you?" said Charlotte, looking at him with affection. "Well, you're a good little pig, and radiant you shall be. I'm in this thing pretty deep now—I might as well go the limit."[14]

Tired from his romp, Wilbur lay down in the clean straw. He closed his eyes. The straw seemed scratchy —not as comfortable as the cow manure, which was always delightfully soft to lie in. So he pushed the straw to one side and stretched out in the manure. Wilbur sighed. It had been a busy day—his first day of being terrific. Dozens of people had visited his yard during the afternoon, and he had had to stand and pose, looking as terrific as he could. Now he was tired.[15] Fern had arrived and seated herself quietly on her stool in the corner.

"Tell me a story, Charlotte!" said Wilbur, as he lay waiting for sleep to come. "Tell me a story!"

Page 101

14. For humorous effect, White employs a writing strategy he learned, perhaps, from Mark Twain: White will begin a sentence or a passage sedately, in standard English, and then suddenly do a rhetorical *volte-face*, or drop into homey colloquialisms.

On one occasion, regarding business pertaining to *TS*, White wrote Ursula Nordstrom, "I'm counting on you to look after my interests in this regard. Look after my hay fever too, while you're at it."[6] And in *TS* he wrote about Louis, the swan, and his beloved Serena, "Louis wearing his trumpet and slate and his chalk pencil and his medal, Serena wearing nothing at all."[7]

Remarkably, even as a child, White was already developing something very like this same stylistic maneuver. In 1910, White wrote to his brother Albert:

> Dear Ally,
>
> Received your letter with much rejoicing. I had to ask ma how to spell rejoicing and I don't know as I have it right yet. Please excuse me if I didn't *or rather excuse ma*. . . . [Italics added][8]

15. Alternation of long, loose sentences with short, pithy ones is another of the stylistic devices advocated by White in *ES*.[9]

Page 102

16. White's source points out that there are well-authenticated instances of spiders' "destruction of small vertebrate animals, including birds, a mouse, a fish, and a snake. . . ."[10]

Gertsch corroborates the point:

> [A] tiny, squirming fish, twice the size of the spider itself, is no more formidable an opponent than a robust grasshopper, and is as easily dispatched. . . . Furthermore, its powerful digestive juices appear fully as effective on the bodies of fishes as on those of the invertebrates that are its habitual food.[11]

In Folder A, Charlotte tells of the exploits of other arachnid relatives too—one spider who found "a heavy concentration of young mosquitoes between window & screen. . . ."

17. White sheds new light on the overly familiar by not using conventional terms to describe it.

So Charlotte, although she, too, was tired, did what Wilbur wanted.

"Once upon a time,"[16] she began, "I had a beautiful cousin who managed to build her web across a small stream. One day a tiny fish leaped into the air and got tangled in the web. My cousin was very much surprised, of course. The fish was thrashing wildly. My

cousin hardly dared tackle it. But she did. She swooped down and threw great masses of wrapping material[17] around the fish and fought bravely to capture it."

"Did she succeed?" asked Wilbur.

"It was a never-to-be-forgotten battle," said Charlotte. "There was the fish, caught only by one fin, and its tail wildly thrashing and shining in the sun. There

was the web, sagging dangerously under the weight of the fish."

"How much did the fish weigh?" asked Wilbur eagerly.

"I don't know," said Charlotte. "There was my cousin, slipping in, dodging out,[18] beaten mercilessly over the head by the wildly thrashing fish, dancing in, dancing out, throwing her threads and fighting hard. First she threw a left around the tail. The fish lashed back. Then a left to the tail and a right to the mid-section. The fish lashed back. Then she dodged to one side and threw a right, and another right to the fin. Then a hard left to the head, while the web swayed and stretched."

"Then what happened?" asked Wilbur.

"Nothing," said Charlotte. "The fish lost the fight. My cousin wrapped it up so tight it couldn't budge."

"Then what happened?" asked Wilbur.

"Nothing," said Charlotte. "My cousin kept the fish for a while, and then, when she got good and ready, she ate it."

"Tell me another story!" begged Wilbur.

So Charlotte told him about another cousin of hers who was an aeronaut.

"What is an aeronaut?" asked Wilbur.[19]

"A balloonist," said Charlotte. "My cousin used to stand on her head and let out enough thread to form a

Page 103

18. Although White cautions writers, "Use figures of speech sparingly,"[12] he is certainly exuberant about this extended boxing analogy.

19. White's source informs us that "long before the invention of balloons or of aeroplanes, spiders had solved the problem of aerial navigation."[13]

Page 104

20. We've seen bits of White's poetry already in these annotations. In 1938, he published the volume *The Fox of Peapack and Other Poems*. For *TS*, he wrote lyrics as well. This euphonious lullaby of Charlotte's ranks among his most pleasing.

For a biographical sketch for his publisher, White once wrote of himself, "He would like, more than anything, to be a poet. The poets, he thinks, are the great ones."[14]

21. This is the last time we see Fern alone with the animals. Henceforth, she pursues new interests.

balloon. Then she'd let go and be lifted into the air and carried upward on the warm wind."

"Is that true?" asked Wilbur. "Or are you just making it up?"

"It's true," replied Charlotte. "I have some very remarkable cousins. And now, Wilbur, it's time you went to sleep."

"Sing something!" begged Wilbur, closing his eyes.

So Charlotte sang a lullaby, while crickets chirped in the grass and the barn grew dark. This was the song she sang.

"Sleep, sleep, my love, my only,
Deep, deep, in the dung and the dark;
Be not afraid and be not lonely!
This is the hour when frogs and thrushes
Praise the world from the woods and the rushes.
Rest from care, my one and only,
Deep in the dung and the dark!"[20]

But Wilbur was already asleep. When the song ended, Fern got up and went home.[21]

Chapter XIV

Dr. Dorian[1]

THE NEXT day was Saturday. Fern stood at the kitchen sink drying the breakfast dishes as her mother washed them. Mrs. Arable worked silently. She hoped Fern would go out and play with other children, instead of heading for the Zuckermans' barn to sit and watch animals.

"Charlotte is the best storyteller I ever heard," said Fern, poking her dish towel into a cereal bowl.

"Fern," said her mother sternly, "you must not invent things. You know spiders don't tell stories. Spiders can't talk."

"Charlotte can," replied Fern. "She doesn't talk very loud, but she talks."

"What kind of story did she tell?" asked Mrs. Arable.

"Well," began Fern, "she told us about a cousin of hers who caught a fish in her web. Don't you think that's fascinating?"

"Fern, dear, how would a fish get in a spider's web?" said Mrs. Arable. "You know it couldn't happen. You're making this up."

Page 105

1. As regards Dr. Dorian's name, in the manuscript drafts he appeared first as Dr. Lacey, Dr. Barton, and Dr. Goudy. It seemed prudent first to discover whether any such gentlemen were real people in the life of E. B. White. Allene White reassures us that her father-in-law would never have used a real person's name. That's surely true, too, for when White was composing *Stuart Little*, he first named the Little family Ade—thus, Stuart Ade. When White edited the *Subtreasury of American Humor*, he included the American humorist George Ade, and it's reasonable to think he changed Stuart's name, not only for the obvious suitability of "Little," but also so as not even to suggest "real life." It does not hurt, either, to stress again White's extraordinary scrupulousness regarding the legal, literary, or simple common-sense rights of privacy of *all* people with whom he had dealings or correspondence.

In fact, the name Dorian fits with White's own designation of the book as "a paean to life, a hymn to the barn"[1] (see page 13), *paean* being an ancient Greek hymn of thanksgiving. The Dorians were the early Greeks who inhabited Arcady, the semihistorical, mythical Greek landscape that has passed into art and literature as the pastoral idyll—a sort of prelapsarian (before Adam and Eve sinned) past when Nature and humankind were in closer harmony. (For further discussions of the pastoral theme, see pages 8–9, 13, 42, 43, and 113.)

Appropriately, then, Dr. Dorian suggests that, perhaps, if adults paid attention closely, as do the children, adults too would hear what the animals have to say. Thus, again, *CW* is an example of the venerable literary form that

Continued on page 106

Page 105 (continued)

harkens to a more innocent age—the pastoral, updated.

Dr. Dorian's name is the clincher that White knew precisely what he was about. And, of course, Mr. Zuckerman's first name, Homer, does not make the argument any weaker.

(Landes suggests that the doctor's name is a combination of the English verb *do* and the French *rien* (nothing), thus, Doctor "do-nothing."[2] This seems extremely doubtful. There would have been nothing to keep White from calling him "Dorien," for one thing.)

Page 106

2. Fern's narrative picks up on the rhythm and the boxing metaphor of Charlotte's original telling.

3. Several times in this novel, White comments indirectly on the gullibility of people (*gullible* being a word Charlotte has earlier defined for Wilbur). Mrs. Arable has forgotten that she thinks Fern is inventing; she's now thoroughly taken in by Fern's story. (On the other hand, if we have suspended *our* own disbelief, all that Fern tells is true, and Mrs. Arable has finally come to her senses.)

"Oh, it happened all right," replied Fern. "Charlotte never fibs. This cousin of hers built a web across a stream. One day she was hanging around on the web and a tiny fish leaped into the air and got tangled in the web. The fish was caught by one fin, Mother; its tail was wildly thrashing and shining in the sun. Can't you just see the web, sagging dangerously under the weight of the fish? Charlotte's cousin kept slipping in, dodging out,[2] and she was beaten mercilessly over the head by the wildly thrashing fish, dancing in, dancing out, throwing . . ."

"Fern!" snapped her mother. "Stop it! Stop inventing these wild tales!"

"I'm not inventing," said Fern. "I'm just telling you the facts."

"What finally happened?"[3] asked her mother, whose curiosity began to get the better of her.

"Charlotte's cousin won. She wrapped the fish up, then she ate him when she got good and ready. Spiders have to eat, the same as the rest of us."

"Yes, I suppose they do," said Mrs. Arable, vaguely.

"Charlotte has another cousin who is a balloonist. She stands on her head, lets out a lot of line, and is carried aloft on the wind. Mother, wouldn't you simply love to do that?"

"Yes, I would, come to think of it," replied Mrs. Arable. "But Fern, darling, I wish you would play out-

doors today instead of going to Uncle Homer's barn. Find some of your playmates[4] and do something nice outdoors. You're spending too much time in that barn —it isn't good for you to be alone so much."

"Alone?" said Fern. "Alone? My best friends are in the barn cellar. It is a very sociable place. Not at all lonely."

Fern disappeared after a while, walking down the road toward Zuckermans'. Her mother dusted the sitting room. As she worked she kept thinking about Fern. It didn't seem natural for a little girl to be so interested in animals. Finally Mrs. Arable made up her mind she would pay a call on old Doctor Dorian and ask his advice. She got in the car and drove to his office in the village.

Dr. Dorian had a thick beard. He was glad to see Mrs. Arable and gave her a comfortable chair.

"It's about Fern," she explained. "Fern spends entirely too much time in the Zuckermans' barn. It doesn't seem normal. She sits on a milk stool in a corner of the barn cellar, near the pigpen, and watches animals, hour after hour. She just sits and listens."

Dr. Dorian leaned back and closed his eyes.

"How enchanting!" he said. "It must be real nice and quiet down there.[5] Homer has some sheep, hasn't he?"

"Yes," said Mrs. Arable. "But it all started with that

Page 107

4. That, of course, is just what Fern will do—as she grows up, away from her sympathy with animals. It's one of the major themes of the story.

The Fern who likes to be alone with animals is more like the boy Sam in *The Trumpet of the Swan*, and like young E. B. White for that matter. The difference is that Sam keeps the faith; Fern "matures."

5. In my view, this rumination by the doctor is one of the finer touches in the book. Observing how such a comment rounds out and deepens the impression made by Dr. Dorian, one appreciates the difference between a stock character and a profound one.

Page 108

6. Dr. Dorian is, of course, echoing Lurvy's earlier comment, "He's quite a pig" (*CW*, page 82).

7. Although Williams said he intended Mrs. Arable to look like Katharine White (see page 201), it's difficult to see the resemblance here.

pig we let Fern raise on a bottle. She calls him Wilbur. Homer bought the pig, and ever since it left our place Fern has been going to her uncle's to be near it."

"I've been hearing things about that pig," said Dr. Dorian, opening his eyes. "They say he's quite a pig.[6]"

7

"Have you heard about the words that appeared in the spider's web?" asked Mrs. Arable nervously.

"Yes," replied the doctor.

"Well, do you understand it?" asked Mrs. Arable.

"Understand what?"

"Do you understand how there could be any writing in a spider's web?"

"Oh, no," said Dr. Dorian. "I don't understand it.

Dr. Dorian

But for that matter I don't understand how a spider learned to spin a web in the first place. When the words appeared, everyone said they were a miracle. But nobody pointed out that the web itself is a miracle."

"What's miraculous about a spider's web?" said Mrs.

Arable. "I don't see why you say a web is a miracle—it's just a web."

"Ever try to spin one?" asked Dr. Dorian.[9]

Mrs. Arable shifted uneasily in her chair. "No," she replied. "But I can crochet a doily and I can knit a sock."

"Sure," said the doctor. "But somebody taught you, didn't they?"[10]

Page 109

8. Landes suggests resemblance between Dr. Dorian and Sigmund Freud.[3] I doubt it. (a) Freud had a trimmed beard—surely within Williams's artistic powers; (b) a beard alone doesn't make a Freud; (c) Dorian's views bear not the slightest relation to those of Freud; and (d) Freud hardly seems Garth Williams's sort of touchstone—or, by any stretch of the imagination, E. B. White's, whose views are suggested in the essay "The Second Tree from the Corner."[4]

(When tempted to draw such inferences merely from the fact of a beard, bear in mind Freud's own caution about overinterpretation, to the effect that sometimes a cigar is merely a cigar [and not a ♂ symbol].)

9. Dr. Dorian's sentiments frequently repeat those expressed by White himself, elsewhere.

10. Gertsch stressed the instinctive nature of the spider's weaving.

> . . . [I]t should be noted that spiders have attained their present position without benefit of so-called intelligence. Endowed with incredibly complicated instincts, the spinning creatures perform their marvels largely as automatons, and show only moderate ability to break the bonds of their behaviour patterns. The baby orb weaver spins a perfect orb web soon after it leaves the egg sac.[5]

Page 110

11. White obviously does. See chapter title and early description, as well as note, page 77. The miracle lies not in the fact of the web itself, but in the fact that nobody ever taught the spider how to weave it.

"My mother taught me."

"Well, who taught a spider? A young spider knows how to spin a web without any instructions from anybody. Don't you regard that as a miracle?"[11]

"I suppose so," said Mrs. Arable. "I never looked at it that way before. Still, I don't understand how those words got into the web. I don't understand it, and I don't like what I can't understand."

"None of us do," said Dr. Dorian, sighing. "I'm a doctor. Doctors are supposed to understand everything. But I don't understand everything, and I don't intend to let it worry me."

Mrs. Arable fidgeted. "Fern says the animals talk to each other. Dr. Dorian, do you believe animals talk?"

"I never heard one say anything," he replied. "But that proves nothing. It is quite possible that an animal has spoken civilly to me and that I didn't catch the remark because I wasn't paying attention. Children pay better attention than grownups. If Fern says that the animals in Zuckerman's barn talk, I'm quite ready to believe her. Perhaps if people talked less, animals would talk more. People are incessant talkers—I can give you my word on that."

"Well, I feel better about Fern," said Mrs. Arable. "You don't think I need worry about her?"

"Does she look well?" asked the doctor.

"Oh, yes."

"Appetite good?"

"Oh, yes, she's always hungry."

"Sleep well at night?"

"Oh, yes."

"Then don't worry," said the doctor.

"Do you think she'll ever start thinking about something besides pigs and sheep and geese and spiders?"

"How old is Fern?"

"She's eight."

"Well," said Dr. Dorian, "I think she will always love animals. But I doubt that she spends her entire life in Homer Zuckerman's barn cellar. How about boys—does she know any boys?"

"She knows Henry Fussy," said Mrs. Arable brightly.

Dr. Dorian closed his eyes again and went into deep thought. "Henry Fussy," he mumbled. "Hmm. Remarkable.[12] Well, I don't think you have anything to worry about. Let Fern associate with her friends in the barn if she wants to. I would say, offhand, that spiders and pigs were fully as interesting as Henry Fussy. Yet I predict that the day will come when even Henry will drop some chance remark that catches Fern's attention. It's amazing how children change from year to year. How's Avery?" he asked, opening his eyes wide.

"Oh, Avery," chuckled Mrs. Arable. "Avery is always fine. Of course, he gets into poison ivy and gets

Page 111

12. Dr. Dorian's comment is marvelously ambiguous. What's he thinking, or recalling, about Henry Fussy? How much subtler than the obviousness of the film, in which Henry Fussy and his mother become loud, bright characters.

Page 112

13. The description of bumptious Avery, followed by "He's fine," is pretty funny. Would Mrs. Arable have thought it "fine" if Fern were getting poison ivy, getting stung by bees, bringing home frogs, and busting up bits of crockery?

stung by wasps and bees and brings frogs and snakes home and breaks everything he lays his hands on. He's fine."[13]

"Good!" said the doctor.

Mrs. Arable said good-bye and thanked Dr. Dorian very much for his advice. She felt greatly relieved.

Chapter XV

The Crickets

THE CRICKETS sang in the grasses. They sang the song of summer's ending, a sad, monotonous song. "Summer is over and gone," they sang. "Over and gone, over and gone. Summer is dying, dying."

The crickets felt it was their duty to warn everybody that summertime cannot last forever. Even on the most beautiful days in the whole year—the days when summer is changing into fall—the crickets spread the rumor of sadness and change.

Everybody heard the song of the crickets. Avery and Fern Arable heard it as they walked the dusty road. They knew that school would soon begin again. The young geese heard it and knew that they would never be little goslings again. Charlotte heard it and knew that she hadn't much time left. Mrs. Zuckerman, at work in the kitchen, heard the crickets, and a sadness came over her, too. "Another summer gone," she sighed. Lurvy, at work building a crate for Wilbur, heard the song and knew it was time to dig potatoes.[1]

Page 113

1. The seasons pass. The lyrical, poetical opening of this chapter sounds all the notes of the conventional pastoral and repeats the melancholy theme of Death finding a place even in mythical Arcady. "*Et in Arcadia ego*" ("I, too, am in Arcadia") read the inscription on eighteenth-century paintings that underlined this theme of Death's presence in the bucolic idyll.[1] (See also page 43.)

The rest of this chapter is one of recapitulation—an authorial catching of breath.

Page 114

2. The maple, personified, turns red; the seasons pass.

Page 115

3. White repeats the theme of friendship with sufficient frequency for there to be no question as to its centrality in the book. Oddly enough, however, whatever the facts of his real life may have been, when one studies all of White's writings closely (including his letters), and when one reads what has been written about him, neither close friendship nor literature is a topic that recurs frequently. As a youngster, White traveled cross-country with a college pal with whom he stayed in touch over the years. We may infer from some of his columns that White was a good neighbor. And professionally, and to a certain degree personally, he was associated closely with James Thurber and collaborated with him on the book *Is Sex Necessary?* But we will look in vain for sustained evidence of emotional involvement in the lives of others, except those of his immediate family. Two partial explanations come to mind, though neither is wholly satisfying: First, White's marriage to Katharine was fully absorbing and all-encompassing; there was neither time nor inclination for sustained engagement in the life of others. (See *Katharine & E. B. White: An Affectionate Memoir* by Isabel Russell.)

Second—and I speak from the experience of having corresponded briefly with him—White's reticence, scrupulousness, and perhaps shyness ever kept inquirers at bay and made documents of his personal life scarce. This scrupulousness, the unwillingness to reveal almost anything that touched on the lives of those associated with him, arose from an educated legal awareness regarding ownership of correspondence as well as from profound thought-

"Summer is over and gone," repeated the crickets. "How many nights till frost?" sang the crickets. "Good-bye, summer, good-bye, good-bye!"

The sheep heard the crickets, and they felt so uneasy they broke a hole in the pasture fence and wandered up into the field across the road. The gander discovered the hole and led his family through, and they walked to the orchard and ate the apples that were lying on the ground. A little maple tree[2] in the swamp heard the cricket song and turned bright red with anxiety.

Wilbur was now the center of attraction on the farm. Good food and regular hours were showing results: Wilbur was a pig any man would be proud of. One day more than a hundred people came to stand at his yard and admire him. Charlotte had written the word RADIANT, and Wilbur really looked radiant as he stood in the golden sunlight. Ever since the spider had befriended him, he had done his best to live up to his reputation. When Charlotte's web said SOME PIG, Wilbur had tried hard to look like some pig. When Charlotte's web said TERRIFIC, Wilbur had tried to look terrific. And now that the web said RADIANT, he did everything possible to make himself glow.

It is not easy to look radiant, but Wilbur threw himself into it with a will. He would turn his head slightly and blink his long eye-lashes. Then he would breathe deeply. And when his audience grew bored, he would

spring into the air and do a back flip with a half twist. At this the crowd would yell and cheer. "How's that for a pig?" Mr. Zuckerman would ask, well pleased with himself. "That pig is radiant."

Some of Wilbur's friends in the barn worried for fear all this attention would go to his head and make him stuck up. But it never did. Wilbur was modest; fame did not spoil him. He still worried some about the future, as he could hardly believe that a mere spider would be able to save his life. Sometimes at night he would have a bad dream. He would dream that men were coming to get him with knives and guns. But that was only a dream. In the daytime, Wilbur usually felt happy and confident. No pig ever had truer friends, and he realized that friendship is one of the most satisfying things in the world.[3] Even the song of the crickets did not make Wilbur too sad. He knew it was almost time for the County Fair, and he was looking forward to the trip. If he could distinguish himself at the Fair, and maybe win some prize money, he was sure Zuckerman would let him live.

Charlotte had worries of her own, but she kept quiet about them. One morning Wilbur asked her about the Fair.

"You're going *with* me, aren't you, Charlotte?" he said.

"Well, I don't know," replied Charlotte. "The Fair

fulness and courtesy. That much may clearly be inferred from unpublished letters.

As for literature, White pays homage to the ideas of Thoreau and for some time carried with him a volume of *Walden*; and often we feel the stylistic influence of Twain. But I cannot think of many writers in whose pages there are fewer references to other writers, past or present. Literary talk and literary theory seem to have interested him not at all.

Page 116

4. Even as she surely senses her approaching end, Charlotte remains Wilbur's teacher.

Elledge relates that E. B. White's father, Samuel White, would send his children to look up the meanings of words in *Webster's Unabridged Dictionary*, kept in brother Albert's room.

comes at a bad time for me. I shall find it inconvenient to leave home, even for a few days."

"Why?" asked Wilbur.

"Oh, I just don't feel like leaving my web. Too much going on around here."

"*Please* come with me!" begged Wilbur. "I need you, Charlotte. I can't stand going to the Fair without you. You've just *got* to come."

"No," said Charlotte, "I believe I'd better stay home and see if I can't get some work done."

"What kind of work?" asked Wilbur.

"Egg laying. It's time I made an egg sac and filled it with eggs."

"I didn't know you could lay eggs," said Wilbur in amazement.

"Oh, sure," said the spider. "I'm versatile."

"What does 'versatile' mean—full of eggs?" asked Wilbur.[4]

"Certainly not," said Charlotte. " 'Versatile' means I can turn with ease from one thing to another. It means I don't have to limit my activities to spinning and trapping and stunts like that."

"Why don't you come with me to the Fair Grounds and lay your eggs there?" pleaded Wilbur. "It would be wonderful fun."

Charlotte gave her web a twitch and moodily watched it sway. "I'm afraid not," she said. "You don't

know the first thing about egg laying, Wilbur. I can't arrange my family duties to suit the management of the County Fair. When I get ready to lay eggs, I have to lay eggs, Fair or no Fair. However, I don't want you to worry about it—you might lose weight. We'll leave it this way: I'll come to the Fair if I possibly can."

"Oh, good!" said Wilbur.[5] "I knew you wouldn't forsake me just when I need you most."

All that day Wilbur stayed inside, taking life easy in the straw. Charlotte rested and ate a grasshopper. She knew that she couldn't help Wilbur much longer. In a few days[6] she would have to drop everything and build the beautiful little sac that would hold her eggs.

Page 117

5. Unwilling to recognize Charlotte's needs, or even to follow up on her hint, Wilbur at this point is still clearly the egocentric child he was at the beginning of the book.

6. White is a master of the authorial technique of showing, rather than telling. However, in this instance, precisely because of Wilbur's obtuseness and unwillingness to inquire further of Charlotte, White is obliged to intrude, to tell the reader.

Page 118

1. White certainly shared his characters' fondness for fairs. In his *New Yorker* piece titled "Good-bye to 48th Street," White despaired of the difficult task of getting rid of possessions. Then he had an idea:

> . . . [W]e should shut the apartment, leave everything to soak for a while, and go to the Fryeburg Fair, in Maine, where we could sit under a tent at a cattle auction and watch somebody else trying to dispose of something. A fair, of course, is a dangerous spot if a man is hoping to avoid acquisition.[1]

White continued, itemizing the pleasures of the occasion—the trotting horses, the calf scramble, the pig scramble, and the baby-beef auction.[2] And there are other dreams a fair offers, such as a new appliance. See page 137.

On the other hand, things did not remain what once they were. Complaining about the cheapening effects of the film version of *Charlotte's Web*, White wrote, "The Blue Hill Fair, which I tried to report faithfully in the book, has become a Disney world, with 76 trombones."[3]

Chapter XVI

Off to the Fair[1]

THE NIGHT before the County Fair, everybody went to bed early. Fern and Avery were in bed by eight. Avery lay dreaming that the Ferris wheel had stopped and that he was in the top car. Fern lay dreaming that she was getting sick in the swings.

Lurvy was in bed by eight-thirty. He lay dreaming that he was throwing baseballs at a cloth cat and winning a genuine Navajo blanket. Mr. and Mrs. Zuckerman were in bed by nine. Mrs. Zuckerman lay dreaming about a deep freeze unit. Mr. Zuckerman lay

dreaming about Wilbur. He dreamt that Wilbur had grown until he was one hundred and sixteen feet long and ninety-two feet high and that he had won all the prizes at the Fair and was covered with blue ribbons and even had a blue ribbon tied to the end of his tail.

Down in the barn cellar, the animals, too, went to sleep early, all except Charlotte. Tomorrow would be Fair Day. Every creature planned to get up early to see Wilbur off on his great adventure.

When morning came, everybody got up at daylight. The day was hot. Up the road at the Arables' house, Fern lugged a pail of hot water to her room and took a sponge bath. Then she put on her prettiest dress because she knew she would see boys at the Fair.[2] Mrs. Arable scrubbed the back of Avery's neck, and wet his hair, and parted it, and brushed it down hard till it stuck to the top of his head—all but about six hairs that stood straight up. Avery put on clean underwear, clean blue jeans, and a clean shirt. Mr. Arable dressed, ate breakfast, and then went out and polished his truck. He had offered to drive everybody to the Fair, including Wilbur.

Bright and early, Lurvy put clean straw in Wilbur's crate and lifted it into the pigpen. The crate was green. In gold letters it said:

ZUCKERMAN'S FAMOUS PIG

Page 119

2. First hint of change in Fern. Dr. Dorian was undoubtedly right.

Page 120

3. In Draft H (the most important one), this was followed by the sentence "The word RADIANT was much admired." This is deleted in the book. Besides being gratuitous commentary, it would violate *ES*'s command "to use the active voice."[4]

4. This is a grammarian's joke, of course. The matter of Wilbur's bedding is one thing, but the misuse of the word *lay* for *lie* is another—a favorite "correction" for the correcting sort of English teachers.

White deals with the confusion of *lie* and *lay* in *ES*.[5]

White is not, however, making fun of farmers generically. Writing to a correspondent who had objected to the farmers' language, he noted that "the characters in 'Charlotte's Web' were not presented as hicks; today's farmer is anything but. Neither were they presented as intellectuals who use the language with precision. Very few people in any walk of life speak and write precisely and correctly, and I don't myself."[6]

5. Originally, in Folder H, this was followed by "'Let's go!' she said." White penciled a box around the sentence—his normal indication to delete.

My California agricultural advisor recommends soap and water, and then a rubbing of fly spray or mineral oil. My Maine informant, on the other hand, reminded me that, after all, "Cleopatra had milk baths, so why not a pig? Buttermilk baths are an old Yankee beauty treatment, as well as a way to use an overabundance of the stuff."

Charlotte had her web looking fine for the occasion.[3] Wilbur ate his breakfast slowly. He tried to look radiant without getting food in his ears.

In the kitchen, Mrs. Zuckerman suddenly made an announcement.

"Homer," she said to her husband, "I am going to give that pig a buttermilk bath."

"A what?" said Mr. Zuckerman.

"A buttermilk bath. My grandmother used to bathe her pig with buttermilk when it got dirty—I just remembered."

"Wilbur's not dirty," said Mr. Zuckerman proudly.

"He's filthy behind the ears," said Mrs. Zuckerman. "Every time Lurvy slops him, the food runs down around the ears. Then it dries and forms a crust. He also has a smudge on one side where he lays in the manure."

"He lays in clean straw," corrected Mr. Zuckerman.[4]

"Well, he's dirty, and he's going to have a bath."

Mr. Zuckerman sat down weakly and ate a doughnut. His wife went to the woodshed. When she returned, she wore rubber boots and an old raincoat, and she carried a bucket of buttermilk and a small wooden paddle.[5]

"Edith, you're crazy," mumbled Zuckerman.

But she paid no attention to him. Together they walked to the pigpen. Mrs. Zuckerman wasted no time. She climbed in with Wilbur and went to work. Dip-

ping her paddle in the buttermilk, she rubbed him all over. The geese gathered around to see the fun, and so did the sheep and lambs. Even Templeton poked his head out cautiously, to watch Wilbur get a buttermilk bath. Charlotte got so interested, she lowered herself

on a dragline so she could see better. Wilbur stood still and closed his eyes. He could feel the buttermilk trickling down his sides. He opened his mouth and some buttermilk ran in. It was delicious. He felt radiant and happy. When Mrs. Zuckerman got through and rubbed him dry, he was the cleanest, prettiest pig you ever saw.

Page 121

6. The illustrator evidently felt a challenge in depicting the human characters in *CW*.

> Stuart was more interesting to illustrate as it was crazier. A little girl the size of Stuart. An invisible car racing around the dentist's office. Stuart driving his car through the country and talking to people.
>
> Charlotte required me to make the people—with the exception of Fern—very ordinary indeed. . . . But the story was just perfect.[7]

Page 122

7. In understated fashion, White renders Charlotte's change of heart.

He was pure white, pink around the ears and snout, and smooth as silk.

The Zuckermans went up to change into their best clothes. Lurvy went to shave and put on his plaid shirt and his purple necktie. The animals were left to themselves in the barn.

The seven goslings paraded round and round their mother.

"Please, please, please take us to the Fair!" begged a gosling. Then all seven began teasing to go.

"Please, please, please, please, please, please . . ." They made quite a racket.

"Children!" snapped the goose. "We're staying quietly-ietly-ietly at home. Only Wilbur-ilbur-ilbur is going to the Fair."

Just then Charlotte interrupted.

"I shall go, too," she said, softly.[7] "I have decided to go with Wilbur. He may need me. We can't tell what may happen at the Fair Grounds. Somebody's got to go along who knows how to write. And I think Templeton better come, too—I might need somebody to run errands and do general work."

"I'm staying right here," grumbled the rat. "I haven't the slightest interest in fairs."

"That's because you've never been to one," remarked the old sheep. "A fair is a rat's paradise. Everybody spills food at a fair. A rat can creep out late at night and

have a feast. In the horse barn you will find oats that the trotters and pacers have spilled. In the trampled grass of the infield you will find old discarded lunch boxes containing the foul remains of peanut butter sandwiches, hard-boiled eggs, cracker crumbs, bits of doughnuts, and particles of cheese. In the hard-packed dirt of the midway, after the glaring lights are out and the people have gone home to bed, you will find a veritable treasure of popcorn fragments, frozen custard dribblings, candied apples abandoned by tired children, sugar fluff crystals, salted almonds, popsicles, partially gnawed ice cream cones, and the wooden sticks of lollypops. Everywhere is loot for a rat—in tents, in booths, in haylofts—why, a fair has enough disgusting leftover food to satisfy a whole army of rats."[8]

Templeton's eyes were blazing.

"Is this true?" he asked. "Is this appetizing yarn of yours true? I like high living, and what you say tempts me."

"It is true," said the old sheep. "Go to the Fair, Templeton.[9] You will find that the conditions at a fair will surpass your wildest dreams. Buckets with sour mash sticking to them, tin cans containing particles of tuna fish, greasy paper bags stuffed with rotten . . ."

"That's enough!" cried Templeton. "Don't tell me any more. I'm going."

"Good," said Charlotte, winking at the old sheep.

Page 123

8. White must have had enormous pleasure compiling this list. The entire paragraph is one of White's finest. It begins with the thematic statement "A fair is a rat's paradise," and moves on a tour through the far reaches of the fair-ground, before ending, climatically, with "a whole army of rats."

9. So the sheep isn't so dumb after all. His suasive powers are impressive after Templeton announced on the previous page, "I haven't the slightest interest in fairs."

Page 124

10. Scientifically, that's how the drag line works for a spider.

Once again, if you read this sentence aloud, you'll find that its rhythm mimics the action it describes. The page renders a rapid sequence of a great deal of action.

"Now then—there is no time to be lost. Wilbur will soon be put into the crate. Templeton and I must get in the crate right now and hide ourselves."

The rat didn't waste a minute. He scampered over to the crate, crawled between the slats, and pulled straw up over him so he was hidden from sight.

"All right," said Charlotte, "I'm next." She sailed into the air,[10] let out a dragline, and dropped gently to the ground. Then she climbed the side of the crate and hid herself inside a knothole in the top board.

The old sheep nodded. "What a cargo!" she said. "That sign ought to say 'Zuckerman's Famous Pig and Two Stowaways'."

"Look out, the people are coming-oming-oming!" shouted the gander. "Cheese it, cheese it, cheese it!"

The big truck with Mr. Arable at the wheel backed slowly down toward the barnyard. Lurvy and Mr. Zuckerman walked alongside. Fern and Avery were standing in the body of the truck hanging on to the sideboards.

"Listen to me," whispered the old sheep to Wilbur. "When they open the crate and try to put you in, struggle! Don't go without a tussle. Pigs always resist when they are being loaded."

"If I struggle I'll get dirty," said Wilbur.

"Never mind that—do as I say! Struggle! If you were to walk into the crate without resisting, Zucker-

man might think you were bewitched. He'd be scared to go to the Fair."

Templeton poked his head up through the straw. [11]"Struggle if you must," said he, "but kindly remember that I'm hiding down here in this crate and I don't want to be stepped on, or kicked in the face, or pummeled, or crushed in any way, or squashed, or buffeted about, or bruised, or lacerated, or scarred, or biffed. Just watch what you're doing, Mr. Radiant, when they get shoving you in!"

"Be quiet, Templeton!" said the sheep. "Pull in your head—they're coming. Look radiant, Wilbur! Lay low, Charlotte! Talk it up, geese!"

The truck backed slowly to the pigpen and stopped. Mr. Arable cut the motor, got out, walked around to the rear, and lowered the tailgate. The geese cheered. Mrs. Arable got out of the truck. Fern and Avery jumped to the ground. Mrs. Zuckerman came walking down from the house. Everybody lined up at the fence and stood for a moment admiring Wilbur and the beautiful green crate. Nobody realized that the crate already contained a rat and a spider.

"That's some pig!" said Mrs. Arable.

"He's terrific," said Lurvy.

"He's very radiant," said Fern,[12] remembering the day he was born.

Page 125

11. Another extraordinary sentence, a fine passage to read aloud. Templeton's salmagundi of terms for abuse may not even be wholly in character, but obviously White is having a grand time.

12. Although "radiant" is typed in the draft, White wrote over it in ink, "precious." He probably then rejected *precious* because, unless Fern was mimicking her mother's speech, it's an unlikely word for a girl her age to use.

Page 126

13. Ever after the precise word, White wrote "butcher" over the typed "kill" (Draft H).

We must not forget that, at this point, there is no reason to think Wilbur will *not* be butchered.

Pages 126–128

14. These pages contain one of the fullest portraits of Avery. He's very much a character in his own right, and here he is rendered in slapstick high good humor.

"Well," said Mrs. Zuckerman, "he's clean, anyway. The buttermilk certainly helped."

Mr. Arable studied Wilbur carefully. "Yes, he's a wonderful pig," he said. "It's hard to believe that he was the runt of the litter. You'll get some extra good ham and bacon, Homer, when it comes time to kill *that* pig."[13]

Wilbur heard these words and his heart almost stopped. "I think I'm going to faint," he whispered to the old sheep, who was watching.

"Kneel down!" whispered the old sheep. "Let the blood rush to your head!"

Wilbur sank to his knees, all radiance gone. His eyes closed.

"Look!" screamed Fern. "He's fading away!"

"Hey, watch me!" yelled Avery, crawling on all fours into the crate. "I'm a pig! I'm a pig!"

Avery's foot touched Templeton under the straw. "What a mess!" thought the rat. "What fantastic creatures boys are! Why did I let myself in for this?"

The geese saw Avery in the crate and cheered.[14]

"Avery, you get out of that crate this instant!" commanded his mother. "What do you think you are?"

"I'm a pig!" cried Avery, tossing handfuls of straw into the air. "Oink, oink, oink!"

"The truck is rolling away, Papa," said Fern.

The truck, with no one at the wheel, had started to

roll downhill. Mr. Arable dashed to the driver's seat and pulled on the emergency brake. The truck stopped. The geese cheered. Charlotte crouched and made herself as small as possible in the knothole, so Avery wouldn't see her.

"Come out at once!" cried Mrs. Arable. Avery crawled out of the crate on hands and knees, making faces at Wilbur. Wilbur fainted away.

"The pig has passed out," said Mrs. Zuckerman. "Throw water on him!"

"Throw buttermilk!" suggested Avery.

The geese cheered.

Lurvy ran for a pail of water. Fern climbed into the pen and knelt by Wilbur's side.

"It's sunstroke," said Zuckerman. "The heat is too much for him."

"Maybe he's dead," said Avery.

"Come out of that pigpen *immediately*!" cried Mrs. Arable. Avery obeyed his mother and[15] climbed into the back of the truck so he could see better. Lurvy returned with cold water and dashed it on Wilbur.

"Throw some on me!" cried Avery. "I'm hot, too."

"Oh, keep quiet!" hollered Fern. "Keep *qui*-ut!" Her eyes were brimming with tears.[16]

Wilbur, feeling the cold water, came to. He rose slowly to his feet, while the geese cheered.

Page 127

15. In Manuscript H, White wrote, "Avery ~~climbed out and then he and Fern~~ climbed into the back of the truck." "Do not explain too much."[8] And so, above the deleted passage, White wrote, "obeyed his mother and."

16. Earlier White had written, "Her eyes had tears in them" (Draft H). Besides being more active, "brimming with tears" implies more water. On this stylistic point, see Beardsley.

Page 128

17. Quite a task, even though Wilbur is only about half a year old. When he's a year old, he might well weigh 400 pounds.

Our Maine authority on pigs instructs us that a pig at 120 pounds is properly called a "hog." A pig being fattened for market weighs about 220 pounds at six months. Six hundred pounds would be extreme. According to Guinness, the record size for a pig is 2,500 pounds and nine feet in length.

Fern isn't involved in the crating of Wilbur, nor does she even comment. She is now far removed from her earlier preoccupations.

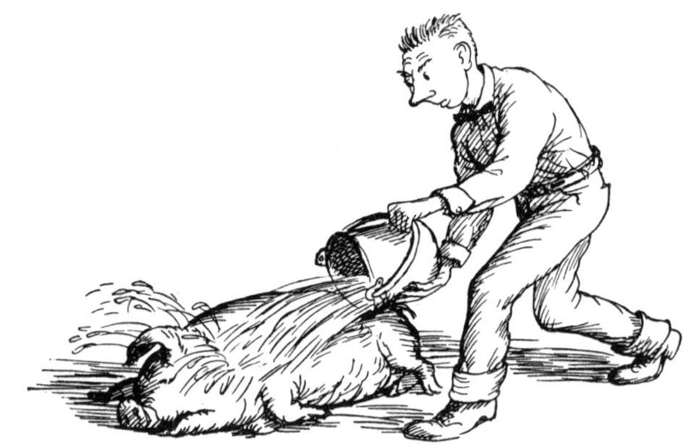

"He's up!" said Mr. Arable. "I guess there's nothing wrong with him."

"I'm hungry," said Avery. "I want a candied apple."

"Wilbur's all right now," said Fern. "We can start. I want to take a ride in the Ferris wheel."

Mr. Zuckerman and Mr. Arable and Lurvy grabbed the pig and pushed him headfirst toward the crate. Wilbur began to struggle. The harder the men pushed, the harder he held back. Avery jumped down and joined the men. Wilbur kicked and thrashed and grunted. "Nothing wrong with *this* pig," said Mr. Zuckerman cheerfully, pressing his knee against Wilbur's behind. "All together, now, boys! Shove!"[17]

With a final heave they jammed him into the crate. The geese cheered. Lurvy nailed some boards across the end, so Wilbur couldn't back out. Then, using all their strength, the men picked up the crate and heaved

it aboard the truck. They did not know that under the straw was a rat, and inside a knothole was a big grey spider. They saw only a pig.

"Everybody in!" called Mr. Arable. He started the motor. The ladies climbed in beside him. Mr. Zuckerman and Lurvy and Fern and Avery rode in back, hanging onto the sideboards. The truck began to move ahead. The geese cheered. The children answered their cheer, and away went everybody to the Fair.[18]

Page 129

18. This is as good a place as any to quote White: "[T]o interpret humor is as futile as explaining a spider's web in terms of geometry."[9]

Page 130

1. The word *uncle* does not appear as chapter title in Draft H.

2. The White family usually attended the Blue Hill Fair. Once, White took his son, Joel, to the Skowhegan Fair—the hottest fair day recorded—where it may be that Joel took a thirteen-year-old girl for a ride on a Ferris wheel.[1] Once or twice, the Whites went to the Fryeburg Fair.

3. In *OMM*, White wrote, "[W]ill the owner of Maine license 3261 please move his car. . . ."[2]

Chapter XVII

Uncle[1]

WHEN they pulled into the Fair Grounds, they could hear music and see the Ferris wheel turning in the sky.[2] They could smell the dust of the race track where the sprinkling cart had moistened it; and they could smell hamburgers frying and see balloons aloft. They could hear sheep blatting in their pens. An enormous voice over the loud speaker said: "Attention, please! Will the owner of a Pontiac car, license number H-2439, please move your car away from the fireworks shed!"[3]

"Can I have some money?" asked Fern.

"Can I, too?" asked Avery.

"I'm going to win a doll by spinning a wheel and it will stop at the right number," said Fern.

"I'm going to steer a jet plane and make it bump into another one."

"Can I have a balloon?" asked Fern.

"Can I have a frozen custard and a cheeseburger and some raspberry soda pop?" asked Avery.

Uncle

"You children be quiet till we get the pig unloaded," said Mrs. Arable.

"Let's let the children go off by themselves," suggested Mr. Arable. "The Fair only comes once a year." Mr. Arable gave Fern two quarters and two dimes. He gave Avery five dimes and four nickels. "Now run along!" he said. "And remember, the money has to last *all day*. Don't spend it all the first few minutes. And be back here at the truck at noontime so we can all have lunch together. And don't eat a lot of stuff that's going to make you sick to your stomachs."[4]

"And if you go in those swings," said Mrs. Arable, "you hang on tight! You hang on *very* tight. Hear me?"

"And don't get lost!" said Mrs. Zuckerman.

"And don't get dirty!"

"Don't get overheated!" said their mother.

"Watch out for pickpockets!" cautioned their father.

"And don't cross the race track when the horses are coming!" cried Mrs. Zuckerman.

The children grabbed each other by the hand and danced off in the direction of the merry-go-round, toward the wonderful music and the wonderful adventure and the wonderful excitement, into the wonderful midway where there would be no parents to guard them and guide them, and where they could be happy and free and do as they pleased. Mrs. Arable stood quietly

Page 131

4. White adeptly renders the litany of prohibitions to which children are subjected by adults. Note, then, the sharp contrast of the bottom paragraph on this page. Using his device of repetition, White shifts perspective to render the children's perceptions of the wonderful music, wonderful adventure, and wonderful excitement of the midway.

Page 132

5. Originally, Garth Williams wrote the word *ices* on the awning of the ice cream stand. Ursula Nordstrom thought that sounded too "English."

In the same letter, Nordstrom said she had asked Williams why he didn't show Wilbur at the fair and Williams had explained that since the focus of the chapter is on the fair, he didn't want to shift the reader's attention back to the farm.[3]

5

and watched them go. Then she sighed. Then she blew her nose.

"Do you really think it's all right?" she asked.

"Well, they've got to grow up some time," said Mr. Arable. "And a fair is a good place to start, I guess."[6]

While Wilbur was being unloaded and taken out of his crate and into his new pigpen, crowds gathered to watch. They stared at the sign ZUCKERMAN'S FAMOUS PIG. Wilbur stared back and tried to look extra good. He was pleased with his new home. The pen was grassy, and it was shaded from the sun by a shed roof.

Charlotte, watching her chance, scrambled out of the crate and climbed a post to the under side of the roof. Nobody noticed her.

Templeton, not wishing to come out in broad daylight, stayed quietly under the straw at the bottom of the crate. Mr. Zuckerman poured some skim milk into Wilbur's trough, pitched clean straw into his pen, and then he and Mrs. Zuckerman and the Arables walked away toward the cattle barn[7] to look at purebred cows and to see the sights. Mr. Zuckerman particularly wanted to look at tractors. Mrs. Zuckerman wanted to see a deep freeze. Lurvy wandered off by himself, hoping to meet friends and have some fun on the midway.

Pages 131–33

6. Fern's growth from a little girl, in harmony with the lives of the animals, to a young girl interested in boys is one of the major themes in the book as we now have it. Fern played a much smaller role in Draft H, which White set aside "to let the body heat go out of it," and the particular and explicit statement of theme we have here does not exist in Draft H at all.

Pages 133

7. In Draft I, White had typed "exhibition building." "Cattle barn" is written over it.

Since this was the version that went to the printer, as well as the last chance to make corrections, any changes White made in Draft I are ones he would have thought important. (As indicated in Appendix B, page 206, it's my opinion that an important draft between H and I is missing. White could not have moved directly and without trace from version H, with its small role for Fern, to the finished version, in which she plays a major role from the start.)

8. For reasons of climate and cost, pigs in northern New England are seldom kept for a full year. However, an "enormous" pig might be one that weighed over eight hundred pounds.

9. True to character, sophisticated Charlotte keeps her cool.

As soon as the people were gone, Charlotte spoke to Wilbur.

"It's a good thing you can't see what *I* see," she said.

"What do you see?" asked Wilbur.

"There's a pig in the next pen and he's enormous.[8] I'm afraid he's much bigger than you are."

"Maybe he's older than I am, and has had more time to grow," suggested Wilbur. Tears began to come to his eyes.

"I'll drop down and have a closer look," Charlotte said. Then she crawled along a beam till she was directly over the next pen. She let herself down on a dragline until she hung in the air just in front of the big pig's snout.

"May I have your name?" she asked, politely.

The pig stared at her. "No name," he said in a big, hearty voice. "Just call me Uncle."

"Very well, Uncle," replied Charlotte. "What is the date of your birth? Are you a spring pig?"

"Sure I'm a spring pig," replied Uncle. "What did you think I was, a spring chicken? Haw, haw—that's a good one, eh, Sister?"

"Mildly funny,[9]" said Charlotte. "I've heard funnier ones, though. Glad to have met you, and now I must be going."

She ascended slowly and returned to Wilbur's pen.

"He claims he's a spring pig," reported Charlotte,

"and perhaps he is. One thing is certain, he has a most unattractive personality. He is too familiar, too noisy, and he cracks weak jokes. Also, he's not anywhere near as clean as you are, nor as pleasant. I took quite a dislike to him in our brief interview. He's going to be a hard pig to beat, though, Wilbur, on account of his size and weight. But with me helping you, it can be done."

"When are you going to spin a web?" asked Wilbur.

"This afternoon, late, if I'm not too tired," said

Page 136

10. As late as Draft I, this read, "She did not look well. Her color wasn't good and she seemed listless." White has followed all his own stylistic advice—specificity, positive language, and the avoidance of qualifiers.

Charlotte. "The least thing tires me these days. I don't seem to have the energy I once had. My age, I guess."

Wilbur looked at his friend. She looked rather swollen and she seemed listless.[10]

"I'm awfully sorry to hear that you're feeling poorly, Charlotte," he said. "Perhaps if you spin a web and catch a couple of flies you'll feel better."

"Perhaps," she said, wearily. "But I feel like the end of a long day." Clinging upside down to the ceiling, she settled down for a nap, leaving Wilbur very much worried.

All morning people wandered past Wilbur's pen. Dozens and dozens of strangers stopped to stare at him and to admire his silky white coat, his curly tail, his kind and radiant expression. Then they would move on to the next pen where the bigger pig lay. Wilbur heard several people make favorable remarks about Uncle's great size. He couldn't help overhearing these remarks, and he couldn't help worrying. "And now, with Charlotte not feeling well . . ." he thought. "Oh, dear!"

All morning Templeton slept quietly under the straw. The day grew fiercely hot. At noon the Zuckermans and the Arables returned to the pigpen. Then, a few minutes later, Fern and Avery showed up. Fern had a monkey doll in her arms and was eating Crackerjack. Avery had a balloon tied to his ear and was chewing a candied apple. The children were hot and dirty.

Uncle

"Isn't it hot?" said Mrs. Zuckerman.

"It's *terribly* hot," said Mrs. Arable, fanning herself with an advertisement of a deep freeze.[11]

One by one they climbed into the truck and opened lunch boxes. The sun beat down on everything. Nobody seemed hungry.

"When are the judges going to decide about Wilbur?" asked Mrs. Zuckerman.

"Not till tomorrow," said Mr. Zuckerman.

Lurvy appeared, carrying an Indian blanket that he had won.

"That's just what we need," said Avery. "A blanket."

"Of course it is," replied Lurvy. And he spread the blanket across the sideboards of the truck so that it was like a little tent. The children sat in the shade, under the blanket, and felt better.

After lunch, they stretched out and fell asleep.

Page 137

11. The evening before the fair, Mrs. Arable had gone to bed early and dreamed "about a deep freeze unit" (*CW*, 118). It's obviously still on her mind.

Page 138

1. The original chapter title, even in the last draft (I), was "EVENING."

The time of day echoes the cycle of the seasons, the rhythm of the story.

2. Earlier, White wrote, "[H]e was annoyed that he had to run errands" in Draft H. The image of a "messenger boy" is more immediate, easier to picture.

Chapter XVIII

The Cool of the Evening[1]

IN THE cool of the evening, when shadows darkened the Fair Grounds, Templeton crept from the crate and looked around. Wilbur lay asleep in the straw. Charlotte was building a web. Templeton's keen nose detected many fine smells in the air. The rat was hungry and thirsty. He decided to go exploring. Without saying anything to anybody, he started off.

"Bring me back a word!" Charlotte called after him. "I shall be writing tonight for the last time."

The rat mumbled something to himself and disappeared into the shadows. He did not like being treated like a messenger boy.[2]

After the heat of the day, the evening came as a welcome relief to all. The Ferris wheel was lighted now. It went round and round in the sky and seemed twice as high as by day. There were lights on the midway, and you could hear the crackle of the gambling machines and the music of the merry-go-round and the voice of the man in the beano booth calling numbers.

The children felt refreshed after their nap. Fern met

her friend Henry Fussy, and he invited her to ride with him in the Ferris wheel.[3] He even bought a ticket for her, so it didn't cost her anything. When Mrs. Arable happened to look up into the starry sky and saw her little daughter sitting with Henry Fussy and going higher and higher into the air, and saw how happy Fern looked, she just shook her head. "My, my!" she said. "Henry Fussy. Think of that!"

Templeton kept out of sight. In the tall grass behind the cattle barn he found a folded newspaper. Inside it were leftovers from somebody's lunch: a deviled ham sandwich, a piece of Swiss cheese, part of a hard-boiled egg, and the core of a wormy apple. The rat crawled in and ate everything. Then he tore a word out of the paper, rolled it up, and started back to Wilbur's pen.[4]

Charlotte had her web almost finished when Templeton returned, carrying the newspaper clipping. She had left a space in the middle of the web. At this hour, no people were around the pigpen, so the rat and the spider and the pig were by themselves.

Page 139

3. This is a critical moment in Fern's life. She is older and her interests have turned completely. As for Ferris wheels, in White's essay "Fall" he wrote: "I love [a fair] early on a rainy morning when the Ferris wheel is wearing its tarpaulins and the phrenologist is just brushing her teeth."[1]

4. Draft H contains a long description of Templeton's feelings at this point. That description was later deleted.

5. "Read it for me—I'm nearsighted." Draft H.

Almost three pages are deleted here from Draft H—the last extant major draft. Sample: Templeton brings a card that had fallen off a tractor and that speaks of "[l]ow cost, all-purpose power unit" and continues, "Take a good look at this handy power package. Plenty of clearance, turns on a dime."

"Well," she said, "I'm not sure Wilbur has plenty of clearance."

Charlotte spoke of her nearsightedness earlier (*CW*, page 37). White's source, probably Gertsch.[2]

"I hope you brought a good one," Charlotte said. "It is the last word I shall ever write."

"Here," said Templeton, unrolling the paper.

"What does it say?" asked Charlotte. "You'll have to read it for me."[5]

"It says 'Humble,' " replied the rat.

"Humble?" said Charlotte. " 'Humble' has two meanings. It means 'not proud' and it means 'near the ground.' That's Wilbur all over. He's not proud and he's near the ground."

"Well, I hope you're satisfied," sneered the rat. "I'm not going to spend all my time fetching and carrying. I came to this Fair to enjoy myself, not to deliver papers."

"You've been very helpful," Charlotte said. "Run along, if you want to see more of the Fair."

The rat grinned. "I'm going to make a night of it," he said. "The old sheep was right—this Fair is a rat's paradise. What eating! And what drinking! And everywhere good hiding and good hunting. Bye, bye, my humble Wilbur! Fare thee well, Charlotte, you old schemer! This will be a night to remember in a rat's life."

He vanished into the shadows.

Charlotte went back to her work. It was quite dark now. In the distance, fireworks began going off—rockets, scattering fiery balls in the sky. By the time the

Arables and the Zuckermans and Lurvy returned from the grandstand, Charlotte had finished her web. The word HUMBLE was woven neatly in the center. Nobody noticed it in the darkness. Everyone was tired and happy.

Fern and Avery climbed into the truck and lay down. They pulled the Indian blanket over them. Lurvy gave Wilbur a forkful of fresh straw. Mr. Arable patted him. "Time for us to go home," he said to the pig. "See you tomorrow."

The grownups climbed slowly into the truck and Wilbur heard the engine start and then heard the truck moving away in low speed. He would have felt lonely and homesick, had Charlotte not been with him. He

never felt lonely when she was near. In the distance he could still hear the music of the merry-go-round.

As he was dropping off to sleep he spoke to Charlotte.

"Sing me that song again, about the dung and the dark," he begged.

"Not tonight," she said in a low voice. "I'm too tired." Her voice didn't seem to come from her web.

"Where are you?" asked Wilbur. "I can't see you. Are you on your web?"

"I'm back here," she answered. "Up in this back corner."

"Why aren't you on your web?" asked Wilbur. "You almost *never* leave your web."

"I've left it tonight," she said.

Wilbur closed his eyes. "Charlotte," he said, after a while, "do you really think Zuckerman will let me live and not kill me when the cold weather comes? Do you really think so?"

"Of course," said Charlotte. "You are a famous pig and you are a good pig. Tomorrow you will probably win a prize. The whole world will hear about you. Zuckerman will be proud and happy to own such a pig. You have nothing to fear, Wilbur—nothing to worry about. Maybe you'll live forever—who knows? And now, go to sleep."

For a while there was no sound. Then Wilbur's voice:

"What are you doing up there, Charlotte?"

"Oh, making something," she said. "Making something, as usual."

"Is it something for me?" asked Wilbur.[6]

"No," said Charlotte. "It's something for *me*, for a change."

"Please tell me what it is," begged Wilbur.

"I'll tell you in the morning," she said. "When the first light comes into the sky and the sparrows stir and the cows rattle their chains, when the rooster crows and the stars fade, when early cars whisper along the highway, you look up here and I'll show you something. I will show you my masterpiece."

Before she finished the sentence, Wilbur was asleep. She could tell by the sound of his breathing that he was sleeping peacefully, deep in the straw.

Miles away, at the Arables' house, the men sat around the kitchen table eating a dish of canned peaches and talking over the events of the day. Upstairs, Avery was already in bed and asleep. Mrs. Arable was tucking Fern into bed.

"Did you have a good time at the Fair?" she asked as she kissed her daughter.

Fern nodded. "I had the best time I have ever had anywhere or any time in all of my whole life."

"Well!" said Mrs. Arable. "Isn't that nice!"[7]

Page 143

6. Wilbur remains self-centered, unable to imagine that anyone else may be suffering. Thus his transformation at book's end is all the more dramatic.

7. Mrs. Arable's abstraction, her essential inattention, is very much part of her.

Page 144

1. White liked this Latin phrase.

Elledge relates that in 1933, when White was hoping to write a longer work, he would refer to it as his "magnum opus."

When I asked the eighty-five-year-old White, in 1984, whether a certain passage in a manuscript was in Katharine's handwriting or in his own, he answered,

> The . . . pages are in *my* handwriting—just a worried little old author talking to himself in an attempt to remove some bugs from his *opus*. [Italics added] [1]

Five years later, in 1989, I was rummaging in the White archives at Cornell. There I found the typed rough draft for that very same note the aged White had sent me. It read:

"in an attempt to ~~get~~ remove some bugs ~~out of~~ from his ~~narration~~ creation [?]"

The draft is remarkable evidence of White's scrupulous and lifetime dedication to word, sense, and nuance. We must wonder, too, why White journeyed from "narration" to "creation" to "opus" when referring to his own writing.

Narration is colorless. As for *creation*, we're apt to think of something grandiose, like a Haydn oratorio.

So how should an author refer to his own "extended prose narrative," which resembles a novel and is beyond question a work of substance, but is for "mere" children? How will he do it without sounding either puffy or self-deprecating? Perhaps the same way he would refer to a great work he dreamed of writing as a young man but doesn't want to go out on a limb for, lest that limb prove brittle.

The answer: the rhetorical flourish of the mock heroic, the grandiloquent self-mockery that forestalls attack. Off and on for fifty years, White played variations on that theme.

Chapter XIX

The Egg Sac

NEXT morning when the first light came into the sky and the sparrows stirred in the trees, when the cows rattled their chains and the rooster crowed and the early automobiles went whispering along the road, Wilbur awoke and looked for Charlotte. He saw her up overhead in a corner near the back of his pen. She was very quiet. Her eight legs were spread wide. She seemed to have shrunk during the night. Next to her, attached to the ceiling, Wilbur saw a curious object. It was a sort of sac, or cocoon. It was peach-colored and looked as though it were made of cotton candy.

"Are you awake, Charlotte?" he said softly.

"Yes," came the answer.

"What is that nifty little thing? Did you make it?"

"I did indeed," replied Charlotte in a weak voice.

"Is it a plaything?"

"Plaything? I should say not. It is my egg sac, my *magnum opus*."[1]

"I don't know what a magnum opus is," said Wilbur.

The Egg Sac

"That's Latin," explained Charlotte. "It means 'great work.' This egg sac is my great work—the finest thing I have ever made."[2]

"What's inside it?" asked Wilbur. "Eggs?"

"Five hundred and fourteen of them,[3]" she replied.

"Five *hundred* and four*teen*?" said Wilbur. "You're kidding."

"No, I'm not. I counted them. I got started counting, so I kept on—just to keep my mind occupied."

"It's a perfectly beautiful egg sac,[4]" said Wilbur, feeling as happy as though he had constructed it himself.

"Yes, it *is* pretty," replied Charlotte, patting the sac with her two front legs. "Anyway, I can guarantee that it is strong. It's made out of the toughest material I have. It is also waterproof. The eggs are inside and will be warm and dry."

Nor is that other phrase in White's note—"*just a worried little old author*" [my italics]—to be dismissed. In 1944, in an almost paradigmatic Whitean sentence, he wrote, "Last week when things were at a low point in Europe, we sat reading the paper, trying to figure out who was going to win—*just a nervous little homebody in a sack suit*, trying to unravel supply lines, spearheads . . . [italics added]."[2]

And, years later, in response to Elledge's letter of condolence after Katharine's death, White wrote, ". . . Right now, I am moving a small oak tree into the desolate gravesite and praying that it will take hold. I am *just a little man in a 10-room house*, with nowhere to go but on [italics added]."[3]

There's a double point to all this: first, the evidence of the self-protective rhetorical, stylistic devices employed by White on subjects very close to him; and second, the persistence and the lifetime indelibility of turns of phrase that are as unchanging and individual as a fingerprint.

Page 145

2. Charlotte is moving from being merely another character to being, in some small degree, a choral commentator, as Dr. Dorian was before. She suggests the miraculous workings of nature that gave title to Chapter XI, "The Miracle," and points ahead to the note of "immortality" the sac will bring about by book's end.

3. Kevin Williams notes that White corrected himself. Originally he gave Charlotte 214 eggs.[4]

4. We love Wilbur at this moment.

5. Perhaps the first time we note a bit of empathy on the part of Wilbur.

A spider egg sack at the White farm

"Charlotte," said Wilbur dreamily, "are you really going to have five hundred and fourteen children?"

"If nothing happens, yes," she said. "Of course, they won't show up till next spring." Wilbur noticed that Charlotte's voice sounded sad.

"What makes you sound so down-hearted? I should think you'd be terribly happy about this."

"Oh, don't pay any attention to me," said Charlotte. "I just don't have much pep any more. I guess I feel sad because I won't ever see my children."

"What do you mean you won't see your children! Of *course* you will. We'll *all* see them. It's going to be simply wonderful next spring in the barn cellar with five hundred and fourteen baby spiders running around all over the place. And the geese will have a new set of goslings, and the sheep will have their new lambs . . ."

"Maybe," said Charlotte quietly. "However, I have a feeling I'm not going to see the results of last night's efforts. I don't feel good at all. I think I'm languishing, to tell you the truth."

Wilbur didn't understand the word "languish" and he hated to bother Charlotte by asking her to explain.[5] But he was so worried he felt he had to ask.

"What does 'languishing' mean?"

"It means I'm slowing up, feeling my age. I'm not young any more, Wilbur. But I don't want you to worry about me. This is your big day today. Look at my web—doesn't it show up well with the dew on it?"

The Egg Sac

Charlotte's web never looked more beautiful than it looked this morning. Each strand held dozens of bright drops of early morning dew.[6] The light from the east struck it and made it all plain and clear. It was a perfect piece of designing and building. In another hour or two, a steady stream of people would pass by, admiring it, and reading it, and looking at Wilbur, and marveling at the miracle.

As Wilbur was studying the web, a pair of whiskers and a sharp face appeared. Slowly Templeton dragged himself across the pen and threw himself down in a corner.

"I'm back," he said in a husky voice. "What a night!"

The rat was swollen to twice his normal size. His stomach was as big around as a jelly jar.

7

Page 147

6. White would have been aware of a beautiful photograph of a dewy web in Gertsch.

7. Garth Williams succeeded in keeping a delicate balance between Templeton as a true rat and as a sort of Falstaffian rogue at rest.

8. Templeton seems truly, deeply, profoundly, irredeemably mean. At times like this, he appears to have no connection to the camaraderie of the barnyard—or perhaps even to the pervasive affirmation of this children's story.

"What a night!" he repeated, hoarsely. "What feasting and carousing! A real gorge! I must have eaten the remains of thirty lunches. Never have I seen such leavings, and everything well-ripened and seasoned with the passage of time and the heat of the day. Oh, it was rich, my friends, rich!"

"You ought to be ashamed of yourself," said Charlotte in disgust. "It would serve you right if you had an acute attack of indigestion."

"Don't worry about my stomach," snarled Templeton. "It can handle anything. And by the way, I've got some bad news. As I came past that pig next door—the one that calls himself Uncle—I noticed a blue tag on the front of his pen. That means he has won first prize. I guess you're licked, Wilbur.[8] You might as well relax —nobody is going to hang any medal on *you*. Furthermore, I wouldn't be surprised if Zuckerman changes his mind about you. Wait till he gets hankering for some fresh pork and smoked ham and crisp bacon! He'll take the knife to you, my boy."

"Be still, Templeton!" said Charlotte. "You're too stuffed and bloated to know what you're saying. Don't pay any attention to him, Wilbur!"

Wilbur tried not to think about what the rat had just said. He decided to change the subject.

"Templeton," said Wilbur, "if you weren't so dopey, you would have noticed that Charlotte has made an egg

sac. She is going to become a mother. For your information, there are five hundred and fourteen eggs in that peachy little sac."

"Is this true?" asked the rat, eyeing the sac suspiciously.

"Yes, it's true," sighed Charlotte.

"Congratulations!" murmured Templeton. "This *has* been a night!" He closed his eyes, pulled some straw over himself, and dropped off into a deep sleep. Wilbur and Charlotte were glad to be rid of him for a while.

At nine o'clock, Mr. Arable's truck rolled into the Fair Grounds and came to a stop at Wilbur's pen. Everybody climbed out.

"Look!" cried Fern. "Look at Charlotte's web! Look what it says!"

The grownups and the children joined hands and stood there, studying the new sign.

" 'Humble,' " said Mr. Zuckerman. "Now isn't that just the word for Wilbur!"

Everyone rejoiced to find that the miracle of the web had been repeated. Wilbur gazed up lovingly into their faces. He looked very humble and very grateful. Fern winked at Charlotte.[9] Lurvy soon got busy. He poured a bucket of warm slops into the trough, and while Wil-

Page 149

9. This sentence is doubly important.

It is added in pen to the typescript of Draft I. Because this is the draft annotated by/for the printer, additions to Draft I are always significant. White was concerned to keep a connection between the secrets of the barnyard and the girl that Fern was at story's outset. Henry Fussy notwithstanding, Fern *has* kept a precious piece of her childhood.

10. Presumably because of Uncle's success, Mrs. Zuckerman cries. Even Lurvy blows his nose loudly. But Fern cries for quite a different reason.

11. It's a good writerly device in passages of high emotion to deflect attention to something as mundane as a buttermilk bath. At Cornell, White had already written his rule for good writing: never to take oneself too damned seriously.[5]

bur ate his breakfast Lurvy scratched him gently with a smooth stick.

"Wait a minute!" cried Avery. "Look at this!" He pointed to the blue tag on Uncle's pen. "This pig has won first prize already."

The Zuckermans and the Arables stared at the tag. Mrs. Zuckerman began to cry. Nobody said a word. They just stared at the tag. Then they stared at Uncle. Then they stared at the tag again. Lurvy took out an enormous handkerchief and blew his nose very loud—so loud, in fact, that the noise was heard by stableboys over at the horse barn.

"Can I have some money?" asked Fern. "I want to go out on the midway."

"You stay right where you are!" said her mother. Tears came to Fern's eyes.[10]

"What's everybody crying about?" asked Mr. Zuckerman. "Let's get busy! Edith, bring the buttermilk!"

Mrs. Zuckerman wiped her eyes with her handkerchief. She went to the truck and came back with a gallon jar of buttermilk.[11]

"Bath time!" said Zuckerman, cheerfully. He and Mrs. Zuckerman and Avery climbed into Wilbur's pen. Avery slowly poured buttermilk on Wilbur's head and back, and as it trickled down his sides and cheeks, Mr. and Mrs. Zuckerman rubbed it into his hair and skin. Passersby stopped to watch. Pretty soon quite a crowd

had gathered. Wilbur grew beautifully white and smooth. The morning sun shone through his pink ears.

"He isn't as big as that pig next door," remarked one bystander, "but he's cleaner. That's what I like."

"So do I," said another man.

"He's humble, too," said a woman, reading the sign on the web.[12]

Everybody who visited the pigpen had a good word to say about Wilbur. Everyone admired the web. And of course nobody noticed Charlotte.

Suddenly a voice was heard on the loud speaker.

"Attention, please!" it said. "Will Mr. Homer Zuckerman bring his famous pig to the judges' booth in front of the grandstand. A special award will be made there in twenty minutes. Everyone is invited to attend. Crate your pig, please, Mr. Zuckerman, and report to the judges' booth promptly!"

For a moment after this announcement, the Arables and the Zuckermans were unable to speak or move. Then Avery picked up a handful of straw and threw it high in the air and gave a loud yell. The straw fluttered down like confetti into Fern's hair. Mr. Zuckerman hugged Mrs. Zuckerman. Mr. Arable kissed Mrs. Arable. Avery kissed Wilbur. Lurvy shook hands with everybody. Fern hugged her mother. Avery hugged Fern. Mrs. Arable hugged Mrs. Zuckerman.

Up overhead, in the shadows of the ceiling, Char-

Page 151

12. Again, people's credulity in the presence of the written word.

lotte crouched unseen, her front legs encircling her egg sac. Her heart was not beating as strongly as usual and she felt weary and old, but she was sure at last that she had saved Wilbur's life,[13] and she felt peaceful and contented.

"We have no time to lose!" shouted Mr. Zuckerman. "Lurvy, help with the crate!"

"Can I have some money?" asked Fern.

"You *wait*!" said Mrs. Arable. "Can't you see everybody is busy?"

"Put that empty buttermilk jar into the truck!" commanded Mr. Arable. Avery grabbed the jar and rushed to the truck.

"Does my hair look all right?" asked Mrs. Zuckerman.

"Looks fine," snapped Mr. Zuckerman, as he and Lurvy set the crate down in front of Wilbur.

"You didn't even *look* at my hair!" said Mrs. Zuckerman.

"You're all right, Edith," said Mrs. Arable. "Just keep calm."

Templeton, asleep in the straw, heard the commotion and awoke. He didn't know exactly what was going on, but when he saw the men shoving Wilbur into the crate he made up his mind to go along. He watched his chance and when no one was looking he

Page 153

13. Folder I reads "she ~~knew now~~ that. . . ."
Since this is the omniscient narrator talking, we are for the first time given certain notice that Wilbur will be saved.

Page 154

14. In *CW*, page 68, "Fern had a crown of daisies in her hair."

Although Fern, with the straw in her hair now, appears to the narrator—and to us, too—as a beautiful rural sprite, her own thoughts are no longer naïve, childish, innocent. This is the moment when Fern has changed—forever.

One critic has viewed the larger context memorably, suggesting that Fern begins her walk, now, into the world of death. Unlike Charlotte, she will not gain immortality, for she is not a writer, as is Charlotte.[6]

crept into the crate and buried himself in the straw at the bottom.

"All ready, boys!" cried Mr. Zuckerman. "Let's go!" He and Mr. Arable and Lurvy and Avery grabbed the crate and boosted it over the side of the pen and up into the truck. Fern jumped aboard and sat on top of the crate. She still had straw in her hair and looked very pretty and excited.[14] Mr. Arable started the motor. Everyone climbed in, and off they drove to the judge's booth in front of the grandstand.

As they passed the Ferris wheel, Fern gazed up at it and wished she were in the topmost car with Henry Fussy at her side.

Chapter XX

The Hour of Triumph[1]

"SPECIAL announcement!" said the loud speaker in a pompous voice.[2] "The management of the Fair takes great pleasure in presenting Mr. Homer L. Zuckerman and his famous pig. The truck bearing this extraordinary animal is now approaching the infield. Kindly stand back and give the truck room to proceed! In a few moments the pig will be unloaded in the special judging ring in front of the grandstand, where a special award will be made. Will the crowd please make way and let the truck pass. Thank you."

Wilbur trembled when he heard this speech. He felt happy but dizzy. The truck crept along slowly in low speed. Crowds of people surrounded it, and Mr. Arable had to drive very carefully in order not to run over anybody. At last he managed to reach the judges' stand. Avery jumped out and lowered the tailgate.

"I'm scared to death," whispered Mrs. Zuckerman.[3] "Hundreds of people are looking at us."

"Cheer up," replied Mrs. Arable, "this is fun."

Page 155

1. In Draft I, this chapter is still titled "THE WINNER," all in caps, but that title is also entirely crossed out and replaced with "The Hour of Triumph." And see page 157.

2. This phrase added in pen in Draft I. Additions to I were presumably last-minute changes.

3. In Draft I, *whispered* is written in pen over a typed, deleted *said*. White ever preferred the precise word.

Page 156

4. It's poignant that Fern, who is responsible for Wilbur's very survival, absents herself so completely in his moment of triumph.

5. At this point, White deleted a good deal of commentary from Draft H, such as "A rat has to be very careful." No ruminations should stall the rapid action at this point, and nothing should distract from sharp focus on the principal characters.

"Unload your pig, please!" said the loud speaker.

"All together, now, boys!" said Mr. Zuckerman. Several men stepped forward from the crowd to help lift the crate. Avery was the busiest helper of all.

"Tuck your shirt in, Avery!" cried Mrs. Zuckerman. "And tighten your belt. Your pants are coming down."

"Can't you see I'm busy?" replied Avery in disgust.

"Look!" cried Fern, pointing. "There's Henry!"

"Don't shout, Fern!" said her mother. "And don't point!"

"Can't I *please* have some money?" asked Fern. "Henry invited me to go on the Ferris wheel again, only I don't think he has any money left. He ran out of money."

Mrs. Arable opened her handbag. "Here," she said. "Here is forty cents. Now don't get lost! And be back at our regular meeting place by the pigpen very soon!"

Fern raced off,[4] ducking and dodging through the crowd, in search of Henry.

"The Zuckerman pig is now being taken from his crate," boomed the voice of the loud speaker. "Stand by for an announcement!"

Templeton crouched under the straw at the bottom of the crate.[5] "What a lot of nonsense!" muttered the rat. "What a lot of fuss about nothing!"

Over in the pigpen, silent and alone, Charlotte rested. Her two front legs embraced the egg sac. Charlotte

could hear everything that was said on the loud speaker. The words gave her courage. This was her hour of triumph.[6]

As Wilbur came out of the crate, the crowd clapped and cheered. Mr. Zuckerman took off his cap and bowed. Lurvy pulled his big handkerchief from his pocket and wiped the sweat from the back of his neck. Avery knelt in the dirt by Wilbur's side, busily stroking him and showing off. Mrs. Zuckerman and Mrs. Arable stood on the running board of the truck.

"Ladeez and gentlemen," said the loud speaker, "we now present Mr. Homer L. Zuckerman's distinguished pig. The fame of this unique animal has spread to the far corners of the earth,[7] attracting many valuable tourists to our great State. Many of you will recall that never-to-be-forgotten day last summer when the writing appeared mysteriously on the spider's web in Mr. Zuckerman's barn, calling the attention of all and sundry to the fact that this pig was completely out of the ordinary. This miracle has never been fully explained, although learned men have visited the Zuckerman pigpen to study and observe the phenomenon. In the last analysis, we simply know that we are dealing with supernatural forces here, and we should all feel proud and grateful. In the words of the spider's web, ladies and gentlemen, this is some pig."

Page 157

6. Charlotte's triumph, not Wilbur's. We see clearly what is the primary focus of White's attention, and we understand why the book is titled *Charlotte's Web*, and not, for example, *The Saving of Wilbur* (or *Piglet Wilbur and His Friends*, as the misconceived German has it). And in retrospect, we see the centrality of The Miracle and of Dr. Dorian's musings.

7. Note that, as always, the miracle of Charlotte's writing is attributed to or transferred to Wilbur by the gullible human beings—just as Charlotte had intended.

Page 158

8. The announcer is, of course, mindlessly using the words that Charlotte wove into the web. From "Do *away* with it?" in *CW*, page 1, to the naming of Charlotte's offspring in the concluding chapter, the uses, misuses, power, and implications of words are often White's theme.

Wilbur blushed. He stood perfectly still and tried to look his best.

"This magnificent animal," continued the loud speaker, "is truly terrific. Look at him, ladies and gentlemen! Note the smoothness and whiteness of the coat, observe the spotless skin, the healthy pink glow of ears and snout."

"It's the buttermilk," whispered Mrs. Arable to Mrs. Zuckerman.

"Note the general radiance of this animal! Then remember the day when the word 'radiant' appeared clearly on the web. Whence came this mysterious writing? Not from the spider, we can rest assured of that. Spiders are very clever at weaving their webs, but needless to say spiders cannot write."

"Oh, they can't, can't they?" murmured Charlotte to herself.

"Ladeez and gentlemen," continued the loud speaker, "I must not take any more of your valuable time. On behalf of the governors of the Fair, I have the honor of awarding a special prize of twenty-five dollars to Mr. Zuckerman, together with a handsome bronze medal suitably engraved, in token of our appreciation of the part played by this pig—this radiant, this terrific, this humble pig[8]—in attracting so many visitors to our great County Fair."

Wilbur had been feeling dizzier and dizzier through

this long, complimentary speech. When he heard the crowd begin to cheer and clap again, he suddenly fainted away. His legs collapsed, his mind went blank, and he fell to the ground, unconscious.

"What's wrong?" asked the loud speaker. "What's going on, Zuckerman? What's the trouble with your pig?"

Avery was kneeling by Wilbur's head, stroking him. Mr. Zuckerman was dancing about, fanning him with his cap.

"He's all right," cried Mr. Zuckerman. "He gets these spells. He's modest and can't stand praise."[9]

"Well, we can't give a prize to a *dead* pig," said the loud speaker. "It's never been done."

"He isn't dead," hollered Zuckerman. "He's fainted. He gets embarrassed easily. Run for some water, Lurvy!"

Lurvy sprang from the judges' ring and disappeared.

Templeton poked his head from the straw. He noticed that the end of Wilbur's tail was within reach. Templeton grinned. "I'll tend to this," he chuckled. He took Wilbur's tail in his mouth and bit it, just as hard as he could bite. The pain revived Wilbur. In a flash he was back on his feet.

"Ouch!" he screamed.

"Hoorray!" yelled the crowd. "He's up! The pig's up! Good work, Zuckerman! That's some pig!" Every-

Page 159

9. White had his own problems with honors. When asked to give a talk for *The Harvard Crimson*, White cabled back, "SORRY CANNOT SPEAK DO NOT KNOW HOW. . . ."[1]

Receiving the Recognition of Merit award of the George G. Stone Center for Children's Books in 1970, White wrote:

> I accept this award, and I send my thanks to the Children's Book Center. I'm sorry I can't be there bodily, to reach out and take the scroll, but perhaps it's just as well; you may recall the story of Charlotte, that when Wilbur, the pig, was given the Award of Merit at the county fair, he fainted dead away and had to be revived by a sharp bite on the tail. I wouldn't want to put the Claremont conference through an ordeal of that sort.[2]

Page 160

10. Not White's view, certainly. His account of what he called "the Hanover ordeal," the receipt of an honorary doctorate at Dartmouth College, is hair-raising and hilarious as he tells of young Bill Pulley, "a very nice boy from Ohio," assigned by Dartmouth to greet the tired, queasy White ("sick as a coot") when he arrived, and not to let him out of his sight thereafter, and of the battle he had donning the academic hood "shaped like a loose-fitting horse collar." As White tells it, when he received the degree, "there was some clapping and a couple of boos," and when he sat down, the hood got caught, pulled over his face, "as in falconry." "Nobody," White wrote, "who has never suffered my peculiar kind of disability can understand the sheer hell of such moments. . . ."[3]

one was delighted. Mr. Zuckerman was the most pleased of all. He sighed with relief. Nobody had seen Templeton. The rat had done his work well.

And now one of the judges climbed into the ring with the prizes. He handed Mr. Zuckerman two ten dollar bills and a five dollar bill. Then he tied the medal around Wilbur's neck. Then he shook hands with Mr. Zuckerman while Wilbur blushed. Avery put out his hand and the judge shook hands with him, too. The crowd cheered. A photographer took Wilbur's picture.

A great feeling of happiness swept over the Zuckermans and the Arables. This was the greatest moment in Mr. Zuckerman's life. It is deeply satisfying to win a prize in front of a lot of people.[10]

As Wilbur was being shoved back into the crate, Lurvy came charging through the crowd carrying a pail of water. His eyes had a wild look. Without hesitating a second, he dashed the water at Wilbur. In his excitement he missed his aim, and the water splashed all over Mr. Zuckerman and Avery. They got soaking wet.

"For goodness' sake!" bellowed Mr. Zuckerman, who was really drenched. "What ails you, Lurvy? Can't you see the pig is all right?"

"You asked for water," said Lurvy meekly.

"I didn't ask for a shower bath," said Mr. Zuckerman. The crowd roared with laughter. Finally Mr. Zuckerman had to laugh, too. And of course Avery was tickled to find himself so wet, and he immediately

started to act like a clown. He pretended he was taking a shower bath; he made faces and danced around and rubbed imaginary soap under his armpits. Then he dried himself with an imaginary towel.

"Avery, stop it!" cried his mother. "Stop showing off!"

But the crowd loved it. Avery heard nothing but the applause. He liked being a clown in a ring, with everybody watching, in front of a grandstand. When he discovered there was still a little water left in the bottom of the pail, he raised the pail high in the air and dumped the water on himself and made faces. The children in the grandstand screamed with appreciation.

At last things calmed down. Wilbur was loaded into the truck. Avery was led from the ring by his mother and placed on the seat of the truck to dry off. The truck, driven by Mr. Arable, crawled slowly back to the pigpen. Avery's wet trousers made a big wet spot on the seat.

Chapter XXI

Last Day[1]

CHARLOTTE and Wilbur were alone. The families had gone to look for Fern. Templeton was asleep. Wilbur lay resting after the excitement and strain of the ceremony. His medal still hung from his neck; by looking out of the corner of his eye he could see it.[2]

"Charlotte," said Wilbur after a while, "why are you so quiet?"

"I like to sit still," she said. "I've always been rather quiet."

"Yes, but you seem specially so today. Do you feel all right?"

"A little tired, perhaps. But I feel peaceful. Your success in the ring this morning was, to a small degree, *my* success. Your future is assured. You will live, secure and safe, Wilbur. Nothing can harm you now. These autumn days will shorten and grow cold. The leaves will shake loose from the trees and fall. Christmas will come, then the snows of winter. You will live to enjoy the beauty of the frozen world, for you mean a great

Page 163

1. Even on the printer's copy, this chapter was still titled "The Death of Charlotte." On April 10, 1952, Nordstrom wrote Katharine White:

> I hope neither of you minded my bringing up the chapter title "Charlotte's Death." I hesitated to mention it but thought it could do no harm. (When I got home last night I looked in my copy of *Little Women*. The chapter in which Jo learns that Beth is going to die is called "Beth's Secret," and the chapter in which Beth does die is called "The Valley of the Shadow.")[1]

White obviously accepted this wise advice not to signal the tragedy in advance.

2. In Draft H, White had written, "But his thoughts were only of Charlotte, and her thoughts were only of him. What a strange friendship, this friendship of the spider and the pig: And how greatly it had enriched their lives."

Deletion of this sort of telling, rather than showing, is fully consistent with White's changes between the expository openings, in the early drafts, and the dramatic beginning of the book in final form.

Page 164

3. Charlotte seems to have the gift of prophecy in this, her valedictory speech.

4. Indeed, Wilbur now, truly, does seem to be "humble."

In Draft B, the word *much* is written between *anything* and *for*.

Originally, actually, it *was* White's intention to have Wilbur save Charlotte when Avery raised his stick to hit her (*CW*, page 72), although that incident was deleted early, and the good deed was given to Templeton when he rolled the rotten goose egg away (*CW*, page 47).

5. We saw such meditations on the brevity of life earlier (see page 43).

deal to Zuckerman and he will not harm you, ever.[3] Winter will pass, the days will lengthen, the ice will melt in the pasture pond. The song sparrow will return and sing, the frogs will awake, the warm wind will blow again. All these sights and sounds and smells will be yours to enjoy, Wilbur—this lovely world, these precious days . . ."

Charlotte stopped. A moment later a tear came to Wilbur's eye. "Oh, Charlotte," he said. "To think that when I first met you I thought you were cruel and bloodthirsty!"

When he recovered from his emotion, he spoke again.

"Why did you do all this for me?" he asked. "I don't deserve it. I've never done anything for you."[4]

"You have been my friend," replied Charlotte. "That in itself is a tremendous thing. I wove my webs for you because I liked you. After all, what's a life, anyway?[5] We're born, we live a little while, we die. A spider's life can't help being something of a mess, with all this trapping and eating flies. By helping you, perhaps I was trying to lift up my life a trifle. Heaven knows anyone's life can stand a little of that."

"Well," said Wilbur. "I'm no good at making speeches. I haven't got your gift for words. But you have saved me, Charlotte, and I would gladly give my life for you—I really would."

"I'm sure you would. And I thank you for your generous sentiments."

"Charlotte," said Wilbur. "We're all going home today. The Fair is almost over. Won't it be wonderful to be back home in the barn cellar again with the sheep and the geese? Aren't you anxious to get home?"

For a moment Charlotte said nothing. Then she spoke in a voice so low Wilbur could hardly hear the words.

"I will not be going back to the barn," she said.

Wilbur leapt to his feet. "Not going back?" he cried. "Charlotte, what are you talking about?"

"I'm done for,"[6] she replied. "In a day or two I'll be dead. I haven't even strength enough to climb down into the crate. I doubt if I have enough silk in my spinnerets to lower me to the ground."

Hearing this, Wilbur threw himself down in an agony of pain and sorrow. Great sobs racked his body. He heaved and grunted with desolation. "Charlotte," he moaned. "Charlotte! My true friend!"

"Come now, let's not make a scene," said the spider. "Be quiet, Wilbur. Stop thrashing about!"

"But I can't *stand* it," shouted Wilbur. "I won't leave you here alone to die. If you're going to stay here I shall stay, too."

"Don't be ridiculous," said Charlotte. "You can't stay here. Zuckerman and Lurvy and John Arable and

Page 165

6. Even on the printer's copy, Draft I, the passage reads, "'I have reached the end of my life,' she replied."

The revised low-key dip in tone is profoundly moving for this dramatic and tragic revelation. Contrast it to the slightly tongue-in-cheek description of Wilbur's histrionics in the next paragraph.

Page 166

7. What a change in Wilbur as he takes command!

the others will be back any minute now, and they'll shove you into that crate and away you'll go. Besides, it wouldn't make any sense for you to stay. There would be no one to feed you. The Fair Grounds will soon be empty and deserted."

Wilbur was in a panic. He raced round and round the pen. Suddenly he had an idea—he thought of the egg sac and the five hundred and fourteen little spiders that would hatch in the spring. If Charlotte herself was unable to go home to the barn, at least he must take her children along.

Wilbur rushed to the front of his pen. He put his front feet up on the top board and gazed around. In the distance he saw the Arables and the Zuckermans approaching. He knew he would have to act quickly.

"Where's Templeton?" he demanded.[7]

"He's in that corner, under the straw, asleep," said Charlotte.

Wilbur rushed over, pushed his strong snout under the rat, and tossed him into the air.

"Templeton!" screamed Wilbur. "Pay attention!"

The rat, surprised out of a sound sleep, looked first dazed then disgusted.

"What kind of monkeyshine is this?" he growled. "Can't a rat catch a wink of sleep without being rudely popped into the air?"

"Listen to me!" cried Wilbur. "Charlotte is very ill.

She has only a short time to live.[8] She cannot accompany us home, because of her condition. Therefore, it is absolutely necessary that I take her egg sac with me. I can't reach it, and I can't climb. You are the only one that can get it. There's not a second to be lost. The people are coming—they'll be here in no time. Please, please, *please*, Templeton, climb up and get the egg sac."

The rat yawned. He straightened his whiskers. Then he looked up at the egg sac.

"So!" he said, in disgust. "So it's old Templeton to the rescue again, is it? Templeton do this, Templeton do that, Templeton please run down to the dump and get me a magazine clipping, Templeton please lend me a piece of string so I can spin a web."

"Oh, hurry!" said Wilbur. "Hurry up, Templeton!"

But the rat was in no hurry. He began imitating Wilbur's voice.

"So it's 'Hurry up, Templeton,' is it?" he said. "Ho, ho. And what thanks do I ever get for these services, I would like to know? Never a kind word for old Templeton, only abuse and wisecracks and side remarks. Never a kind word for a rat."

"Templeton," said Wilbur in desperation, "if you don't stop talking and get busy, all will be lost, and I will die of a broken heart. Please climb up!"

Templeton lay back in the straw. Lazily he placed

Page 167

8. A number of teachers, librarians, and parents objected to the subject of death in a children's book. (In fact, some may still do so.) Probably White was thinking of them when he wrote to Ursula Nordstrom,

> I am working on a new book about a boa constrictor and a litter of hyenas. The boa constrictor swallows the babies one by one, and the mother hyena dies laughing.[2]

Page 168

9. Up to now it has been Wilbur who has acted like a spoiled child.

10. The first act of real selflessness on the part of Wilbur.

his forepaws behind his head and crossed his knees, in an attitude of complete relaxation.

"Die of a broken heart," he mimicked. "How touching! My, my! I notice that it's always me you come to when in trouble. But I've never heard of anyone's heart breaking on *my* account. Oh, no. Who cares anything about old Templeton?"

"Get up!" screamed Wilbur. "Stop acting like a spoiled child!"[9]

Templeton grinned and lay still. "Who made trip after trip to the dump?" he asked. "Why, it was old Templeton! Who saved Charlotte's life by scaring that Arable boy away with a rotten goose egg? Bless my soul, I believe it was old Templeton. Who bit your tail and got you back on your feet this morning after you had fainted in front of the crowd? Old Templeton. Has it ever occurred to you that I'm sick of running errands and doing favors? What do you think I am, anyway, a rat-of-all-work?"

Wilbur was desperate. The people were coming. And the rat was failing him. Suddenly he remembered Templeton's fondness for food.

"Templeton," he said, "I will make you a solemn promise. Get Charlotte's egg sac for me, and from now on I will let you eat first, when Lurvy slops me. I will let you have your choice of everything in the trough and I won't touch a thing until you're through."[10]

The rat sat up. "You mean that?" he said.

"I promise. I cross my heart."

"All right, it's a deal," said the rat. He walked to the wall and started to climb. His stomach was still swollen from last night's gorge. Groaning and com-

plaining, he pulled himself slowly to the ceiling. He crept along till he reached the egg sac. Charlotte moved aside for him. She was dying, but she still had strength enough to move a little. Then Templeton bared his long ugly teeth and began snipping the threads that fastened the sac to the ceiling. Wilbur watched from below.

Page 169

11. Look well at this marvelous picture. Charlotte has moved aside so Templeton can get the eggs.

Page 170

12. One psychologically sensitive critic has noted that "the ever-oral Wilbur had to grow up before he could transport Charlotte's 514 spider-daughters into a safe corner."[3]

Not all Charlotte's 514 children are necessarily "daughters," but Knoepflmacher is correct in calling our attention to Wilbur's orality.

Page 171

13. In Box 2, in the folder dealing with the proposed film version, White wrote:

> When Charlotte dies, the story teller should be heard saying those words that begin, "She never moved again." I cannot tell you why or how those words have the power to move people, but is has been clearly established they do. Librarians, schoolteachers, mothers, fathers and children all seem to break apart when they hear those words. I had no idea what I was up to when I was writing them, but I wouldn't want to see them omitted from the script. *You would be passing up the single most telling paragraph of the book.* [Italics added]

In fact, the words "She never moved again" were *not* included in the film.

14. Even in the printer's copy, Draft I, the passage reads, "No one knew it when she died." One can only speculate that "being with" someone is a more vivid and immediate concept than the abstract "knowing," thus underscoring her aloneness.

Commenting on the projected film version of *CW*, White wrote his friend and agent J. G. Gude:

> Charlotte's death, and later the hatching of the young spiders in spring should be turned over to Mozart, for background music. There is an old Columbia Masterworks record . . . "Quartet in F Major, for oboe, violin, and violoncello—Leon Goosens on oboe." The adagio movement of that

"Use extreme care!" he said. "I don't want a single one of those eggs harmed."

"Thith thtuff thticks in my mouth," complained the rat. "It'th worth than caramel candy."

But Templeton worked away at the job, and managed to cut the sac adrift and carry it to the ground, where he dropped it in front of Wilbur. Wilbur heaved a great sigh of relief.

"Thank you, Templeton," he said. "I will never forget this as long as I live."

"Neither will I," said the rat, picking his teeth. "I feel as though I'd eaten a spool of thread. Well, home we go!"

Templeton crept into the crate and buried himself in the straw. He got out of sight just in time. Lurvy and John Arable and Mr. Zuckerman came along at that moment, followed by Mrs. Arable and Mrs. Zuckerman and Avery and Fern. Wilbur had already decided how he would carry the egg sac—there was only one way possible. He carefully took the little bundle in his mouth and held it there on top of his tongue.[12] He remembered what Charlotte had told him—that the sac was waterproof and strong. It felt funny on his tongue and made him drool a bit. And of course he couldn't say anything. But as he was being shoved into the crate, he looked up at Charlotte and gave her a

wink. She knew he was saying good-bye in the only way he could. And she knew her children were safe.

"Good-bye!" she whispered. Then she summoned all her strength and waved one of her front legs at him.

She never moved again.[13] Next day, as the Ferris wheel was being taken apart and the race horses were being loaded into vans and the entertainers were packing up their belongings and driving away in their trailers, Charlotte died. The Fair Grounds were soon deserted. The sheds and buildings were empty and forlorn. The infield was littered with bottles and trash. Nobody, of the hundreds of people that had visited the Fair, knew that a grey spider had played the most important part of all. No one was with her when she died.[14]

quartet (just a strain or two) would be the perfect accompaniment for the death of the spider, interlarded with the distant music of the Fair. . . . The oboe has a flutelike sound that would be just right for this pastoral story. . . . Mozart clearly had the "Web" in mind when he wrote "Quartet in F Major." Take heart! In the Year of the Rat, anything can happen. I could even smuggle Mozart into Hollywood.[4]

That was a futile hope.

Page 172

1. Wilbur now fully believes the truth of what Charlotte told him (*CW*, page 164).

Chapter XXII

A Warm Wind

AND SO Wilbur came home to his beloved manure pile in the barn cellar. His was a strange homecoming. Around his neck he wore a medal of honor; in his mouth he held a sac of spider's eggs. There is no place like home, Wilbur thought, as he placed Charlotte's five hundred and fourteen unborn children carefully in a safe corner. The barn smelled good. His friends the sheep and the geese were glad to see him back.

The geese gave him a noisy welcome.

"Congratu-congratu-congratulations!" they cried. "Nice work."

Mr. Zuckerman took the medal from Wilbur's neck and hung it on a nail over the pigpen, where visitors could examine it. Wilbur himself could look at it whenever he wanted to.

In the days that followed, he was very happy. He grew to a great size. He no longer worried about being killed, for he knew that Mr. Zuckerman would keep him as long as he lived.[1] Wilbur often thought of Char-

lotte. A few strands of her old web still hung in the doorway. Every day Wilbur would stand and look at the torn, empty web, and a lump would come to his throat. No one had ever had such a friend—so affectionate, so loyal, and so skillful.

The autumn days grew shorter, Lurvy brought the squashes and pumpkins in from the garden and piled them on the barn floor, where they wouldn't get nipped on frosty nights. The maples and birches turned bright colors and the wind shook them and they dropped their leaves one by one to the ground. Under the wild apple trees in the pasture, the red little apples lay thick on the ground, and the sheep gnawed them and the geese gnawed them and foxes came in the night and sniffed them. One evening, just before Christmas, snow began falling. It covered house and barn and fields and woods. Wilbur had never seen snow before. When morning came he went out and plowed the drifts in his yard, for the fun of it. Fern and Avery arrived, dragging a sled. They coasted down the lane and out onto the frozen pond in the pasture.

"Coasting is the most fun there is," said Avery.

"The most fun there is,"[2] retorted Fern, "is when the Ferris wheel stops and Henry and I are in the top car and Henry makes the car swing and we can see everything for miles and miles and miles."

"Goodness, are you still thinking about that ol' Fer-

Page 173

2. White shared this opinion. Ruminating about space satellites, he wrote: "I see nothing in space as promising as the view from a Ferris wheel."[1]

Page 174

3. As usual, White's editing renders scenes specific. In Draft B, White had written, "[C]old weather settled on the world."

4. Specificity may come as close to being a universal rule for good writing as there is.

Even the final printer's version read "grain." White had obtained better information, and changed the word to "corn."

Beatrix Potter is another author with a similar insistence on precision, as, in *Peter Rabbit*, she particularizes that when Mrs. Rabbit went to the baker's, "she bought a loaf of brown bread and five currant buns,"[2] and when Peter invaded Mr. McGregor's garden: "First he ate some lettuces and some French beans; and then he ate some radishes."[3]

5. An excellent passage for observing how White streamlined his prose. In Draft B the passage reads: "as a result of this overeating ~~treatment arrangement.~~"

ris wheel?" said Avery in disgust. "The Fair was weeks and weeks ago."

"I think about it all the time," said Fern, picking snow from her ear.

After Christmas the thermometer dropped to ten below zero.[3] Cold settled on the world. The pasture was bleak and frozen. The cows stayed in the barn all the time now, except on sunny mornings when they went out and stood in the barnyard in the lee of the straw pile. The sheep stayed near the barn, too, for protection. When they were thirsty they ate snow. The geese hung around the barnyard the way boys hang around a drug store, and Mr. Zuckerman fed them corn and turnips to keep them cheerful.[4]

"Many, many, many thanks!" they always said, when they saw food coming.

Templeton moved indoors when winter came. His ratty home under the pig trough was too chilly, so he fixed himself a cozy nest in the barn behind the grain bins. He lined it with bits of dirty newspapers and rags, and whenever he found a trinket or a keepsake he carried it home and stored it there. He continued to visit Wilbur three times a day, exactly at mealtime, and Wilbur kept the promise he had made. Wilbur let the rat eat first. Then, when Templeton couldn't hold another mouthful, Wilbur would eat. As a result of overeating,[5] Templeton grew bigger and fatter than

any rat you ever saw. He was gigantic. He was as big as a young woodchuck.

The old sheep spoke to him about his size one day. “You would live longer,” said the old sheep, “if you ate less.”

“Who wants to live forever?” sneered the rat. “I am naturally a heavy eater[6] and I get untold satisfaction from the pleasures of the feast.” He patted his stomach, grinned at the sheep, and crept upstairs to lie down.

All winter Wilbur watched over Charlotte’s egg sac as though he were guarding his own children. He had

Page 175

6. In earlier drafts, this was “~~I am a natural~~ [~~gourmand~~] ~~glutton.~~”

“Avoid fancy words.”[4]

In spite of the fact that White wrote Deitch that Templeton was “a great gourmand”[5] (see page 46), White crossed out the fancy French for Templeton’s speech because, after all, only sophisticated Charlotte spoke in that tone. Since White expressed his distaste for high-falutin diction, one can ask why he allowed it to Charlotte. Perhaps it was partly that she might better serve as Wilbur’s (lexical) mentor. Perhaps it was partly that she was modeled on Don Marquis’s cat mehitabel, whose soul had once inhabited Cleopatra herself.

7. The year has come full circle since the beginning of the story.

We can think of a number of stories that are cyclical or "circular," as opposed to those that seem linear or progressive, and the implication and symbolism of this "shape" of story is profound. Virginia Lee Burton's *The Little House* is one of the prime examples of the rendering of cycles—cycles of seasons, cycles of families, cycles of the protagonist, the Little House herself.

On the other hand, a picaresque tale such as *Stuart Little* seems, definitely, linear—a fact that upset terribly all those critics who, like Anne Carroll Moore, objected to the ending, which they felt "inconclusive."

"The shape of story" is, of course, a metaphorical phrase, but it is one that connotes profoundly. In *The Little House*, the curvilinear lines of the illustrations represent not only the gender of the female Little House, and her surroundings in good times, but also the cycles, return, and renewal, the generation and the continuity, and the affirmations of life that are the theme of the book.

The would-be censors who wanted to evade the death of Charlotte never understood that affirmation and intimations of renewal underlie the entire tale.

8. Since White was fond of musical reference, we may liken the change from the euphonious mellifluousness of the warm wind blowing to the brisk accents of "[o]ne fine sunny morning" to a progression from andante to allegro.

scooped out a special place in the manure for the sac, next to the board fence. On very cold nights he lay so that his breath would warm it. For Wilbur, nothing in life was so important as this small round object—nothing else mattered. Patiently he awaited the end of winter and the coming of the little spiders. Life is always a rich and steady time when you are waiting for something to happen or to hatch. The winter ended at last.

"I heard the frogs today," said the old sheep one evening. "Listen! You can hear them now."

Wilbur stood still and cocked his ears. From the pond, in shrill chorus, came the voices of hundreds of little frogs.

"Springtime," said the old sheep, thoughtfully. "Another spring." As she walked away, Wilbur saw a new lamb following her. It was only a few hours old.

The snows melted and ran away.[7] The streams and ditches bubbled and chattered with rushing water. A sparrow with a streaky breast arrived and sang. The light strengthened, the mornings came sooner. Almost every morning there was another new lamb in the sheepfold. The goose was sitting on nine eggs. The sky seemed wider and a warm wind blew. The last remaining strands of Charlotte's old web floated away and vanished.[8]

One fine sunny morning, after breakfast, Wilbur

stood watching his precious sac. He wasn't thinking of anything much. As he stood there, he noticed something move. He stepped closer and stared. A tiny spider crawled from the sac. It was no bigger than a grain of sand, no bigger than the head of a pin. Its body was grey with a black stripe underneath. Its legs were grey and tan. It looked just like Charlotte.

Wilbur trembled all over when he saw it. The little spider waved at him. Then Wilbur looked more closely. Two more little spiders crawled out and waved. They climbed round and round on the sac, exploring their new world. Then three more little spiders. Then eight. Then ten. Charlotte's children were here at last.

Wilbur's heart pounded. He began to squeal. Then he raced in circles, kicking manure into the air. Then he turned a back flip. Then he planted his front feet and came to a stop in front of Charlotte's children.

"Hello, there!" he said.

The first spider said hello, but its voice was so small Wilbur couldn't hear it.

"I am an old friend of your mother's," said Wilbur. "I'm glad to see you. Are you all right? Is everything all right?"

The little spiders waved their forelegs at him. Wilbur could see by the way they acted that they were glad to see him.

9. The miracle, as Dr. Dorian pointed out, is that as soon as they hatch, the tiny spiders know how to weave a web.

10. Comstock describes the phenomenon as follows:

> [G]reat numbers of young spiders . . . climb each to the top of some object. This may be a fence post, the top of a twig, the upper part of some herb, or merely the summit of a clod of earth. Here the spider lifts up its abdomen and spins out a thread, which if there is a mild upward current of air is carried away by it. . . . This spinning process is continued until the friction of the air upon the silk is sufficient to buoy up the spider. It then lets go its hold with its feet and is carried off by the wind.

Such ballooning spiders, Comstock notes, have been encountered by ships at sea "hundreds of miles from land."[6]

"Is there anything I can get you? Is there anything you need?"

The young spiders just waved. For several days and several nights they crawled here and there, up and down, around and about, waving at Wilbur, trailing tiny draglines behind them, and exploring their home. There were dozens and dozens of them. Wilbur couldn't count them, but he knew that he had a great many new friends. They grew quite rapidly. Soon each was as big as a BB shot. They made tiny webs near the sac.[9]

Then came a quiet morning when Mr. Zuckerman opened a door on the north side. A warm draft of rising air blew softly through the barn cellar. The air smelled of the damp earth, of the spruce woods, of the sweet springtime. The baby spiders felt the warm updraft. One spider climbed to the top of the fence. Then it did something that came as a great surprise to Wilbur. The spider stood on its head, pointed its spinnerets in the air, and let loose a cloud of fine silk. The silk formed a balloon.[10] As Wilbur watched, the spider let go of the fence and rose into the air.

"Good-bye!" it said, as it sailed through the doorway.

"Wait a minute!" screamed Wilbur. "Where do you think you're going?"

But the spider was already out of sight. Then another

baby spider crawled to the top of the fence, stood on its head, made a balloon, and sailed away. Then another spider. Then another. The air was soon filled with tiny balloons, each balloon carrying a spider.

Wilbur was frantic. Charlotte's babies were disappearing at a great rate.

11

"Come back, children!" he cried.

"Good-bye!" they called. "Good-bye, good-bye!"

At last one little spider took time enough to stop and talk to Wilbur before making its balloon.

"We're leaving here on the warm updraft.[12] This is our moment for setting forth. We are aeronauts[13] and we

Page 179

11. Ursula Nordstrom wrote White that she had thought there would be more little spiders in this illustration, "but perhaps it is all right as it is now."[7]

12. Even on the printer's copy (Draft I), the sentence read, "We're leaving here on the warm breeze." The more specific and accurate *updraft* is written in.

As for "setting forth," that (just like cycles and recurrence) is the theme of much of the world's great literature—the stories of Adam and Eve, of Gawain and the Green Knight, of Huckleberry Finn, and of Stuart Little, who, at story's end,

> climbed into his car, and started up the road that led toward the north. The sun was just coming up over the hills on his right. As he peered ahead into the great land that stretched before him, the way seemed long. But the sky was bright, and he somehow felt he was headed in the right direction.[8]

As White put it, "Stuart's journey symbolizes the continuing journey that everybody takes—in search of what is perfect and unattainable. This is perhaps too elusive an idea to put into a book for children, but I put it in anyway."[9]

13. Gertsch refers to balloon spiders as "these tiny aeronauts."[10]

Page 180

14. The fact that Charlotte's daughters repeat the very word she herself first used to greet Wilbur underlines the cyclical continuity of life—and plot.

are going out into the world to make webs for ourselves."

"But *where?*" asked Wilbur.

"Wherever the wind takes us. High, low. Near, far. East, west. North, south. We take to the breeze, we go as we please."

"Are *all* of you going?" asked Wilbur. "You can't *all* go. I would be left alone, with no friends. Your mother wouldn't want that to happen, I'm sure."

The air was now so full of balloonists that the barn cellar looked almost as though a mist had gathered. Balloons by the dozen were rising, circling, and drifting away through the door, sailing off on the gentle wind. Cries of "Good-bye, good-bye, good-bye!" came weakly to Wilbur's ears. He couldn't bear to watch any more. In sorrow he sank to the ground and closed his eyes. This seemed like the end of the world, to be deserted by Charlotte's children. Wilbur cried himself to sleep.

When he woke it was late afternoon. He looked at the egg sac. It was empty. He looked into the air. The balloonists were gone. Then he walked drearily to the doorway, where Charlotte's web used to be. He was standing there, thinking of her, when he heard a small voice.

"Salutations!"[14] it said. "I'm up here."

"So am I," said another tiny voice.

"So am I," said a third voice. "Three of us are staying. We like this place, and we like *you.*"

Wilbur looked up. At the top of the doorway three small webs were being constructed. On each web, working busily was one of Charlotte's daughters.

"Can I take this to mean," asked Wilbur, "that you have definitely decided to live here in the barn cellar, and that I am going to have *three* friends?"

"You can indeed," said the spiders.

"What are your names, please?" asked Wilbur, trembling with joy.

15. *Aranea* is the Latin word for spider, and was the name of the genus of orb-weaving spiders to which Charlotte belonged, and which used to be called *Epeira* (see page 37). Today, the spider in question is called *Araneus cavaticus*, according to the International Commission of Zoological Nomenclature. The specific name (*cavatica*) has been changed to agree in gender with *Araneus*. This masculinizing of the name might have caused White some difficulty.[11]

"I'll tell you my name," replied the first little spider, "if you'll tell me why you are trembling."

"I'm trembling with joy," said Wilbur.

"Then my name is Joy," said the first spider.

"What was my mother's middle initial?" asked the second spider.

"A," said Wilbur.

"Then my name is Aranea,[15]" said the spider.

"How about me?" asked the third spider. "Will you just pick out a nice sensible name for me—something not too long, not too fancy, and not too dumb?"

Wilbur thought hard.

"Nellie?" he suggested.

"Fine, I like that very much," said the third spider. "You may call me Nellie." She daintily fastened her orb line to the next spoke of the web.

Wilbur's heart brimmed with happiness. He felt that he should make a short speech on this very important occasion.

"Joy! Aranea! Nellie!" he began. "Welcome to the barn cellar. You have chosen a hallowed doorway from which to string your webs. I think it is only fair to tell you that I was devoted to your mother. I owe my very life to her. She was brilliant, beautiful, and loyal to the end. I shall always treasure her memory. To you, her daughters, I pledge my friendship, forever and ever."

"I pledge mine," said Joy.

"I do, too," said Aranea.

"And so do I," said Nellie, who had just managed to catch a small gnat.

It was a happy day for Wilbur. And many more happy, tranquil days followed.

As time went on, and the months and years came and went, he was never without friends. Fern did not come regularly to the barn any more. She was growing up, and was careful to avoid childish things, like sitting on a milk stool near a pigpen. But Charlotte's children and grandchildren and great grandchildren, year after year, lived in the doorway. Each spring there were new little spiders hatching out to take the place of the old. Most of them sailed away, on their balloons. But always two or three stayed and set up housekeeping in the doorway.

Mr. Zuckerman took fine care of Wilbur all the rest of his days, and the pig was often visited by friends and admirers, for nobody ever forgot the year of his triumph and the miracle of the web. Life in the barn was very good—night and day, winter and summer, spring and fall, dull days and bright days. It was the best place to be,[16] thought Wilbur, this warm delicious cellar, with the garrulous geese, the changing seasons, the heat of the sun, the passage of swallows, the nearness of rats, the sameness of sheep, the love of spiders, the smell of manure, and the glory of everything.

Page 183

16. White's sentiments, stated explicitly at the very beginning of an earlier draft and later moved to the start of Chapter III.

17. For years, I had been pointing out White's artistry in creating the beautiful rhythm of those last two sentences—the balanced, periodic first one, and the quiet, falling note of the brief concluding one. Consider my amazement to learn that in 1943 (six years before he wrote *Charlotte's Web*), when White was attacked in a letter to *The New York Times*, Katharine White wrote,

> [Those] are not words that should be applied to anyone who is an honest man and an honest writer. Andy is both.[12]

There are those who say a novel should be a work of art solely, and you must not preach in it. That may be true as regards novels but it is not true as regards humor. Humor must not professedly teach, and it must not professedly preach, but it must do both if it would live forever. By forever, I mean thirty years.[13]

Wilbur never forgot Charlotte. Although he loved her children and grandchildren dearly, none of the new spiders ever quite took her place in his heart. She was in a class by herself. It is not often that someone comes along who is a true friend and a good writer. Charlotte was both.[17]

THE END

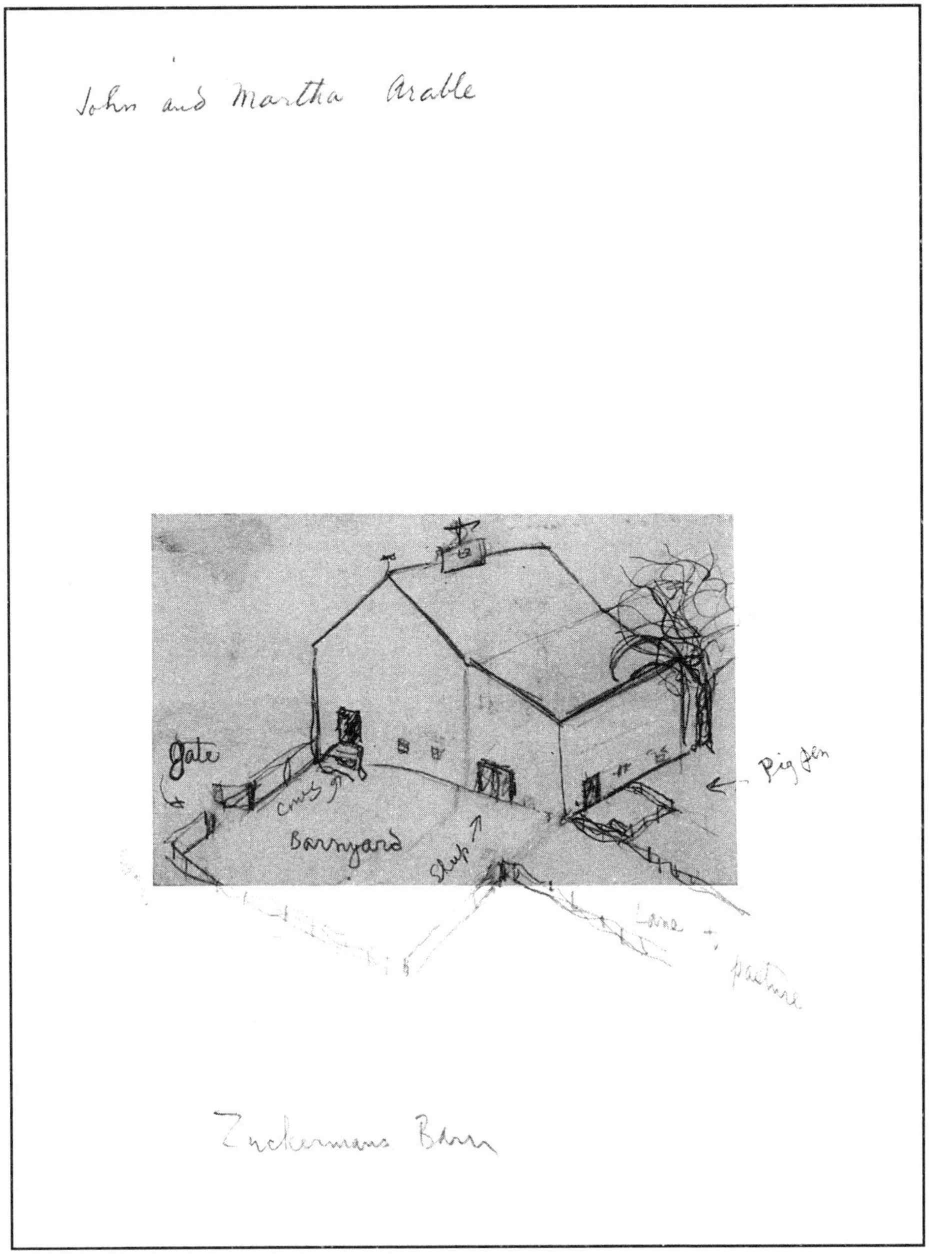

Plate 1. "Zuckerman's Barn," which White modeled on his own

STYLE SHEET

1. Possessive singular of nouns – Louis – Louis's

2. Serial comma. Red, white, and blue.

3. Place a comma before a conjunction introducing an independent clause.

'The situation is perilous, but there is still .....

When the subject is the same for both clauses =

use comma before "but"

omit comma before "and"

4. Trumpeter Swan is upper case

Swan is lower case

In general, all specific creatures are u.c.

Redwinged Blackbird, Polar Bear,

Plate 2. E. B. White's handwritten chart of punctuation style

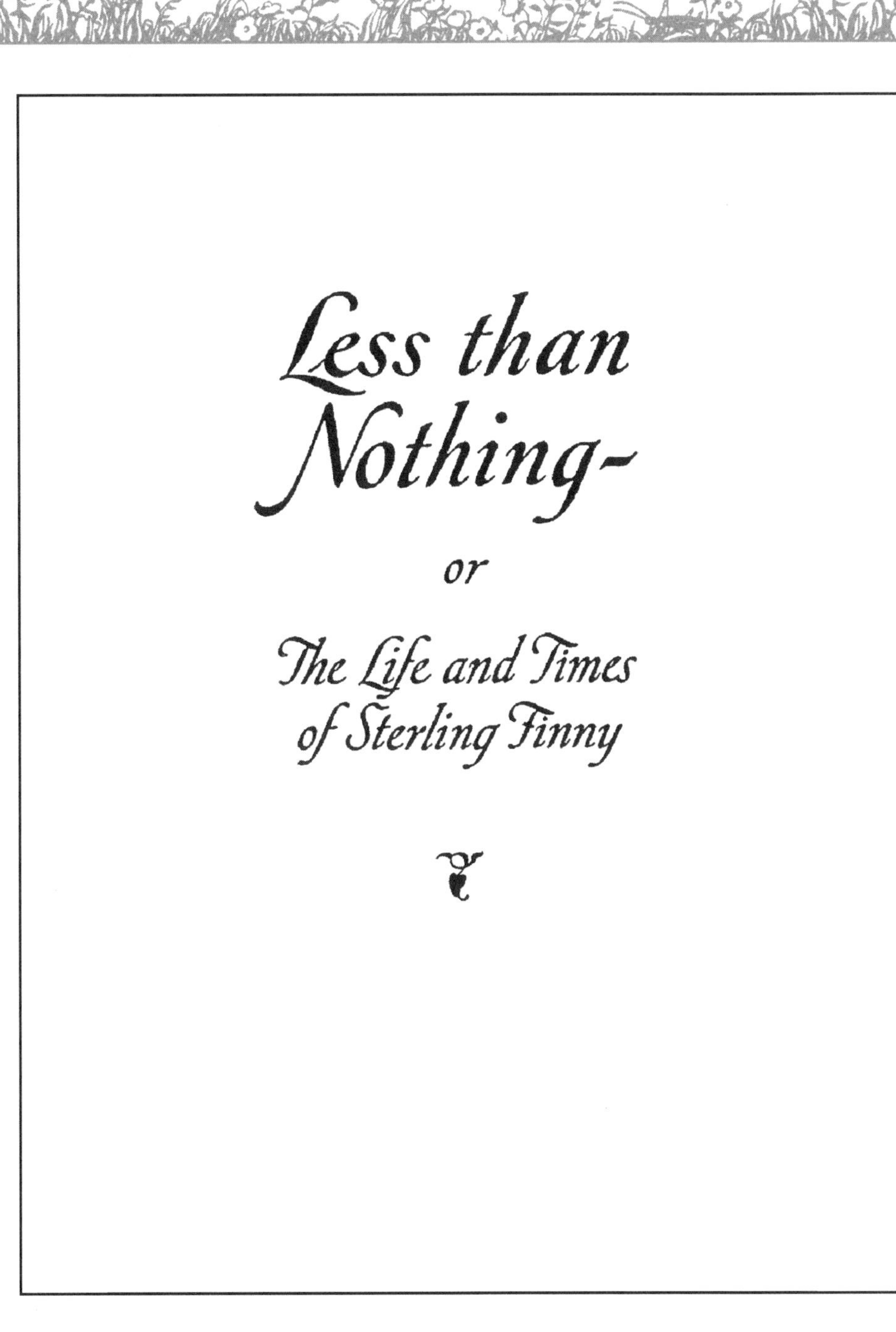

Less than Nothing—

or

The Life and Times of Sterling Finny

Plate 3. Half title page of E. B. White's first publication

Wilbur was merely suffering the doubts and fears that often go with finding a new friend. In good time he was to discover that he was mistaken about Charlotte. Underneath her rather bold and cruel exterior, she had ~~a~~ kind heart, ~~Once she~~ as you ~~bestowed her friendship~~ and ~~she was~~ loyal ~~and true to the very end~~. ~~and her whole life was~~ will presently see.

It is doubtful that anyone ever had a truer friend.

Plate 4. Revised draft for Charlotte's Web, *page 41*

caput
thorax
mandible
palpus or palpi
palpal claw

forehead
sternum (plate)
falx

fang
hair
labium

Legs have 7 joints.

1. coxa
2. trochanter
3. femur
4. patella
5. tibia
6. metatarsus

(Charlotte ~~[illegible]~~ names them for Wilbur, who likes to hear her run over the names.)

Last 5 of the joints are lined with spines, bristles, and hair.

"You have awfully hairy legs, Charlotte"

The spines on the hind legs are like the "flyers" of a spinning wheel. They are used for the flocculation of the threads as they pass from the spinning ~~tubes~~.

Plate 5. E. B. White's notes on spider anatomy

Illus. for Note 70 p55

22

"Well," said Charlotte, "you and I lead different lives. You don't have to spin a web. That takes real leg work."

"I ~~might be able to~~ could spin a web if I tried," said Wilbur, boasting. "I've just never tried."

"Let's see you do it," said Charlotte.

~~what would you use for a spinneret?~~

"OK," replied Wilbur. "You coach me and I'll spin one. It must be a lot of fun to spin a web. How do I start?" 3

Plate 6. Revised draft for Charlotte's Web, *page 56*

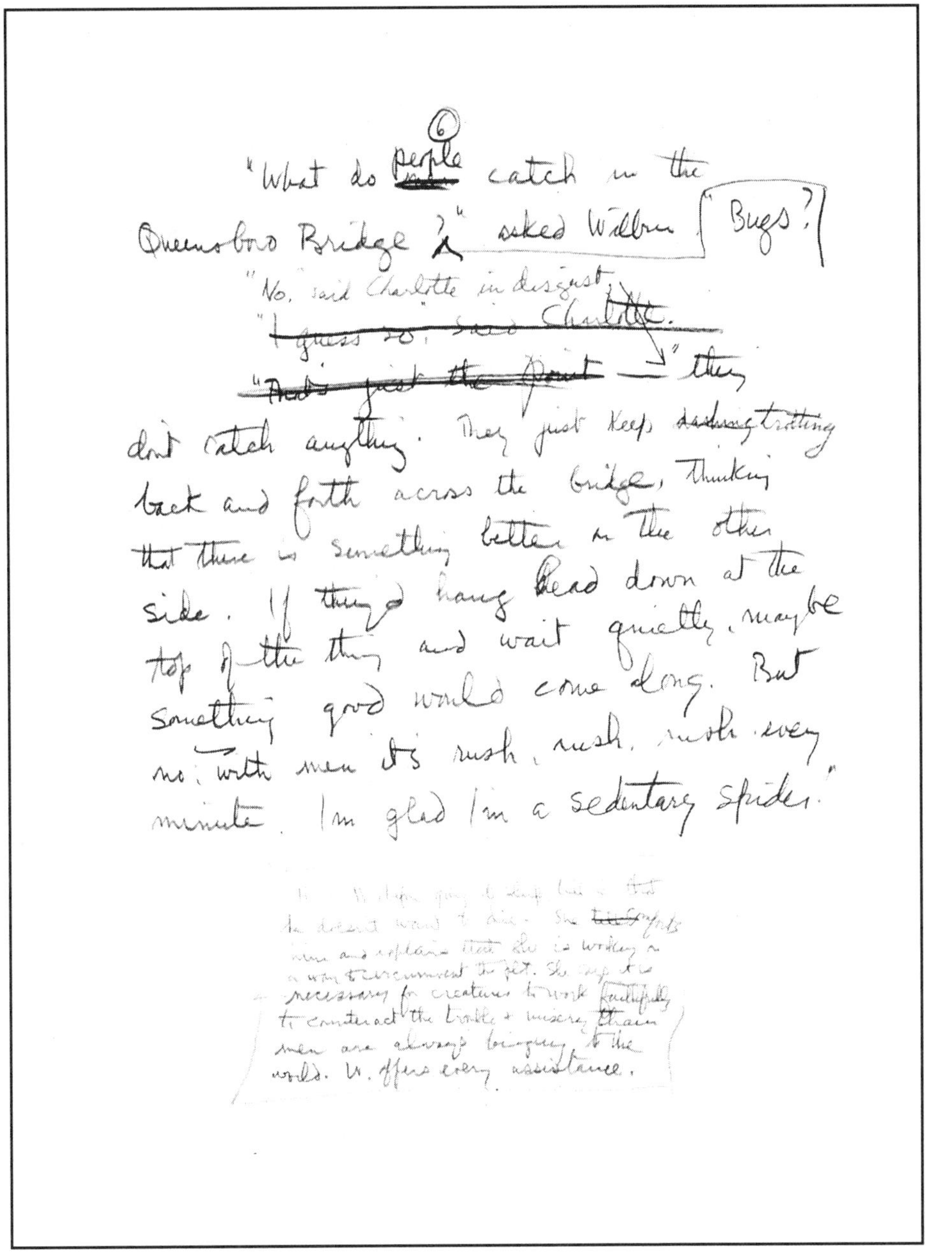

"What do people catch in the Queensboro Bridge?" asked Wilbur. "Bugs?"

"No," said Charlotte in disgust. ~~"I guess so," said Charlotte.~~ ~~"That's just the point"~~ — "they don't catch anything. They just keep ~~dashing~~ trotting back and forth across the bridge, thinking there is something better on the other side. If they'd hang head down at the top of the thing and wait quietly, maybe something good would come along. But no, with men it's rush, rush, rush every minute. I'm glad I'm a sedentary spider."

Plate 7. Revised draft for Charlotte's Web, *page 60*

Chapter ~~XI~~ X

~~THE PLAN~~

Day after day the spider waited, head down, for an idea to come to her. Hour by hour she sat motionless, deep in thought. Having promised Wilbur that she would save his life, she was determined to keep her promise.

Charlotte was naturally patient. She knew from experience that if she waited long enough, a fly would come to her web; and she felt sure that if she thought ~~steadily~~ long enough about Wilbur's problem, an idea would come to her mind.

Finally, one morning toward the middle of July, the idea came. "Why, how perfectly simple!" she said to herself. "The way to save Wilbur's life is to ~~make~~ Zuckerman ~~think his pig is a very unusual pig~~. ~~If I can~~ ~~convince him~~ make Zuckerman think that ~~Wilbur is no ordinary~~ pig, he will not want to kill ~~him~~ and eat him, he will want to keep him and show him off to his friends and neighbors."

Charlotte knew that men were very vain, and that almost every man liked to think he owned something that was better than anybody else's.

"If I can fool a fly," thought Charlotte, "I can surely fool a man. People are not as smart as bugs."

Wilbur walked into his yard just at this moment.

"What are you thinking about, Charlotte?" he asked.

"I was just thinking," said the spider, "that people are very gullible."

"What does 'gullible' mean?"

"Easy to fool," said Charlotte.

"That's a blessing," replied Wilbur, and he lay

Plate 8. Revised draft for Charlotte's Web, *page 66*

"Methinks you protest too much, Wilbur."

"Well, I don't want to stay alive under false pretenses."

man of distinction (pig of distinction)

Sum pig

prepotent

Crunchy

With more

Terrific

Hygrade

pre shrunk (argument about this) (label for a shirt)

the slogan on Ivory flakes "with new Radiant Action" they settle for just the word RADIANT

delicious, nutritious (nutritious is out)

Pig Supreme. (Sounds like a dessert)

Plate 9. Manuscript page in which E. B. White enumerates possibilities for Charlotte's web writings

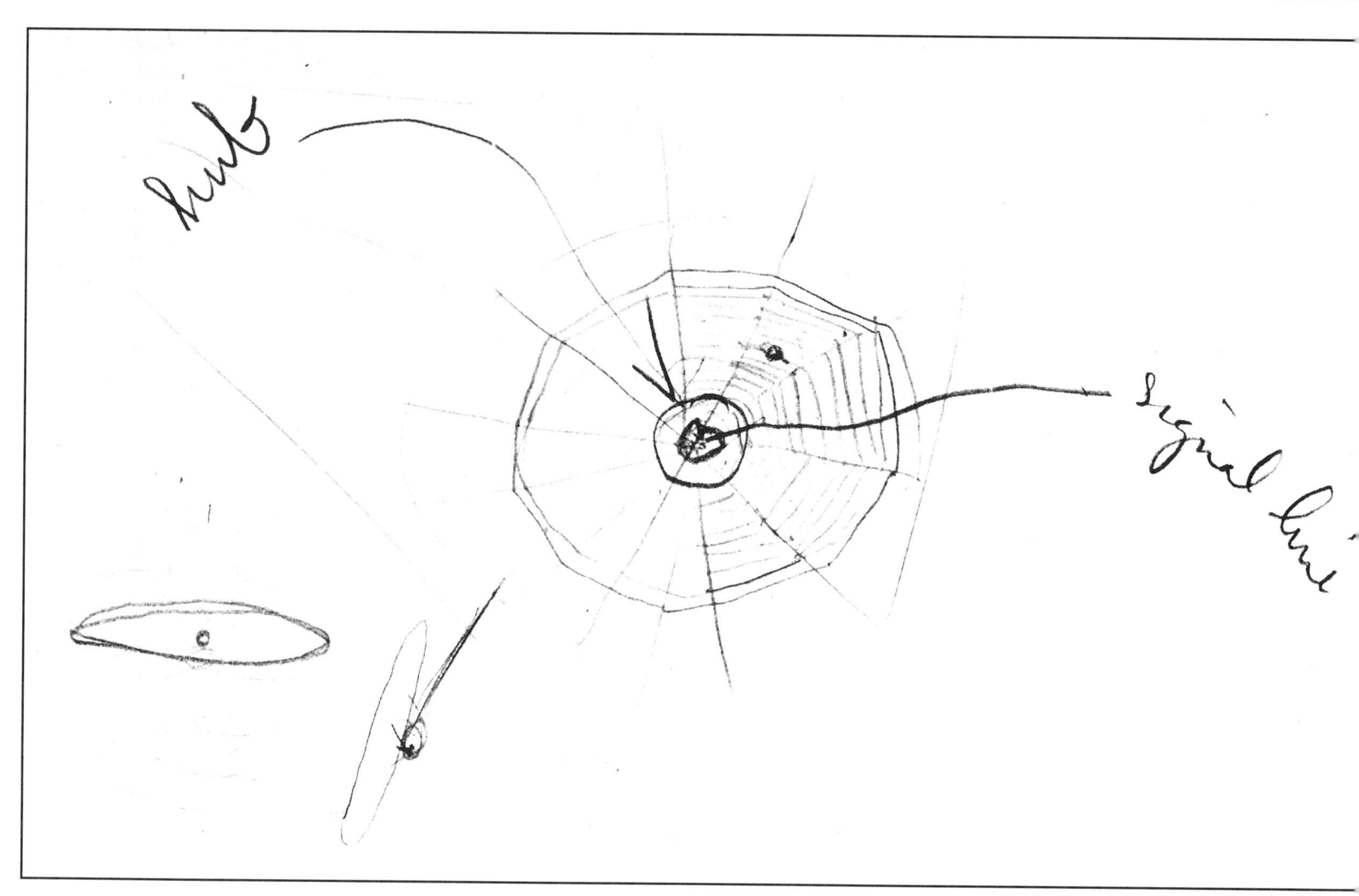

Plate 10. E. B. White's drawing of the vectors of the web-spinning process

First they anchor a drag line.
The foundation is an irregular polygon.
The swinging basket
The trial cables.

A spider needs eight legs. She uses
2 sets of forelegs for antennae when
she is at work laying out lines

A

From the foundation line, the spider makes an attachment
and drops down, paying out cable as she goes.
She ~~fo~~ makes this fast to the ground or
Something, then climbs back to here and
runs a diagonal
across by ascending
the dropline and
carrying another
line along in hind feet up & over
to point A

Plate 11. E. B. White's notes on web weaving

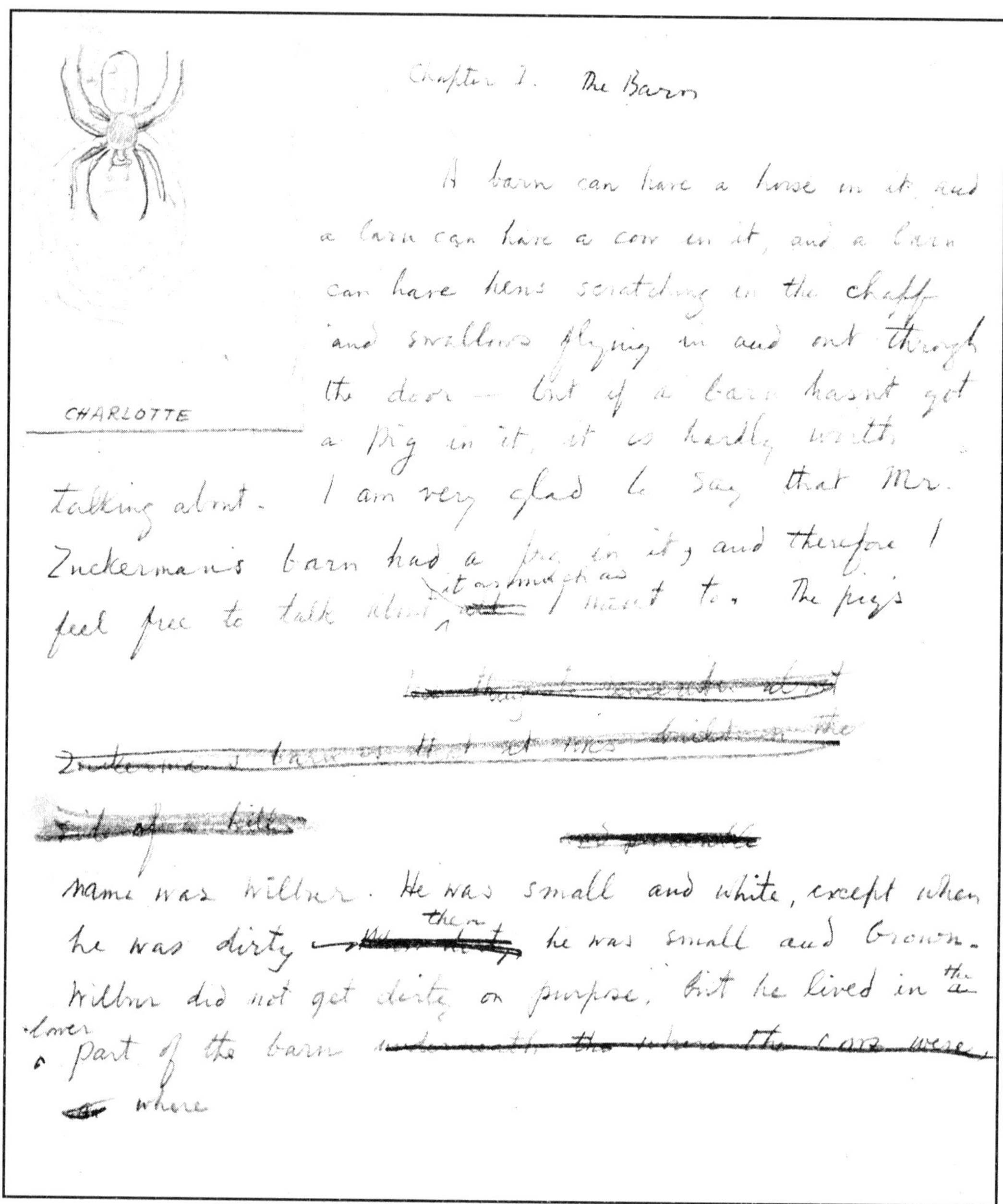

Chapter I. The Barn

A barn can have a horse in it and a barn can have a cow in it, and a barn can have hens scratching in the chaff and swallows flying in and out through the door — but if a barn hasn't got a pig in it, it is hardly worth talking about. I am very glad to say that Mr. Zuckerman's barn had a pig in it, and therefore I feel free to talk about it as much as I want to. The pig's

name was Wilbur. He was small and white, except when he was dirty — then he was small and brown. Wilbur did not get dirty on purpose, but he lived in the lower part of the barn where

Plate 12. Second draft for the beginning of Charlotte's Web

Appendix A

GARTH WILLIAMS, THE ILLUSTRATOR

I had always hoped that Williams and White would be as indestructible as ham and eggs, Scotch and soda, Gilbert and Sullivan. (EBW)[1]

Garth Williams was born on April 16, 1912, in New York City. Both his parents were artists, and the child was early taken to Europe but soon returned to the United States, where his early years were spent in New Jersey. He returned to study art in London, traveled widely in Europe, won the Prix de Rome for sculpture in 1936, and served in the British Red Cross when war was declared in 1939.

After his return to the United States, Williams first became affiliated with *The New Yorker* in 1943. Since then, Williams has lived in Canada, Mexico, and the United States, both writing and illustrating more than a half dozen children's books as well as illustrating more than seventy for other writers. His *The Rabbits' Wedding*, once a *cause célèbre*,* has been in print for more than thirty-five years.

Williams's book-illustrating career began with that unforgettable, dapper, mouse-shaped little boy Stuart Little. Williams gained further recognition with his renderings for Laura Ingalls Wilder's Little House series, George Selden's *The Cricket in Times Square*, and, of course, our Charlotte.

Williams illustrated at a prodigious rate, notwithstanding trips between domiciles in Mexico and in the United States. And still today, Williams continues to work prolifically, indefatigably, and humorously. Even as I write this, I have before me his joyous, zestful, original, and bold paintings for Jack Prelutsky's collection of lamely humorous verse *Beneath a Blue Umbrella*

*Some readers interpreted the marriage of a black rabbit and a white one as a covert argument for miscegenation. Williams maintained that he had simply written a story of two rabbits.

(1990)—one of those instances of the illustrations making the book.

For the beginning of the felicitous association with E. B. White, by way of Ursula Nordstrom, Williams's own description merits repeating. Williams had been attempting to establish his artistic reputation in New York. Carrying a diverse portfolio from publisher to publisher, he sought entrance into the world of book illustration. One day, out of the blue, he received a call from Ursula Nordstrom at Harper. She had the manuscript for *Stuart Little*, and as Williams tells it:

> . . . [W]hen the MSS arrived, it had a note pinned to it—"please try Garth Williams as illustrator." A good omen.
>
> E. B. White wanted me to read it at once and let him know if I liked it. So I sat down in Harper & Brothers['s] office and read it, and I was delighted.[2]

As it happened, on the very day White's *Stuart Little* arrived, Williams was drawing the portrait of a mouse befriended by his daughter, Fiona. Williams used the visiting rodent as a model, giving him, however, "un-mouse-like ears and a variety of small other details to comply with the first paragraphs of the story."

By way of Nordstrom, White and Williams remained in touch, and occasionally small adjustments were made in the drawings. In May of 1945, White wrote Nordstrom that he liked Stuart's crawl stroke very much (*SL*, p. 116), but that the lovely little Harriet Ames, just a trifle shorter than Stuart's own "two inches nothing and a quarter," wasn't quite right. "Her hair should be smoother and neater, also her legs should look more attractive . . . and her skirt should be fuller."[3] White enclosed a clipping from a Sears, Roebuck catalogue, and also one from the Montgomery Ward catalogue, pointing out that model number 21 was how he envisioned Miss Ames.

Although other illustrators had been considered for *Stuart Little*[4]—Robert Lawson (*Ferdinand*), James Daugherty (*Andy and the Lion*), and Ernest H. Shepard (*Winnie the Pooh*)—Williams proved himself worthy of that illustrious company. The text and Williams's illustrations, as they stand, are a veritable duet.

White, too, approved heartily, noting that "I think Garth Williams deserves all the bouquets that could be handed him for a brilliant and imaginative job. He has made the pictures enhance and add to the text in the way only the very best illustrators can and has made the book his book too in every way."[5]

Charlotte's Web presented a different challenge from *Stuart Little*, as Williams stated in his

letter to me—the animals having "to be very real, with the sole peculiarity that they talked to themselves and to some people. But the story," Williams, said, "was just perfect."

In point of fact, there is evidence of some discussion back and forth between White and Williams. Williams's preliminary drawings of Charlotte showed the spider with a woman's face. White was concerned about this, and in March 1952, he wrote to Ursula Nordstrom:

> Under sep cov I am sending you "American Spiders" by Willis J. Gertsch, of the Natural History Museum staff. Will you be kind enough to pass it along to Garth Williams for his amusement. Aranea Cavatica is not shown in this book, but there is a spider in Plate 23 called Neoscona that looks like Charlotte, pretty much. Charlotte, however, has a rather nice little design, or engraving, on top of her abdomen—sort of like a keystone.
>
> There is a very funny picture in this book that I think Garth should see. It is "A" on the unnumbered page preceding P. 85. The eyes and hair are quite fetching.
>
> Plate I shows an orb web covered with dew.[6]

In the end, White was thoroughly pleased, writing to the filmmaker Louis de Rochemont in June 1961 (long after the book's publication):

> When Garth Williams tried to dream up a spider that had human characteristics, the results were awful. He tried and tried, but we ended up with a Charlotte that was practically right out of a natural history book, or, more precisely, out of my own brain.[7]

Garth Williams's own recollections in his letter to me confirm the evidence in White's published letters.

> White gave me the two enormous tomes on spiders, about 30,000 different kinds, all with different faces, all gruesome. I struggled to invent a loveable spider-face. They all have 8 eyes. Mouth like pincers. So I used the wooly spider-type, placing 6 eyes in the hair, leaving two as we are accustomed to finding them. Finally I gave her a Mona Lisa face, as she is, after all, the heroine of the story.
>
> White accepted the accurate rendition of the Aranea Cavatica and suggested we skip a full-face. He put two dots on the edge of her face looking down and put 3 strokes to suggest hair on top of her head—and the problem was solved. But I contend he cheated. (See page 66.)

One interesting speculation about Garth Williams's contribution to the story of Charlotte and Wilbur has been put forth by the Canadian

Charlotte's Web, 5

Came after I had illustrated many other books. It was most welcome. Stuart was more interesting to illustrate as it was crazier. A little girl the size of Stuart. An invisible car racing around the dentist's office. Stuart driving his car through the country and talking to people.

Charlotte required me to make the people—with the exception of Fern—<u>very</u> ordinary indeed. The animals had to be very real, with the sole peculiarity that they talked to themselves and to some people. But the story was just perfect.

White gave me the two enormous tomes on spiders about 30,000. different kinds, all with different faces, all gruesome. I struggled to invent a loveable spider-face. They all have 8 eyes. Mouth like pincers So I used the wooly spider-type, placing 6 eyes in the hair, leaving two as we are accustomed to finding them. Finally I gave her a Mona Lisa face, as she is, after all, the heroine of the story.

White accepted the accurate rendition of the Aranea Cavatica and suggested we skip a full-face. He put two dots on the edge of her face looking down and put 3 strokes to suggest hair on top of her head—and the problem was solved. But I contend he cheated.

contd: on p.6.

Letter from Garth Williams to the annotator, relating how he came to be involved in Charlotte's Web. *(Since the Arables do not look like E. B. and Katharine White, and since Mr. and Mrs. Little do look like them, probably Williams forgot he was now writing about* Charlotte's Web *and not about* Stuart Little.*)*

Charlotte's Web contd: 6

My only worry was what to make Mr and Mrs Little look like After pondering some time on this problem I decide to make them rather like Andy and Katherine White. Mr White passed the frontisp without comment.

critic Perry Nodelman. Nodelman sees *Charlotte's Web* as a static novel in which action is retarded by poetic descriptions. And so Nodelman suggests that Williams's "energetic" drawings balance "the often dreamy music of the text."[8] They ensure that there is not a surfeit of inactive exposition. (Mark Twain termed prolonged descriptive passages "weather," and in *The American Claimant* he hilariously assembled all the book's description in one appendix, so that the reader could read for action, uninterrupted.) By 1969, discussions began between White and Nordstrom regarding an illustrator for White's last novel, *The Trumpet of the Swan*. But that is another story.

It's worth attending more closely the workings of a well-illustrated book. Earlier, I referred to the collaboration as a "duet." That is to say, in a well-illustrated book, the pictures do not act as fingerprints of the text; they do not merely reproduce what the words say. Rather, they more or less tell their own story, sometimes, in fact, commenting ironically or even negating the words.

Thus, see for example, the earlier cited instance (page 88) in which Beatrix Potter showed the blackbirds looking with puzzlement at the jacket on the scarecrow hung up to frighten them away."[9]

Similarly, *Charlotte's Web* is a collaboration of text and picture, in which Garth Williams has his own things to say. We've already pointed out in the notes that Fern's presence in Chapter XII on *CW*, page 88, is entirely Williams's idea. White says nothing about her being there for that amusing barnyard planning session, and it is solely because Williams put her in the illustration that we know she was there.

Likewise, the facial expressions on the animals—Templeton's Falstaffian self-satisfaction (*CW*, p. 147), Wilbur's dubious anxiety (*CW*, p. 58), and his expression of humility mixed with some-pig-ness as he has his news photos taken (*CW*, p. 163)—those are interpretations by Williams, only elliptically suggested by the text.

Many fine books, like some of Beatrix Potter's, or like John Burningham's *Come Away from the Water, Shirley*, actually *subvert* or contradict the text, making for a delicious sort of irony or duplicity. It's a trick easiest to carry out when author and illustrator are the same.* Williams didn't go *that* far, but certainly most of the moments of the story he illustrated were his own choice, and even the image of Fern that most of us carry with us today must surely derive from

*A remarkable example of an illustrator who is *not* the author having ironically subverted the author's text is in the illustrations Edward Gorey drew for my hum drum text in the two books *Donald and the . . .* and *Donald Has a Difficulty*.

the graceful child madonna nursing Wilbur (*CW*, p. 6), the ponytailed farm kid in unselfconscious happiness (*CW*, p. 11), or the absorbed, smiling child sitting in a happy trance "next to Wilbur's pen . . . during the long afternoons, thinking and listening and watching Wilbur" (*CW*, p. 15).

All the more shocking the Hollywood cutie pie–nymphet of the animated Hanna-Barbera production.*

---

*Davis (p. 243) relates that Katherine "had for several years felt deeply guilty about the terrible animated film version of *Charlotte's Web*, Andy having sold the book in order to help pay [her] enormous medical bills. (When the movie was televised, Katharine was more upset about it than Andy—'That's not the way our barn looks!')"

Isabel Russell (p. 79), Katharine's secretary at the time, reports that White returned from his viewing of the film saying, "Well, frankly, it was just about what I expected. Not really good but perhaps not as bad as I had anticipated."

The Hanna-Barbera production makes much of what White called the "boy-girl story" of Henry Fussy and Fern, to the magnification of which the author objected. All in all, it is clear that White's own suggestions about the film (*L.*, p. 629) were ignored.

Appendix B

THE MANUSCRIPTS

"Revise and rewrite. . . . Remember, it is no sign of weakness or defeat that your manuscript ends up in need of major surgery."[1]

E.B. White claimed that when he donated his papers to the Division of Rare & Manuscript Collections at the library of Cornell University, his alma mater, his fire insurance rate dropped precipitously. Today, the White papers, letters, and manuscripts are stored in a room in the basement of that library, in handsome blue boxes.* They compose a vast collection, perhaps the largest collection of any American writer in that library.[2] The manuscripts and letters pertaining to CW brought Mr. White an IRS tax gift allowance of $4,817.50. As Mr. White said, "[I]f I could pick up forty-eight hundred bucks for a children's book, think what I could do with something written for adults!"[3]

Since there are frequent references to additions, deletions, and changes in the annotations, it's important that I clarify the sources for such information—the nine folders and two boxes of drafts. There is, however, little reason for the general reader to attempt to keep the various manuscripts in mind. Enough to say that, in early drafts, *Charlotte's Web* was an animal story, primarily of Wilbur and Charlotte. All the early drafts began with a description either of the barn, of Charlotte, or of Wilbur, or—in one instance—of Mr. Arable going out to the barn to find the eleven pigs. The fast-moving opening and the parallel plot of Fern developed only after White had set aside the book for a time to "let the body heat out of it," as he wrote to Ursula Nordstrom (see page 218).[4]

---

*Working with all these manuscript boxes led me to a curious discovery that may be relevant to the author of *Charlotte's Web*. Through much of his life, White complained of severe hay fever—clogged head, runny eyes, and so forth. In October 1989, I planned to spend four days working with the manuscript collection at Cornell. However, at the end of the third day of burying my nose in White's papers, I was so congested, and my eyes were running so badly, that I was obliged to stop work. I've never had an allergy before or since. Could it be that White's paper, or the attic in which it was stored, was responsible for his suffering? Isabel Russell (p. 145) recounts that foraging in his attic had brought on one of White's allergy attacks in 1976.

The *CW* materials are in folders in two boxes. One box contains eight successive drafts (more or less) for the book; the other contains scripts and materials presumably pertaining to the screenplay projected by Gene Deitch, who had done a Bemelmans *Madeline* short that White liked[5] but about whose *Charlotte* he quickly had misgivings.[6]

Ten years after publication, White wrote a covering description about the manuscript in Folder B shortly before it was donated to Cornell.

> a note about the manuscript
>
> I began writing "Charlotte's Web" in 1949, worked at it in spare moments, and finished it about two years later, January 1951. The completed manuscript consisted of seventeen chapters. When I was on the point of submitting it to my publisher, I decided that I was dissatisfied with the story as it stood. So I set it aside and later reworked it. I added five chapters, starting the narrative with the birth of the pig on the John Arable farm and giving the little girl a more important place in the story. The book was published during the following year, 1952.
>
> [signed] E B White
> 13 Nov 1961

In addition to that cover note, White wrote an inventory of the draft folders in Box One, loosely reconstructing the evolution of the book. That inventory and reconstruction is fairly accurate, and I reproduce it below. In brackets, I've added my own commentary or additions to White's reconstruction.

A. Contains notes, sketches, memoranda, miscellany, false starts, discarded pages.

> [First attempt begins, "Charlotte was a big grey spider," and is succeeded with other starts beginning with descriptions of Wilbur and of the barn. Fern was not in the story.]

B. First draft. Longhand. Finished 19 January 1951.

> [Begins, "I shall speak first of Wilbur." Lurvy is named "Larry."
> [This is the draft about which White wrote Ursula Nordstrom on March 1, 1951, that he had "put it away for a while to ripen (let the body heat go out of it). It doesn't satisfy me the way it is and I think eventually I shall rewrite it pretty much, in order to shift the emphasis and make other reforms."][7]

C. An attempt to start story a new way, with John Arable pulling on boots and going to the hoghouse. Much of this draft was never used.

The name of the Arable boy has become Avery.

[This is the version in which Fern is set an arithmetic problem about feeding a baby. The scene does not appear in the final version of the book—but it has been transposed to *TS* p. 64. The pages, even with Fern's name still in the manuscript, are at the Morgan Library, with the *TS* manuscripts.]

D. Another attempt at a new start. Second draft apparently.

[Begins with John Arable, then p. 2, "Chapter II FERN." Largely a clean-typed version of folder C.]

E. Another attempt at a new start. Some pages missing from this version turn up in the final typescript. Pages 1 through 4 were dropped.

[Since it begins with "Where's Papa going with that ax?" it is possible that this is one of the missing working pages that were written between Draft H and the printer's copy, Draft I.]

F. Draft of a new Chapter I. Close to the final version.

G. Draft of a new Chapter II.

H. This draft was the book I was ready to submit for publication when I realized something was wrong with it.

[Intermediate draft of the whole book, pages numbered 1 through 134, a few sheets missing. Some of the missing pages became part of the final typescript. White did put it aside, then rewrote it to give Fern a leading role.]

I. Final draft, with printer's marks.

Regarding the sequence, I believe we must consider the typed Draft H to have followed Draft B. More importantly, the crucial draft (and notes) for the final printer's version (Draft I) seems to be missing. Draft H begins:

~~CHARLOTTE'S WEB~~

~~Chapter I~~

ESCAPE

~~I shall speak first of Wilbur..~~

~~Wilbur was what farmers call a spring pig~~, which simply means that he was born in springtime. When he was four weeks old he was taken from his mother and went to live in a manure pile

in the cellar of Zuckerman's barn.

~~The barn was very large. It was very old. It smelled of manure. . . . .~~

(Usually, when White drew a box around a text, he meant to delete it.)

The printer's version, Draft I, is obviously a final, perfectly typed copy. It contains five more chapters than does the version in Draft H, which White had set aside. And it begins with Fern setting the breakfast table, just as in the published book. It follows that all White's working papers between Draft H, finished January 1951, and the final version are missing.

Roughly, and in brief, White started the book in 1949 and finished the first version in 1951. He had seventeen chapters. He put the manuscript aside for close to a year, then added the new chapters giving prominence to Fern. On March 29, 1952, White turned in the manuscript to Harper, and that year the book was published.

White's extraordinary efforts to get started are best seen in three false starts in the first folder. The first attempt reads as follows:

> Charlotte was a big grey spider who lived in a ~~beautiful web~~ doorway. But there is no use talking about Charlotte until we have talked about her best friend—a pig named Wilbur.

The second version, having a drawing of a spider in the upper-left-hand corner, is titled "Chapter I. The Barn," and begins:

> A barn can have a horse in it, and a barn can have a cow in it, and a barn can have hens scratching in the chaff . . . but if a barn hasn't got a pig in it, it is hardly worth talking about.

[See plate 12, page 196.]

The next version kept the same focus on the barn:

> CHAPTER I. THE BARN
>
> The best part of Zuckerman's barn was the ~~part under the shed on the south side cellar~~ part underneath the where the cows were cow on the south side. ~~Mr. Zuckerman had a trap door in the main floor and twice a day he would take his shovel and open the trapdoor~~ It was warm because the sun shone in through the door, and it was warm because of the ~~cow~~

The draft in Folder B begins with firm resolve to focus:

> CHAPTER I. ESCAPE
>
> I shall speak first of Wilbur.
>
> Wilbur was a small beautifully nicely-behaved pig living in a manure pile in the symmetrical cellar of a barn. He

> was what farmers call a spring pig—which simply means he ~~happened to be~~ was born in springtime. But there is no use talking about Wilbur until we have looked into the matter of the barn itself. The barn was very large. It was very old. It smelled of hay and it smelled of manure.

This way of commencing by setting forth what he believes his main subject will be, and then digressing as he attempts to incorporate his other topics, is typical of White's mode of composition. It is the identical method he employed in writing the successive drafts of his third children's book, *The Trumpet of the Swan*.[8]

White is aware that, in order to capture the attention of a child, a story should start with action. Thus the designation of an "Introduction"—an attempt to begin before the real story begins, perhaps.

> INTRODUCTION
>
> At midnight, John Arable pulled his boots on, lit a lantern, and walked out through the woods to the hog house. The sow ~~heaved~~ lay on her side; her eyes were closed. In the corner stood the newborn pigs, ten of them. They had their heads together, in a circle, like football players . . . before a play. Mr. Arable set his lantern down, leaned on the rail, and smiled.
>
> "Ten of them," he whispered. "Nine full-size, and one little runty pig. Little Wilbur: Funny there's always one that's smaller than the others."

The published book, of course, begins with action and suspense:

> "Where's Papa going with that ax?"

Given these labors, it's not surprising that White wrote me:

> I was interested to see again my early attempts to get *Charlotte's Web* started. I recall quite well my difficulty in putting it in a shape that satisfied me. From the evidence, I had as much trouble getting off the ground as did the Wright Brothers.[9]

In addition to the draft folders in the first box, there is a second box of materials relevant exclusively to the projected film version. This box contains, first, one copy of the Dell Yearling paperback, annotated in two different handwritings—White's in ink and someone else's printed in pencil. There are red lines in the margin for expository (nondialogue) passages.

The first folder in the box is labeled "Film Version," dated 1970, and consists of ninety-five pages of White's usual yellow draft paper. Perhaps the most significant passage is that in which (once again) White states his own view of his book, as follows:

> STORY TELLER'S VOICE
>
> This is a story of miracles—the miracle of birth, the miracle of friendship, the miracle of death.

There are a few White gems, such as the line of dialogue White wrote for the script:

> "You <u>would</u> have eleven of them, when you only have ~~room~~ accommodations to feed ten!"

In the script, the word *teat* is changed to *breast*, as Mrs. Arable explains the newborn Wilbur's problem to Fern.

In the second folder, there is a note presumably to the director: "Bulls don't touch noses of cows. You know what they touch."

In a third folder, titled Television Scenario, dated about 1973, White enumerates the chapters by whether they are essentially live action or mostly narration. Otherwise, the folder is of no importance.

Finally, there is another folder titled Television Scenario containing five pages, and one containing brief comments by White on Earl Hamner's screenplay.

Appendix C

SPIDERS

Writing an affectionate poem to Katharine in 1929, White early suggested a fondness for spiders. After he had his own barn, he had ample incentive and opportunity to inform himself about arachnids at close quarters. Once White actually decided to write about a word-weaving spider, he relied on two basic reference works, one by the distinguished Cornell entomologist John Henry Comstock and one by Willis J. Gertsch. Gertsch was Associate Curator, Department of Insects and Spiders, at the American Museum of Natural History, as well as the reviser of the Comstock book. White actually approached Dr. Gertsch with a list of questions about the life of the spider.[1] He also sent Ursula Nordstrom a New York Public Library slip to pass on to Garth Williams so that Williams might consult the three-volume turn-of-the-century work *Spiders and Their Spinningwork* by H. C. McCook.[2]

FIGURE 1

A typical research page from the early stages of preparation for the writing of *Charlotte's Web*. There are many such pages, as there also were years later about trumpeter swans, when White was preparing to write *The Trumpet of the Swan*. On this page, White seems just to have learned of the existence of the Comstock book, for the information—"Eating their prey–p. 23"—refers to the book by Gertsch.

FIGURE 2

Seemingly addressed to the interested layman, the beginning of Gertsch's book is eminently readable. Since White refers to page 23 for information on the eating habits of spiders, it's likely that he derived his correctly ordered list of the segments of a spider's leg from Gertsch's illustration.

FIGURE 3

This could be a page from the list of questions with which White approached Gertsch. Note that the answers were written with a different pencil (presumably at a different time) than the questions.

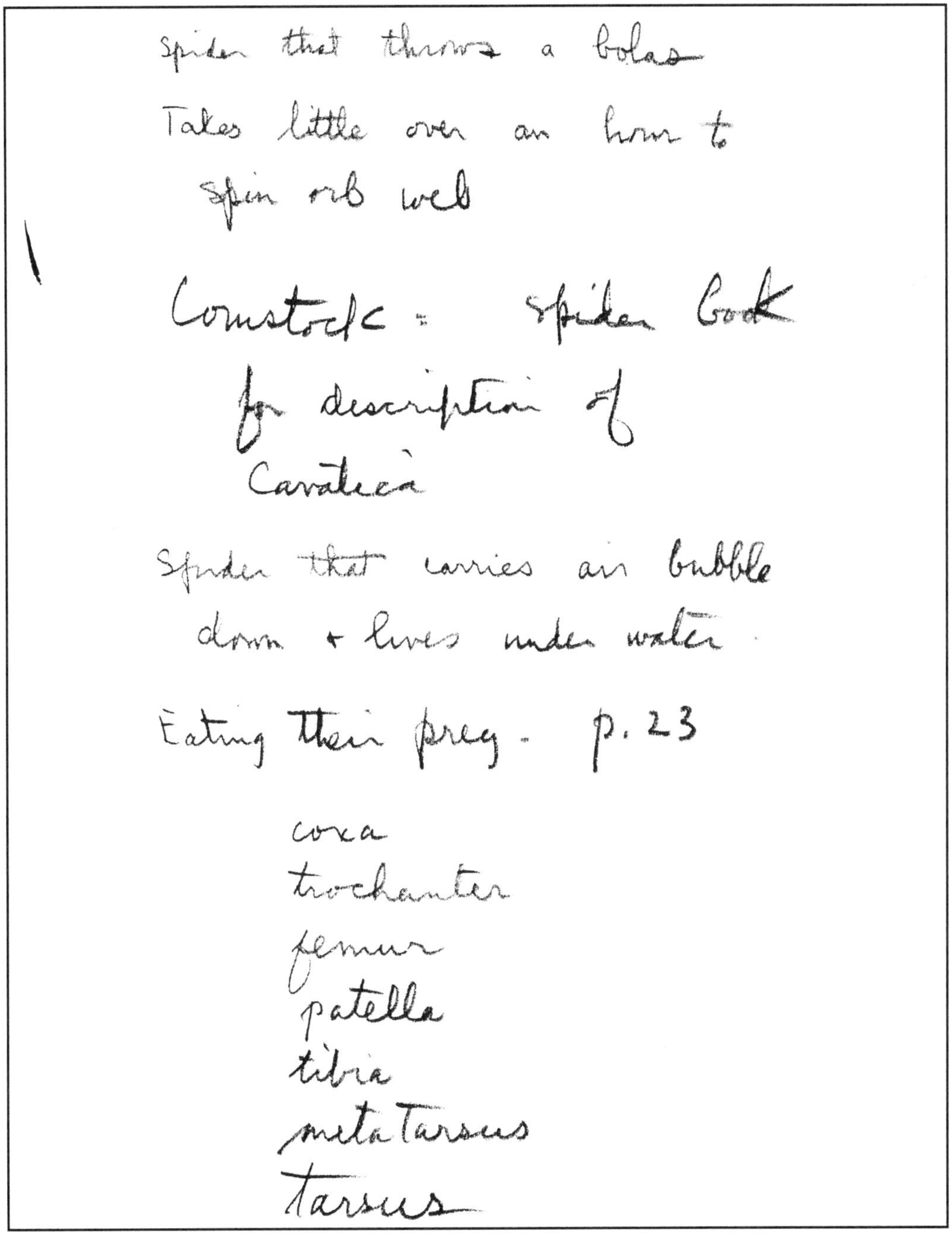

spider that throws a bolas

Takes little over an hour to spin orb web

Comstock: spider book for description of Caratecca

Spider that carries air bubble down + lives under water

Eating their prey - p. 23

coxa
trochanter
femur
patella
tibia
metaTarsus
tarsus

Figure 1

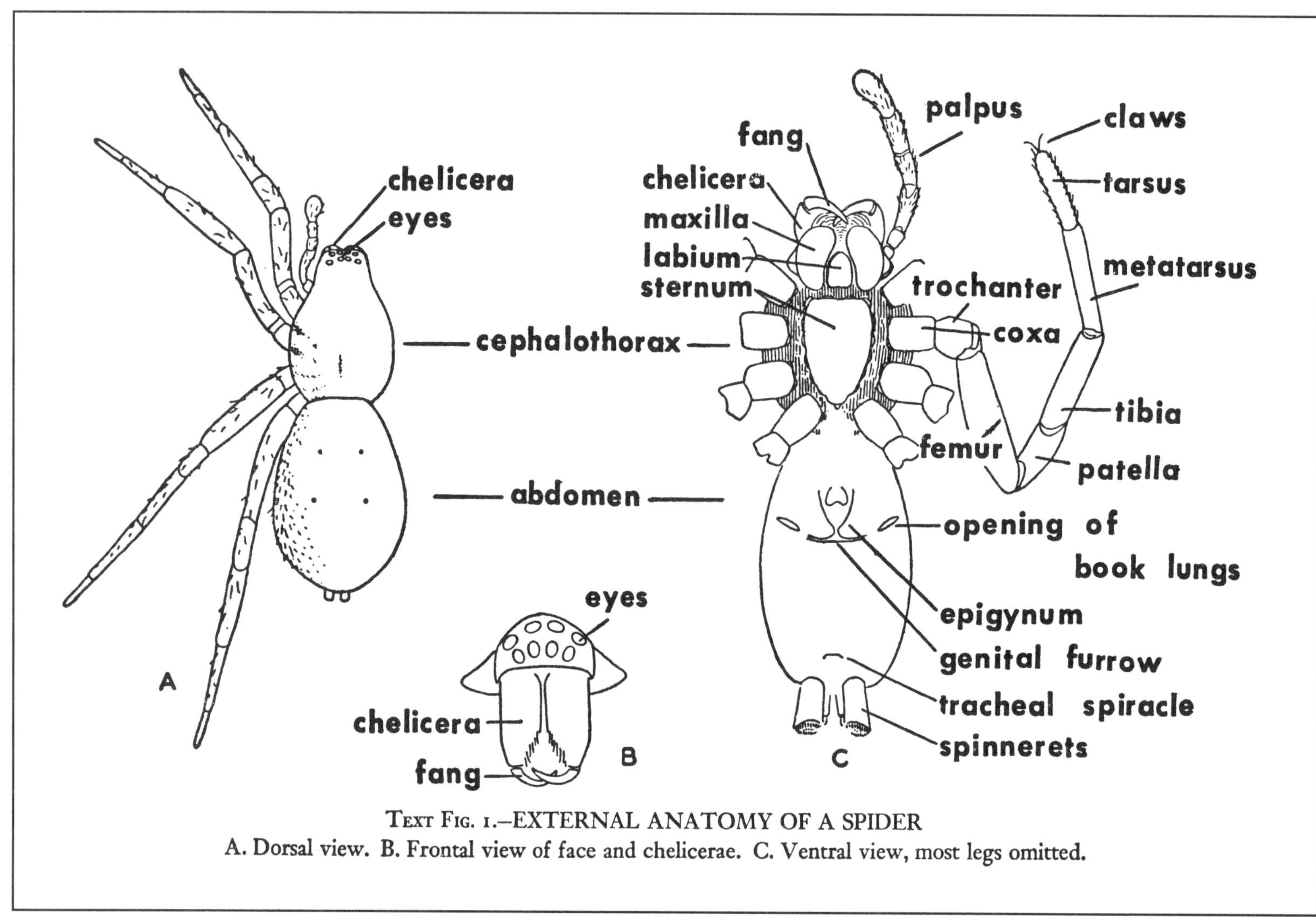

TEXT FIG. 1.–EXTERNAL ANATOMY OF A SPIDER
A. Dorsal view. B. Frontal view of face and chelicerae. C. Ventral view, most legs omitted.

Figure 2

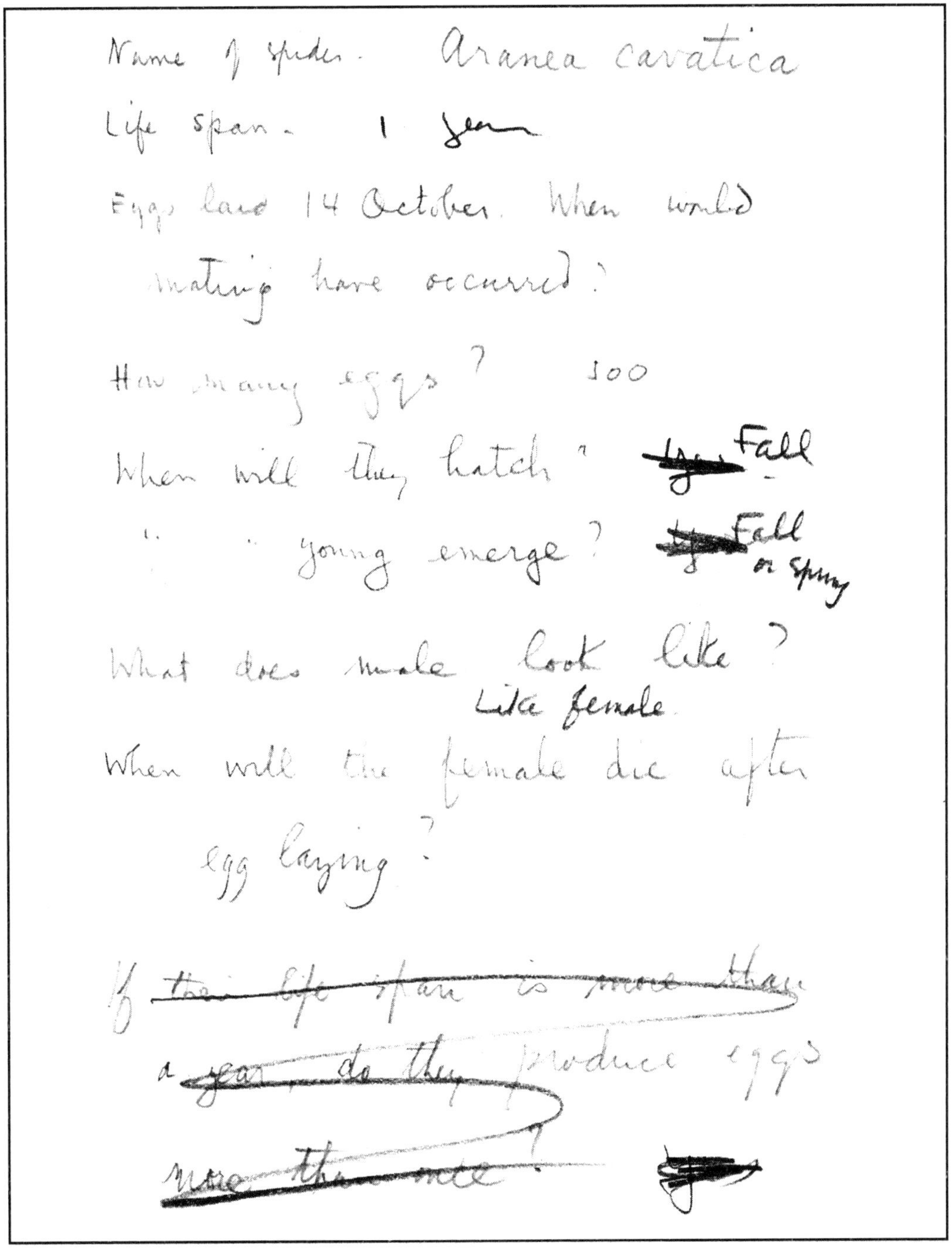

Name of spider. Aranea cavatica

Life span. 1 year

Eggs laid 14 October. When would mating have occurred?

How many eggs? 500

When will they hatch? ~~Spr~~ Fall

" " young emerge? ~~Sp~~ Fall or Spring

What does male look like? Like female

When will the female die after egg laying?

If ~~their life span is more than a year, do they~~ produce eggs ~~more than once~~? ~~Sp~~

Figure 3

A. Letter to Cass Canfield: Concern for scientific accuracy and the non-Disneyfication of Charlotte. The articulation of a spider's legs continues to impress White.

[North Brooklin, Me.]
20 May 1952

Dear Cass:

Thanks for the encouraging letter. I'm awfully glad that my spider has been well received locally—or shall I say internally? Am worried, though, at not having seen the Garth Williams picture that Ursula said was being put in the works for use in the catalogue. I would like to see the picture, because I feel that the book must at all odds have a beguiling Charlotte. The solution, I am quite sure, is for the artist to depict attitudes and postures, rather than facial expression. Spiders don't have much of any face—in fact they hardly have any head, or at least the head is relatively inconspicuous. But they have eight wonderfully articulated legs (arms), which offer a great chance for ballet treatment. Garth is such a wonderful artist that I am sure he will succeed; but for a while there he was bogged down in an attempt to produce a face.

As for my collecting some poems, or some prose, or both—I have it in mind and hope to get at it soon. Will be in New York for about a week in June—10th to 16th. Hope to see you.

Best regards,
Andy

B. Letter to Ursula Nordstrom: Probably few authors have as much say about the illustration of their books as did E. B. White—a function both of his reputation and of the sensitive and individual treatment the great editor gave her authors.

North Brooklin, Maine
24 May 1952

Dear Ursula:

Thanks for the dummy cuts and the jacket design. I like everything. The group on the jacket is charming. My only complaint is that the goose looks, for some reason, a bit snakelike. Perhaps this is because its beak is open, or pehaps because the eye is round like a snake's. You sound so rushed that I presume you don't want to make any revisions, and I would be satisfied to have the jacket go as is, if it seems right to you. But no goose-lover in this house is satisfied.

The web effect is OK for the purposes of jacket design, but the type of rather mussy Charles Addams attic web is not

right for the illustrations. I'm sure that Garth realizes that. Charlotte weaves quite an orderly, symmetrical web, and Garth has it right in the picture of Charlotte thinking—which, incidentally, I like. Smooth legs and smooth abdomen are correct. (Actually, Charlotte's legs are equipped with fine hairs, and these are mentioned in the book, but the overall effect is of smooth, silk-stocking legs.)

I think Fern is delightful in both pictures, and I couldn't be happier about her. Wilbur, also, is perfect on the jacket—very beguiling. In the dummy picture, where he is lying flat, weeping, I got a momentary shock because when I first glanced at the picture, it looked as though his right front foot were his snout. If there is time, I think it would be helpful simply to remove that foot entirely, leaving his snout nicely outlined against the straw. (I've tried this, by blocking it out with my fingernail, and it looks fine with just one front leg showing.) And by the way, I think Harper & Brothers should take Charlotte's advice: Never hurry and never worry. What's all this rosh, rosh, rosh?

On the whole, I am very pleased with developments, and have complete confidence that Garth will handle everything beautifully. If this letter isn't helpful or doesn't answer what is necessary to know, call me up. Our number here is Sedgwick (Me.) 106.

Sincerely,
Andy

C. Letter to Ursula Nordstrom: In March, White had asked Nordstrom whether she knew of any other case in literature of a spider weaving words in a web. "I'm not well read in juvenile literature, or any other kind . . ." he wrote,[3] and Nordstrom obviously countered by telling him of Scotland's king Robert the Bruce, who learned patience in battle by watching a spider spin its web.

North Brooklin, Maine
23 July 1952

Dear Ursula:

The corrected drawings are fine and I am very grateful to Garth for his trouble. I don't think it is necessary to do anything about Mrs. Arable in #3. She looks all right.

Thanks for the tall tales of Robert the Bruce. Spiders expect to have their webs busted, and they take it in their stride. One of Charlotte's daughters placed her web in the tie-ups, right behind my bull calf, and I kept forgetting about it and would bust

one of her foundation lines in my trips to and from the trapdoor where I push the manure into the cellar. After several days of this, during which she had to rebuild the entire web each evening, she solved the matter neatly by changing the angle of the web so that the foundation line no longer crossed my path. Her ingenuity has impressed me, and I am now teaching her to write SOME BOOK, and will let Brentano have her for their window. . . .

FIGURE 4

"There is a very funny picture in [Gertsch] that I think Garth should see. It is 'A' on the unnumbered page preceding P. 85. The eyes and hair are quite fetching," White wrote to Nordstrom:[4]

North Brooklin, Maine
28 March [1952]

Under sep cov I am sending you "American Spiders" by Willis J. Gertsch, of the Natural History Museum staff. Will you be kind enough to pass it along to Garth Williams for his amusement. Aranea Cavatica is not shown in this book, but there is a spider in Plate 23 called Neoscona that looks like Charlotte, pretty much. Charlotte, however, has a rather nice little design, or engraving, on top of her abdomen—sort of like a keystone.

There is a very funny picture in this book that I think Garth should see. It is "A" on the unnumbered page preceding P. 85. The eyes and hair are quite fetching.

Plate I shows an orb web covered with dew.

Am also enclosing a N.Y. Public Library slip giving name and class mark of the McCook work on spiders. [See page 210.] This is in three volumes, containing hundreds and hundreds of pictures. Garth might find it helpful to thumb through these majestic tomes. He'd better watch out, though—once a man gets interested in spiders, there's no time left for art. [See page 199.]

Yrs,
Andy

TEXT FIG. 2.—COURTSHIP POSTURES OF MALE WOLF AND JUMPING SPIDERS

A. *Pardosa milvina* Hentz. B. *Habronattus viridipes* Hentz. C. *Peckhamia noxiosa* Hentz. D. *Hyctia pikei* Peckham. E. *Peckhamia picata* Peckham. F. *Euophrys monadnock* Emerton.

(Redrawn from Kaston, Emerton and Peckham).

Figure 4

Appendix D

E. B. WHITE'S LETTERS AND COMMENTS ABOUT CHARLOTTE'S WEB

LETTERS

To Ursula Nordstrom.[1] White is referring to Draft B. At this point, the story began with Wilbur and the barn. (See pages 196 and 207.) Eventually, these false starts were moved to Chapter III.

25 West 43rd Street
March 1, 1951

Dear Miss Nordstrom:

Thanks for the report. . . .

I've recently finished another children's book, but have to put it away for a while to ripen (let the body heat go out of it). It doesn't satisfy me the way it is and I think eventually I shall rewrite it pretty much, in order to shift the emphasis and make other reforms.

Sincerely,
E. B. White

To Mrs. Kaston.[2] Similar to the description White wrote later for Harper's "Dear Reader" release (see pages 239–40).

[New York]
April 10, 1953

Dear Mrs. Kaston:

Thanks for the letter and the picture of Charlotte's cousin, which is very pretty.

The idea of writing in Charlotte's Web came to me one day when I was on my way down through the orchard carrying a pail of slops to my pig. I had made up my mind to write a children's book about animals, and I needed a way to save a pig's life, and I had been watching a large spider in the backhouse, and what with one thing and another, the idea came to me.

Sincerely,
E. B. White

To Louis de Rochemont.[3] De Rochemont proposed an animated version of *Charlotte's Web.*

[North Brooklin, Me.]
28 June 1961

Dear Mr. de Rochemont:

Here is the letter I threatened to write. I'll try to keep it from turning into a trilogy.

While animation is a perfect device for satire, *Charlotte's Web* is not really a satire. It has a thread of fantasy, but essentially it is a hymn to the barn. It is pastoral, seasonal, and is concerned with ordinary people in, for the most part, ordinary situations. The heroine dies, the summer ends, and when the story comes to a close the girl, Fern, is a different girl—she has matured a little. Her interest has shifted from the barnyard animals to a boy who gives her a ride on the Ferris wheel.

Because of this, it has occurred to me that the book, if handled with imagination, might make a motion picture in live action—real girl, real barn, real creatures. A good deal of the action in the book would present no problem whatever to the camera. . . . And then there are the parts that are out of the question for the camera and would need an assist from the drawing board. The critical problem would be to arrive at a smooth transition between live scenes and animated scenes. If this problem can be solved at all, I believe the key lies in narration—in particular, narration by Fern herself.

Fern, in the story, often runs home and tells her mother about the goings-on in the barn cellar. Her mother is uneasy about the whole business and she presses Fern for details. In a film, this happy accident could be greatly useful. Fern could even turn out to be something of a sketch artist, and when grilled, could draw pictures for her mother showing what the barn cellar looks like—the spider, the rat, the pig. These rough sketches would be the germ of the animated characters, and the action could then go quickly from narration to dramatic animation. The most difficult scenes in the book would thus be presented in retrospect and in animation—as recaptured by the little girl. . . . The thing that would make the real spider interchangeable with the drawing-board spider, the real pig with the drawing-board pig, would be the voice always the same, and unmistakeable. . . .

I also think a small amount of general narrative would be useful—a narrator speaking directly to the audience, using words from the book. Children rather like to be told something in plain words, and although the movie maker usually regards narration as a sign of weakness, I think in the case of "Charlotte's Web" it might be appropriate. It could be the intimate, relaxed kind of scene-setting that Thornton Wilder's

narrator did so effectively in "Our Town."

An experience I had with the problem of illustrating the book is perhaps what gives me the courage to propose this live-action method of filming. When Garth Williams tried to dream up a spider that had human characteristics, the results were awful. He tried and tried, but we ended up with a Charlotte that was practically right out of a natural history book, or, more precisely, out of my own brain. And I pulled no punches in the story: the spider in the story is not prettified in any way, she is merely endowed with more talent than usual. This natural Charlotte was accepted at face value, and I came out ahead because of not trying to patronize an arachnid. I think a film maker might have the same good results by sticking with nature and with the barn. . . . I saw a spider spin the egg sac described in the story, and I wouldn't trade the sight for all the animated chipmunks in filmland. I watched the goslings hatch every spring, and I feel the same about that.

Anyway, I hope I've given you the gist of this idea. It could easily be a very sour idea, but it has stuck in my head for a long while, and I'd love to know whether you think it has any merit.

Sincerely,
E. B. White

To Alexander Lindey.[4] Lindey was White's lawyer in negotiations with John and Faith Hubley, who had hoped to film *Charlotte's Web*. The letter is important because it makes clear that White would consider a saccharine ending, without the death of Charlotte, as a "gross violation" of the spirit of the book.

[North Brooklin, Me.]
May 24, 1967

Dear Al:

The purpose of the "right of approval" clause is two-fold: it should protect me from a motion picture version of "Charlotte's Web" that violates the spirit and meaning of the story, and it should protect the Hubleys from obstructive behavior of an author. The movie will be their creation, not mine, and they will naturally want to get on with it in the way they feel it should go. I believe they are sympathetic with and agreeable to my desire to have a look at the screenplay, see sketches of the principal characters, and hear the principal voices. This shouldn't be either difficult or expensive.

I want the chance to edit the script wherever anything turns up that is a gross departure or a gross violation. I would also like to be protected against the insertion of wholly new material—songs, jokes, capers, episodes. I don't anticipate trouble of this sort; the Hubleys have already expressed to me in a letter (as well as verbally) their desire to produce a faithful adaptation, and I believe them to be sincere in this.

This approval business is sensitive, though. Artistic temperaments and pride can easily get on a collision course. In the elaborate papers sent me by Jap Gude, for instance, it says "Owner shall have the right of approval, *not to be unreasonably withheld.*" (Italics mine.) I don't know at what point a man's opinion, or stricture, becomes "unreasonable." What may seem reasonable to me may seem unreasonable to the Hubleys. This is the joker. We will just have to work it out between us as best we can.

I will give you an example of what I call a "gross" violation. In my book, Charlotte dies. If in the screenplay, she should turn up alive at the end of the story in the interests of a happier ending, I would consider this a gross violation and I would regard my disapproval as reasonable.

Good luck!
Andy

To Ursula Nordstrom.[5] The letter is about finding an illustrator for White's last novel, *The Trumpet of the Swan*. Edward Frascino won the assignment.

North Brooklin, Maine
October 7, 1969

Dear Ursula:

Thanks for your very generous letter. It frightens me to think that a publishing house is willing to put up large sums of money for something it hasn't even seen, but everything scares me these days.

I can't let you have a copy of the manuscript, as there *is* no copy and I never use carbon paper when I write, and I stay away from Xerox because I don't like the way it smells. I have a title and am pleased with it but you'll have to wait until I turn the thing in. . . .

About the illustrator, the choice will be up to you. I have no preconceptions but simply want my book to enjoy the best drawings we can get. The ideal way, I would imagine, would be to ask two or three of the likeliest candidates for the job to submit a sketch or two after reading some of the script, and see which fellow comes up with the happiest drawing. But I don't suppose artists—particularly those who are well-established, like Garth Williams—are willing to perform any such antics. Whoever is chosen will have a lot of support and help from me. Garth's Stuart was superb and did much to elevate the book. His Charlotte (until we abandoned everything and just drew a spider) was horrible and would have wrecked the book. I have no idea what Garth is up to, these days. I do not feel committed to him, but I feel grateful to him. I have no reason to want to change illustrators unless you, after reading the script, think you know somebody who could do the job better. More than anything else, the drawings will need

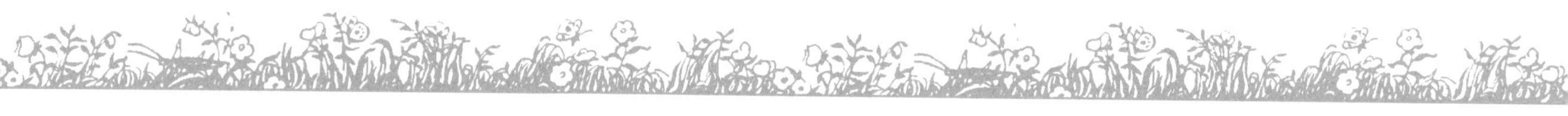

someone's touch who is humorous and can make them amusing as well as charming.

May God be with us at all times in this fantastic venture.

Yrs,
Andy

To Ursula Nordstrom.[6] The film was eventually produced in 1973, a Hanna-Barbera–Sagittarius Production.[7]

North Brooklin, Maine
October 28, 1969

Dear Ursula:

. . .

The reason the story has never been made into a film is because I won't sign a contract unless it gives me the right to see and approve the general shape and appearance of the main characters, and the Hollywood big shots won't sign a contract that *does* give me this right. This has been going on for seventeen years.

Last winter, John and Faith Hubley had the book under option and were most anxious to do a picture. They had no objection to my proviso, but when they went out to Hollywood to raise the money, they met with resistance. Just as soon as a Hollywood producer stumbles on the clause in the contract that gives the author of the book the right of approval, he chucks up his dinner and abandons the deal. The standard procedure in the movies is to knock off the author with one clean blow, and then proceed with the picture. I am just stubborn enough to stand my ground. It causes nothing but trouble, but *somebody* has to stand up to Hollywood. It's such fun. (All it costs me is $75,000—a bargain.)

Yrs,
Andy

P.S. The Disney organization tried for years to beat me down. I didn't beat, and Disney is dead. But he's still trying from the grave.

To Gene Deitch.[8] White wrote his attorney, Milton Greenstein, that he was favorably impressed by Deitch, who "has had 25 years in cartoon film production," and whose version of three Bemelmans *Madeline* shorts he enjoyed. "I feel fairly happy about Deitch—happy as I can ever be in never-never land, which still gives me the shakes."[9] White became increasingly disillusioned with the project.[10]

North Brooklin
January 12 [1971]

Dear Gene:

It was generous of you to send me such a detailed report of your scheme for the picture. This afternoon I sent you a few more photographs—they were taken in Canada, but they

are close to New England in form and spirit.

You said in your letter (about my script) "how I wish I had the whole thing." You have everything I wrote; there wasn't any more.

I've studied your letter very carefully and find myself in sympathy, or agreement, with most of it. I do hope, though, that you are not planning to turn "Charlotte's Web" into a moral tale. It is not that at all. It is, I think, an *appreciative* story, and there is quite a difference. It celebrates life, the seasons, the goodness of the barn, the beauty of the world, the glory of everything. But it is essentially amoral, because animals are essentially amoral, and I respect them, and I think this respect is implicit in the tale. I discovered, quite by accident, that reality and fantasy make good bedfellows. I discovered that there was no need to tamper in any way with the habits and characteristics of spiders, pigs, geese, and rats. No "motivation" is needed if you remain true to life and true to the spirit of fantasy. I would hate to see Charlotte turned into a "dedicated" spider: she is, if anything, more the Mehitabel type—toujours gai. She is also a New Englander, precise and disciplined. She does what she does. Perhaps she is magnifying herself by her devotion to another, but essentially she is just a trapper. . . .

As for Templeton, he's an old acquaintance and I know him well. He starts as a rat and he ends as a rat—the perfect opportunist and a great gourmand. I devoutly hope that you are not planning to elevate Templeton to sainthood. . . .

An aura of magic is essential, because this is a magical happening. Much can be done by music of the right kind, as when the moment arrives when communication takes place between the little girl and the animals in the barn cellar. This is truly a magical moment and should be so marked by the music. (I hear it as a sort of thrumming, brooding sound, like the sound of crickets in the fall, or katydids, or cicadas. It should be a haunting, quiet, steady sound—subdued and repetitive.)

Even more can be done by *words*, if you are able to use them. (You'll have to forgive me for being a word man, but that's what I am.)

In writing of a spider, I did not make the spider adapt her ways to my scheme. I spent a year studying spiders before I ever started writing the book. In this, I think I found the key to the story. I hope you will, in your own medium, be true to Charlotte and to nature in general. My feeling about animals is just the opposite of Disney's. He made them dance to his tune and came up with some great creations, like Donald Duck. I preferred to dance to *their* tune and came up with Charlotte and Wilbur. It would be futile and unfair to compare the two approaches,

but you are stuck with my scheme and will probably come out better if you go along with it. Both techniques are all right, each in its own way, but I have a strong feeling that you can't mix them. It just comes natural to me to keep animals pure and not distort them or take advantage of them.

Interdependence? I agree that the film should be a paean to life, a hymn to the barn, an acceptance of dung. But I think it would be quite untrue to suggest that barnyard creatures are dependent on each other. The barn is a community of rugged individualists, everybody mildly suspicious of everybody else, including me. Friendships sometimes develop, as between a goat and a horse, but there is no sense of true community or cooperation. Heaven forfend! Joy of life, yes. Tolerance of other creatures, yes. Community, no.

I just want to add that there is no symbolism in "Charlotte's Web." And there is no political meaning in the story. It is a straight report from the barn cellar, which I dearly love, having spent so many fine hours there, winter and summer, spring and fall, good times and bad times, with the garrulous geese, the passage of swallows, the nearness of rats, and the sameness of sheep.

K sends her best to you and Zdenka.

Yrs,
Andy

To Gene Deitch.[11] Ever, White fought against the trivializing of Charlotte.

North Brooklin
February 3, 1971

Dear Gene:

. . . It is all very well to say that "Charlotte's Web was a web of love which extended beyond her own lifespan." But you should never lose sight of the fact that it was a web spun by a true arachnid, not by a *de facto* person. One has eight legs and has been around for an unbelievably long time on this earth; the other has two legs and has been around just long enough to raise a lot of hell, drain the swamps, and bring the planet to the verge of extinction.

. . . As you say, spiders do not talk to pigs, except in the world of the fable. But when conversation does finally take place, in that fabulous and pure world, it is indeed a spider who talks, indeed a pig. It is not a woman in spider's clothing, or a boy in a pig's skin. Be true to animals, O Good Gene, and you will live forever. When you enter the barn cellar, remove your hat. . . .

Yrs,
Andy

To J. G. Gude, who was White's agent for film rights.[12] A month after this letter, the project was taken over by Hanna-Barbera.

[North Brooklin, Me.]
April 10, 1971

Dear Jap:

I saw only a tiny fragment of Deitch's treatment, but it was enough to make me uneasy. And I've been uneasy from the very start because of the Czech locale. Sagittarius has spent enough in airplane fares alone to have offset any gain.

If Deitch plans to make "Charlotte's Web" a picture for adults, then he doesn't understand the story and should be dropped. If he has taken the joy out of the tale, he already has two strikes against him. If he is groping for conflict, he is groping in the dark. If he is phasing Fern out of the story he might as well be phasing Scarlett out of "Gone With the Wind." Fern is built-in, and nobody in his right mind would want to yank her. . . .

The first letter I had from Deitch unnerved me. He seemed to be searching for moral implications. He was analyzing the bejesus out of the story instead of *accepting* it, the way children do. He seemed to want to make the story serve some ends of his own—I'm not sure what. Anybody who can't accept the miracle of the web shouldn't try to film it. . . .

As for music, I agree with you that music is very important, but Deitch seems to want to introduce a lot of songs and turn the thing into a sort of musical. I'm distrustful of this, and the one song he sent me was way off base. You could, of course, weave "Charlotte's Web" into a musical comedy, and maybe some day it will be done. But right now, I think the most promising approach is to keep the story right on course and not interrupt it every few minutes with a song. . . .

Yrs,
Andy

To Childhood Revisited Class.[13] "'Charlotte' was a story of friendship, life, death, salvation."

March 9, 1973

. . .

"Charlotte's Web" was different. I had moved to the country, had experienced the pleasures of a barnyard and a barn, and had introduced sheep, geese, and a pig into the scene. (The rat and the spider moved in without help from me.) I conceived the idea for the story, and by that time I was well acquainted with the principal characters. Before attempting the book, however, I studied spiders and boned up on them. I watched Charlotte at work, here on my place, and I also read books about the life of spiders, to inform myself about their habits, their capabilities, their temperament. It took me two years to write the story. Having finished it, I found I was dissatisfied with it, so instead of

submitting it to my publisher, I laid it aside for a while, then rewrote it, introducing Fern and other characters. This took a year, but it was a year well spent.

I can't say whether my style and attitude changed between the writing of "Charlotte's Web" and the writing of "The Trumpet of the Swan." I was almost seventy when I began "The Trumpet." Like Louis, I needed money. Perhaps a man loses his innocence at seventy—I don't know. I had to do a great deal of research for the book because I had never seen a trumpeter swan and, in fact, would not have dared write about the swans at all if I had not been familiar with geese. A man who is dealing in fantasy doesn't worry about contradictions or inconsistencies. It is true, as you point out, that a swan, equipped as he is with an inflexible bill, would be unable to blow a trumpet. But I leapt lightly over that hurdle: I wanted a Trumpeter Swan who could play like Louis Armstrong, and I simply created him and named him Louis. The cutting of the webs between his toes is also fantastical, just as the bird itself is; I introduced it partly to tell a little bit about the horn and its valves, partly because I thought it an amusing incident. It showed, moreover, that Louis was willing to make a personal sacrifice in order to achieve his goal.

I don't think there is any more violence in "The Trumpet of the Swan" than in my other books. You can't have a big bird crashing his way into a music store to steal a horn without stirring up a bit of trouble. The episode is essentially violent in its very nature. As for whether realism and honesty are "good for a young child," I don't pretend to know what is good, what is bad. I go by my instinct. I write largely for myself and am content to believe that what is good enough for me is good enough for a youngster. If "The Trumpet" differs from the other two books, I think it is because perhaps it presupposes a greater maturity in the reader. (I am always distressed when I hear of a second grade teacher reading "The Trumpet" to her class—it really belongs more in the fourth and fifth grade level.) It is a love story. "Charlotte" was a story of friendship, life, death, salvation. "Stuart Little" was a story of a quest—the quest for beauty.

As for the emphasis on money, I think it was Jane Austen who said there were only two things in the world worth writing about—love and money. Louis had both problems. I offer no apology.

Thanks for your letter. I hope I've answered some of your questions.

Sincerely,
E. B. White

COMMENTS ABOUT *CHARLOTTE'S WEB*

1. "Death of a Pig"[14]
In the January 1948 *Atlantic Monthly*, White published the article in which he described his empathetic attendance on his ailing pig. Elledge notes that both the event and writing about it had a healing effect on White.[15] Although the connection to *Charlotte's Web* seems obvious, White claimed not to have thought of it (see page xxviii).

2. "Children's Books"[16]
This piece appeared first in *Harper's* in January 1939. Earlier in the essay, White referred to the arrival of children's books for Katharine to review as "an annual emergency" as they came by tens and twenties, inundating the house. The article is collected in *OMM*. (See page xxii.)

3. "Pigs and Spiders"[17]
This succinct description of the origin of *Charlotte's Web* is an expansion of a piece that appeared first in *The Saturday Review*.

4. "Dear Reader:"
To answer some of the hundreds of questions asked by Mr. White's admirers, Harper designed a brochure that included this letter. The third paragraph is very similar to a description in one of White's letters (see page 239).[18] Around the borders are illustrations from White's books.

5. "Security"[19]
From this excerpt from *Harper's* (November 1938), we may understand why White wrote with such empathy of Fern's and Avery's delight in the fair. The last sentence evokes memories of the first illustration in Chapter I of *Stuart Little*.

6. "On Writing for Children"[20]
From interviews with writers, in *Paris Review*. White's view that to write for children one must write *up*, not down, coincides with that expressed by a number of the best-loved children's authors—and may well account for their success. As C. S. Lewis said, one writes a children's story, simply, because it is the best art form for saying something one has to say.[21]

7. "The Future of Reading"[22]
Published first in *The New Yorker*, March 1951, the piece seems at least as timely today as it must have been then.

8. "The Cornfield"[23]
Cycles, new lives from the old, were on White's mind long before he wrote *Charlotte's Web*, as in this poem to his young son, Joel.

1. DEATH OF A PIG

I spent several days and nights in mid-September with an ailing pig and I feel driven to account for this stretch of time, more particularly since the pig died at last, and I lived, and things might easily have gone the other way round and none left to do the accounting. Even now, so close to the event, I cannot recall the hours sharply and am not ready to say whether death came on the third night or the fourth night. This uncertainty afflicts me with a sense of personal deterioration; if I were in decent health I would know how many nights I had sat up with a pig.

The scheme of buying a spring pig in blossomtime, feeding it through summer and fall, and butchering it when the solid cold weather arrives, is a familiar scheme to me and follows an antique pattern. It is a tragedy enacted on most farms with perfect fidelity to the original script. The murder, being premeditated, is in the first degree but is quick and skillful, and the smoked bacon and ham provide a ceremonial ending whose fitness is seldom questioned.

Once in a while something slips—one of the actors goes up in his lines and the whole performance stumbles and halts. My pig simply failed to show up for a meal. The alarm spread rapidly. The classic outline of the tragedy was lost. I found myself cast suddenly in the role of pig's friend and physician—a farcical character with an enema bag for a prop. I had a presentiment, the very first afternoon, that the play would never regain its balance and that my sympathies were now wholly with the pig. This was slapstick—the sort of dramatic treatment that instantly appealed to my old dachshund, Fred, who joined the vigil, held the bag, and, when all was over, presided at the interment. When we slid the body into the grave, we both were shaken to the core. The loss we felt was not the loss of ham but the loss of pig. He had evidently become precious to me, not that he represented a distant nourishment in a hungry time, but that he had suffered in a suffering world. But I'm running ahead of my story and shall have to go back.

My pigpen is at the bottom of an old orchard below the house. The pigs I have raised have lived in a faded building that once was an icehouse. There is a pleasant yard to move about in, shaded by an apple tree that overhangs the low rail fence. A pig couldn't ask for anything better—or none has, at any rate. The sawdust in the icehouse makes a comfortable bottom in which

to root, and a warm bed. This sawdust, however, came under suspicion when the pig took sick. One of my neighbors said he thought the pig would have done better on new ground—the same principle that applies in planting potatoes. He said there might be something unhealthy about that sawdust, that he never thought well of sawdust.

It was about four o'clock in the afternoon when I first noticed that there was something wrong with the pig. He failed to appear at the trough for his supper, and when a pig (or a child) refuses supper a chill wave of fear runs through any household, or ice-household. After examining my pig, who was stretched out in the sawdust inside the building, I went to the phone and cranked it four times. Mr. Dameron answered. "What's good for a sick pig?" I asked. (There is never any identification needed on a country phone; the person on the other end knows who is talking by the sound of the voice and by the character of the question.)

"I don't know, I never had a sick pig," said Mr. Dameron, "but I can find out quick enough. You hang up and I'll call Henry."

Mr. Dameron was back on the line again in five minutes. "Henry says roll him over on his back and give him two ounces of castor oil or sweet oil, and if that doesn't do the trick give him an injection of soapy water. He says he's almost sure the pig's plugged up, and even if he's wrong, it can't do any harm."

I thanked Mr. Dameron. I didn't go right down to the pig, though. I sank into a chair and sat still for a few minutes to think about my troubles, and then I got up and went to the barn, catching up on some odds and ends that needed tending to. Unconsciously I held off, for an hour, the deed by which I would officially recognize the collapse of the performance of raising a pig; I wanted no interruption in the regularity of feeding, the steadiness of growth, the even succession of days. I wanted no interruption, wanted no oil, no deviation. I just wanted to keep on raising a pig, full meal after full meal, spring into summer into fall. I didn't even know whether there were two ounces of castor oil on the place.

Shortly after five o'clock I remembered that we had been invited out to dinner that night and realized that if I were to dose a pig there was no time to lose. The dinner date seemed a familiar conflict: I move in a desultory society and often a week or two will roll by without my going to anybody's house to dinner or anyone's coming to mine, but when an occasion does arise, and I am summoned, something usually turns up (an hour or two in advance) to make all human intercourse seem vastly inappropriate. I have come to believe that there is in hostesses a special power of divination, and that they deliberately arrange

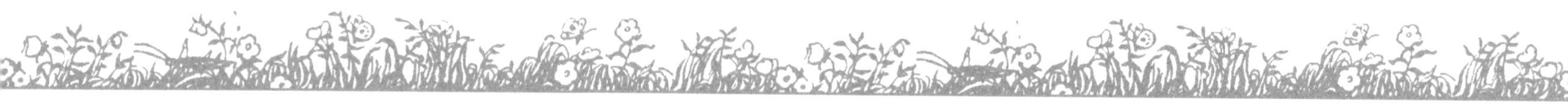

dinners to coincide with pig failure or some other sort of failure. At any rate, it was after five o'clock and I knew I could put off no longer the evil hour.

When my son and I arrived at the pigyard, armed with a small bottle of castor oil and a length of clothesline, the pig had emerged from his house and was standing in the middle of his yard, listlessly. He gave us a slim greeting. I could see that he felt uncomfortable and uncertain. I had brought the clothesline thinking I'd have to tie him (the pig weighed more than a hundred pounds) but we never used it. My son reached down, grabbed both front legs, upset him quickly, and when he opened his mouth to scream I turned the oil into his throat—a pink, corrugated area I had never seen before. I had just time to read the label while the neck of the bottle was in his mouth. It said Puretest. The screams, slightly muffled by oil, were pitched in the hysterically high range of pig-sound, as though torture were being carried out, but they didn't last long: it was all over rather suddenly, and, his legs released, the pig righted himself.

In the upset position the corners of his mouth had been turned down, giving him a frowning expression. Back on his feet again, he regained the set smile that a pig wears even in sickness. He stood his ground, sucking slightly at the residue of oil; a few drops leaked out of his lips while his wicked eyes, shaded by their coy little lashes, turned on me in disgust and hatred. I scratched him gently with oily fingers and he remained quiet, as though trying to recall the satisfaction of being scratched when in health, and seeming to rehearse in his mind the indignity to which he had just been subjected. I noticed, as I stood there, four or five small dark spots on his back near the tail end, reddish brown in color, each about the size of a housefly. I could not make out what they were. They did not look troublesome but at the same time they did not look like mere surface bruises or chafe marks. Rather they seemed blemishes of internal origin. His stiff white bristles almost completely hid them and I had to part the bristles with my fingers to get a good look.

Several hours later, a few minutes before midnight, having dined well and at someone else's expense, I returned to the pighouse with a flashlight. The patient was asleep. Kneeling, I felt his ears (as you might put your hand on the forehead of a child) and they seemed cool, and then with the light made a careful examination of the yard and the house for sign that the oil had worked. I found none and went to bed.

We had been having an unseasonable spell of weather—hot, close days, with the fog shutting in every night, scaling for a few hours in midday, then creeping back again at dark, drifting in first over the trees on the point, then suddenly blowing across the fields, blotting out the world and

taking possession of houses, men, and animals. Everyone kept hoping for a break, but the break failed to come. Next day was another hot one. I visited the pig before breakfast and tried to tempt him with a little milk in his trough. He just stared at it, while I made a sucking sound through my teeth to remind him of past pleasures of the feast. With very small, timid pigs, weanlings, this ruse is often quite successful and will encourage them to eat; but with a large, sick pig the ruse is senseless and the sound I made must have made him feel, if anything, more miserable. He not only did not crave food, he felt a positive revulsion to it. I found a place under the apple tree where he had vomited in the night.

At this point, although a depression had settled over me, I didn't suppose that I was going to lose my pig. From the lustiness of a healthy pig a man derives a feeling of personal lustiness; the stuff that goes into the trough and is received with such enthusiasm is an earnest of some later feast of his own, and when this suddenly comes to an end and the food lies stale and untouched, souring in the sun, the pig's imbalance becomes the man's, vicariously, and life seems insecure, displaced, transitory.

As my own spirits declined, along with the pig's, the spirits of my vile old dachshund rose. The frequency of our trips down the footpath through the orchard to the pigyard delighted him, although he suffers greatly from arthritis, moves with difficulty, and would be bedridden if he could find anyone willing to serve him meals on a tray.

He never missed a chance to visit the pig with me, and he made many professional calls on his own. You could see him down there at all hours, his white face parting the grass along the fence as he wobbled and stumbled about, his stethoscope dangling—a happy quack, writing his villainous prescriptions and grinning his corrosive grin. When the enema bag appeared, and the bucket of warm suds, his happiness was complete, and he managed to squeeze his enormous body between the two lowest rails of the yard and then assumed full charge of the irrigation. Once, when I lowered the bag to check the flow, he reached in and hurriedly drank a few mouthfuls of the suds to test their potency. I have noticed that Fred will feverishly consume any substance that is associated with trouble—the bitter flavor is to his liking. When the bag was above reach, he concentrated on the pig and was everywhere at once, a tower of strength and inconvenience. The pig, curiously enough, stood rather quietly through this colonic carnival, and the enema, though ineffective, was not as difficult as I had anticipated.

I discovered, though, that once having given a pig an enema there is no turning back, no chance of resuming one of life's more stereo-

typed roles. The pig's lot and mine were inextricably bound now, as though the rubber tube were the silver cord. From then until the time of his death I held the pig steadily in the bowl of my mind; the task of trying to deliver him from his misery became a strong obsession. His suffering soon became the embodiment of all earthly wretchedness. Along toward the end of the afternoon, defeated in physicking, I phoned the veterinary twenty miles away and placed the case formally in his hands. He was full of questions, and when I casually mentioned the dark spots on the pig's back, his voice changed its tone.

"I don't want to scare you," he said, "but when there are spots, erysipelas has to be considered."

Together we considered erysipelas, with frequent interruptions from the telephone operator, who wasn't sure the connection had been established.

"If a pig has erysipelas can he give it to a person?" I asked.

"Yes, he can," replied the vet.

"Have they answered?" asked the operator.

"Yes, they have," I said. Then I addressed the vet again. "You better come over here and examine this pig right away."

"I can't come myself," said the vet, "but McFarland can come this evening if that's all right. Mac knows more about pigs than I do anyway. You needn't worry too much about the spots. To indicate erysipelas they would have to be deep hemorrhagic infarcts."

"Deep hemorrhagic what?" I asked.

"Infarcts," said the vet.

"Have they answered?" asked the operator.

"Well," I said, "I don't know what you'd call these spots, except they're about the size of a housefly. If the pig has erysipelas I guess I have it, too, by this time, because we've been very close lately."

"McFarland will be over," said the vet.

I hung up. My throat felt dry and I went to the cupboard and got a bottle of whiskey. Deep hemorrhagic infarcts—the phrase began fastening its hooks in my head. I had assumed that there could be nothing much wrong with a pig during the months it was being groomed for murder; my confidence in the essential health and endurance of pigs had been strong and deep, particularly in the health of pigs that belonged to me and that were part of my proud scheme. The awakening had been violent and I minded it all the more because I knew that what could be true of my pig could be true also of the rest of my tidy world. I tried to put this distasteful idea from me, but it kept recurring. I took a short drink of the whiskey and then, although I wanted to go down to the yard and look for fresh signs, I was scared to. I was certain I had erysipelas.

It was long after dark and the supper dishes had been put away when a car drove in and McFarland got out. He had a girl with him. I could just make her out in the darkness—she seemed young and pretty. "This is Miss Owen," he said. "We've been having a picnic supper on the shore, that's why I'm late."

McFarland stood in the driveway and stripped off his jacket, then his shirt. His stocky arms and capable hands showed up in my flashlight's gleam as I helped him find his coverall and get zipped up. The rear seat of his car contained an astonishing amount of paraphernalia, which he soon overhauled, selecting a chain, a syringe, a bottle of oil, a rubber tube, and some other things I couldn't identify. Miss Owen said she'd go along with us and see the pig. I led the way down the warm slope of the orchard, my light picking out the path for them, and we all three climbed the fence, entered the pighouse, and squatted by the pig while McFarland took a rectal reading. My flashlight picked up the glitter of an engagement ring on the girl's hand.

"No elevation," said McFarland, twisting the thermometer in the light. "You needn't worry about erysipelas." He ran his hand slowly over the pig's stomach and at one point the pig cried out in pain.

"Poor piggledy-wiggledy!" said Miss Owen.

The treatment I had been giving the pig for two days was then repeated, somewhat more expertly, by the doctor, Miss Owen and I handing him things as he needed them—holding the chain that he had looped around the pig's upper jaw, holding the syringe, holding the bottle stopper, the end of the tube, all of us working in darkness and in comfort, working with the instinctive teamwork induced by emergency conditions, the pig unprotesting, the house shadowy, protecting, intimate. I went to bed tired but with a feeling of relief that I had turned over part of the responsibility of the case to a licensed doctor. I was beginning to think, though, that the pig was not going to live.

He died twenty-four hours later, or it might have been forty-eight—there is a blur in time here, and I may have lost or picked up a day in the telling and the pig one in the dying. At intervals during the last day I took cool fresh water down to him and at such times as he found the strength to get to his feet he would stand with head in the pail and snuffle his snout around. He drank a few sips but no more; yet it seemed to comfort him to dip his nose in water and bobble it about, sucking in and blowing out through his teeth. Much of the time, now, he lay indoors half buried in sawdust. Once, near the last, while I was attending him I saw him try to make a bed for himself but he lacked the strength, and when

he set his snout into the dust he was unable to plow even the little furrow he needed to lie down in.

He came out of the house to die. When I went down, before going to bed, he lay stretched in the yard a few feet from the door. I knelt, saw that he was dead, and left him there: his face had a mild look, expressive neither of deep peace nor of deep suffering, although I think he had suffered a good deal. I went back up to the house and to bed, and cried internally—deep hemorrhagic intears. I didn't wake till nearly eight the next morning, and when I looked out the open window the grave was already being dug, down beyond the dump under a wild apple. I could hear the spade strike against the small rocks that blocked the way. Never send to know for whom the grave is dug, I said to myself, it's dug for thee. Fred, I well knew, was supervising the work of digging, so I ate breakfast slowly.

It was a Saturday morning. The thicket in which I found the gravediggers at work was dark and warm, the sky overcast. Here, among alders and young hackmatacks, at the foot of the apple tree, Lennie had dug a beautiful hole, five feet long, three feet wide, three feet deep. He was standing in it, removing the last spadefuls of earth while Fred patrolled the brink in simple but impressive circles, disturbing the loose earth of the mound so that it trickled back in. There had been no rain in weeks and the soil, even three feet down, was dry and powdery. As I stood and stared, an enormous earthworm which had been partially exposed by the spade at the bottom dug itself deeper and made a slow withdrawal, seeking even remoter moistures at even lonelier depths. And just as Lennie stepped out and rested his spade against the tree and lit a cigarette, a small green apple separated itself from a branch overhead and fell into the hole. Everything about this last scene seemed overwritten—the dismal sky, the shabby woods, the imminence of rain, the worm (legendary bedfellow of the dead), the apple (conventional garnish of a pig).

But even so, there was a directness and dispatch about animal burial, I thought, that made it a more decent affair than human burial: there was no stopover in the undertaker's foul parlor, no wreath nor spray; and when we hitched a line to the pig's hind legs and dragged him swiftly from his yard, throwing our weight into the harness and leaving a wake of crushed grass and smoothed rubble over the dump, ours was a businesslike procession, with Fred, the dishonorable pallbearer, staggering along in the rear, his perverse bereavement showing in every seam in his face; and the post mortem performed handily and swiftly right at the edge of the grave, so that the inwards that had caused the pig's death preceded him into the ground and he lay at last rest-

ing squarely on the cause of his own undoing.

I threw in the first shovelful, and then we worked rapidly and without talk, until the job was complete. I picked up the rope, made it fast to Fred's collar (he is a notorious ghoul), and we all three filed back up the path to the house, Fred bringing up the rear and holding back every inch of the way, feigning unusual stiffness. I noticed that although he weighed far less than the pig, he was harder to drag, being possessed of the vital spark.

The news of the death of my pig travelled fast and far, and I received many expressions of sympathy from friends and neighbors, for no one took the event lightly and the premature expiration of a pig is, I soon discovered, a departure which the community marks solemnly on its calendar, a sorrow in which it feels fully involved. I have written this account in penitence and in grief, as a man who failed to raise his pig, and to explain my deviation from the classic course of so many raised pigs. The grave in the woods is unmarked, but Fred can direct the mourner to it unerringly and with immense good will, and I know he and I shall often revisit it, singly and together, in seasons of reflection and despair, on flagless memorial days of our own choosing.

2.
FROM "CHILDREN'S BOOKS"

. . .

Close physical contact with the field of juvenile literature leads me to the conclusion that it must be a lot of fun to write for children—reasonably easy work, perhaps even important work. One side of it which must be exciting is finding a place, a period, or a thing that hasn't already been written about. This season's list indicates that the authors set about their task with a will. One of them, as I said before, hit upon the valley of the Euphrates. Another one shut his eyes, opened an atlas, and let his finger fall on the Louisiana bayous. Another, with enviable prescience, managed to turn out the third book of a trilogy on Czechoslovakia. Munro Leaf, scouring the earth for another *Ferdinand*, wound up in the Scotland of the MacGregors and the Maxine Sullivans. (Such is the staying power of success, you can have this rather flat tale in either the standard or the special deluxe edition.)

. . .

Not less impressive than its geographical scope is the polygot character of this literature. A child who romps around in the juvenile field today picks up a smattering of many tongues and dialects. I have just been browsing hit and miss in a deep pile of books, opening them in the middle and reading a page or two. The experience has left me gibbering.

The first book I opened was *Exploring With Andrews*. "Shortly after we left," I began, "torrential downpours swept away half a dozen *yurts* pitched at the bottom of a steep bluff."

Without going back to find out what a yurt was, I drifted on into the next book, *Soomoon, Boy of Bali*. It was my luck to alight on page 40, where, from somewhere in the village, "came the deep, hollow tones of a *gamelang*."

Yurts to you, gamelang, I thought to myself, and picked up the next book.

3.
PIGS AND SPIDERS
MY FRIENDS IN THE ANIMAL WORLD
by E. B. WHITE, author of *CHARLOTTE'S WEB*

I have been asked to tell how I came to write *Charlotte's Web*. Well, I like animals, and it would be odd if I failed to write about them. Animals are a weakness with me, and when I got a place in the country I was quite sure animals would appear, and they did.

A farm is a particular problem for a man who likes animals, because the fate of most livestock is that they are murdered by their benefactors. The creatures may live serenely but they end violently, and the odor of doom hangs about them always. I have kept several pigs, starting them in spring as weanlings and carrying trays to them all through the summer and fall. The relationship bothered me. Day by day I became better acquainted with my pig, and he with me, and the fact that the whole adventure pointed toward an eventual piece of double-dealing on my part lent an eerie quality to the thing. I do not like to betray a person or a creature, and I tend to agree with Mr. E. M. Forster that in these times the duty of a man, above else, is to be reliable. It used to be clear to me, slopping a pig, that as far as the pig was concerned I could not be counted on, and this, as I say, troubled me. Anyway, the theme of *Charlotte's Web* is that a pig shall be saved, and I have an idea that somewhere deep inside me there was a wish to that effect.

As for Charlotte herself, I had never paid much attention to spiders until a few years ago. Once you begin watching spiders, you haven't time for much else—the world is really loaded with them. I do not find them repulsive or revolting, any more than I find anything in nature repulsive or revolting, and I think it is too bad that children are often corrupted by their elders in this hate campaign. Spiders are skillful, amusing, and only in rare instances has anybody ever come to grief because of a spider.

One cold October evening I was lucky enough to see Aranea Cavatica spin her egg sac and deposit her eggs. (I did not know her name at the time, but I admired her, and later Mr. Willis J. Gertsch of the American Museum of Natural History told me her name.) When I saw that she was fixing to become a mother, I got a stepladder and and extension light and had an excellent view of the whole business. A few days

later, when it was time to return to New York, not wishing to part with my spider, I took a razor blade, cut the sac adrift from the underside of the shed roof, put spider and sac in a candy box, and carried them to town. I tossed the box on my dresser. Some weeks later I was surprised and pleased to find that Charlotte's daughters were emerging from the air holes in the cover of the box. They strung tiny lines from my comb to my brush, from my brush to my mirror, and from my mirror to my nail scissors. They were very busy and almost invisible, they were so small. We all lived together happily for a couple of weeks, and then somebody whose duty it was to dust my dresser balked, and I broke up the show.

At the present time, three of Charlotte's granddaughters are trapping at the foot of the stairs in my barn cellar, where the morning light, coming through the east window, illuminates their embroidery and makes it seem even more wonderful than it is.

I haven't told why I wrote the book, but I haven't told why I sneeze, either. A book is a sneeze.

4.
HARPER PUBLICITY FLIER FOR *CHARLOTTE'S WEB*

Dear Reader:

I receive many letters from children and can't answer them all—there wouldn't be time enough in a day. That is why I am sending you this printed reply to your letter. I'll try to answer some of the questions that are commonly asked.

Where did I get the idea for *Stuart Little* and for *Charlotte's Web*? Well, many years ago I went to bed one night in a railway sleeping car, and during the night I dreamed about a tiny boy who acted rather like a mouse. That's how the story of Stuart Little got started.

As for *Charlotte's Web*, I like animals and my barn is a very pleasant place to be, at all hours. One day when I was on my way to feed the pig, I began feeling sorry for the pig because, like most pigs, he was doomed to die. This made me sad. So I started thinking of ways to save a pig's life. I had been watching a big grey spider at her work and was impressed by how clever she was at weaving. Gradually I worked the spider into the story that you know, a story of friendship and salvation on a farm. Three years after I started writing it, it was published. (I am not a fast worker, as you can see.)

I don't know how or when the idea for *The Trumpet of the Swan* occurred to me. I guess I must have wondered what it would be like to be a Trumpeter Swan and not be able to make a noise.

Sometimes I'm asked how old I was when I started to write, and what made me want to write. I started early—as soon as I could spell. In fact, I can't remember any time in my life when I wasn't busy writing. I don't know what caused me to do it, or why I enjoyed it, but I think children often find pleasure and satisfaction in trying to set their thoughts down on paper, either in words or in pictures. I was no good at drawing, so I used words instead. As I grew older, I found that writing can be a way of earning a living.

Some of my readers want me to visit their school. Some want me to send a picture, or an autograph, or a book. And some ask questions about my family and my animals and my pets. Much as I'd like to, I can't go visiting. I can't send books, either—you can find them in a bookstore or a library. Many children assume that a writer owns (or even makes) his own books. This is not true—books are made by the publisher. If the writer wants a copy, he must buy it. That's why I can't send books. And I do not

send autographs—I leave that to the movie stars. You will find a picture of me on the first page of this folder. I live most of the year in the country, in New England. From our windows we can look out at the sea and the mountains. I have a wife, a married son, and three grandchildren.

Are my stories true, you ask? No, they are imaginary tales, containing fantastic characters and events. In *real* life, a family doesn't have a child who looks like a mouse; in *real* life, a spider doesn't spin words in her web. In *real* life, a swan doesn't blow a trumpet. But real life is only one kind of life—there is also the life of the imagination. And although my stories are imaginary, I like to think that there is some truth in them, too—truth about the way people and animals feel and think and act.

Thank you all for your wonderful letters—I love to get them even though I cannot answer each one personally.

Yours sincerely,

E B White

E.B. White

5.
SECURITY

September 1938

It was a fine clear day for the fair this year, and I went up early to see how the Ferris wheel was doing and to take a ride. It pays to check up on Ferris wheels these days: by noting the volume of business one can get some idea which side is ahead in the world—whether the airborne freemen outnumber the earthbound slaves. It was encouraging to discover that there were still quite a few people at the Fair who preferred a feeling of high, breezy insecurity to one of solid support. My friend Healy surprised me by declining to go aloft; he is an unusually cautious man, however—even his hat was insured.

I like to watch the faces of people who are trying to get up their nerve to take to the air. You see them at the ticket booths in amusement parks, in the waiting room at the airport. Within them two irreconcilables are at war—the desire for safety, the yearning for a dizzy release. My *Britannica* tells nothing about Mr. G. W. G. Ferris, but he belongs with the immortals. From the top of the wheel, seated beside a small boy, windswept and fancy free, I looked down on the Fair and for a moment was alive. Below us the old harness drivers pushed their trotters round the dirt track, old men with their legs still sticking out stiffly round the rumps of horses. And from the cluster of loud speakers atop the judges' stand came the "Indian Love Call," bathing heaven and earth in jumbo tenderness.

This silvery wheel, revolving slowly in the cause of freedom, was only just holding its own, I soon discovered; for farther along in the midway, in a sideshow tent, a tattoo artist was doing a land-office business, not with anchors, flags, and pretty mermaids, but with Social Security Numbers, neatly pricked on your forearm with the electric needle. He had plenty of customers, mild-mannered pale men, asking glumly for the sort of indelible ignominy that was once reserved for prisoners and beef cattle. Drab times these, when the bravado and the exhibitionism are gone from tattooing and it becomes simply a branding operation. I hope the art which produced the bird's eye view of Sydney will not be forever lost in the routine business of putting serial numbers on people who are worried about growing old.

The sight would have depressed me had I not soon won a cane by knocking over three cats with three balls. There is no moment when a man so surely has the world by the tail as when he strolls down the midway swinging a prize cane.

6.
"ON WRITING FOR CHILDREN"

[When E. B. White was once asked if there was any shifting of gears in writing books for children, he replied:]

Anybody who shifts gears when he writes for children is likely to wind up stripping his gears. But I don't want to evade your question. There is a difference between writing for children and for adults. I am lucky, though, as I seldom seem to have my audience in mind when I am at work. It is as though they didn't exist.

Anyone who writes down to children is simply wasting his time. You have to write up, not down. Children are demanding. They are the most attentive, curious, eager, observant, sensitive, quick, and generally congenial readers on earth. They accept, almost without question, anything you present them with, as long as it is presented honestly, fearlessly, and clearly. I handed them, against the advice of experts, a mouse-boy, and they accepted it without a quiver. In *Charlotte's Web*, I gave them a literate spider, and they took that.

Some writers for children deliberately avoid using words they think a child doesn't know. This emasculates the prose and, I suspect, bores the reader. Children are game for anything. I throw them hard words, and they backhand them over the net. They love words that give them a hard time, provided they are in a context that absorbs their attention. I'm lucky again; my own vocabulary is small, compared to most writers, and I tend to use the short words. So it's no problem for me to write for children. We have a lot in common.

7.
THE FUTURE OF READING

In schools and colleges, in these audio-visual days, doubt has been raised as to the future of reading—whether the printed word is on its last legs. One college president has remarked that in fifty years "only five per cent of the people will be reading." For this, of course, one must be prepared. But how prepare? To us it would seem that even if only one person out of a hundred and fifty million should continue as a *reader*, he would be the one worth saving, the nucleus around which to found a university. We think this not impossible person, this Last Reader, might very well stand in the same relation to the community as the queen bee to the colony of bees, and that the others would quite properly dedicate themselves wholly to his welfare, serving special food and building special accommodations. From his nuptial, or intellectual, flight would come the new race of men, linked perfectly with the long past by the unbroken chain of the intellect, to carry on the community. But it is more likely that our modern hive of bees, substituting a coaxial cable for spinal fluid, will try to perpetuate the race through audio-visual devices, which ask no discipline of the mind and which are already giving the room the languor of an opium parlor.

Reading is the work of the alert mind, is demanding, and under ideal conditions produces finally a sort of ecstasy. As in the sexual experience, there are never more than two persons present in the act of reading—the writer, who is the impregnator, and the reader, who is the respondent. This gives the experience of reading a sublimity and power unequalled by any other form of communication. It would be just as well, we think, if educators clung to this great phenomenon and did not get sidetracked, for although books and reading may at times have played too large a part in the educational process, that is not what is happening today. Indeed, there is very little true reading, and not nearly as much writing as one would suppose from the towering piles of pulpwood in the dooryards of our paper mills. Readers and writers are scarce, as are publishers and reporters. The reports we get nowadays are those of men who have not gone to the scene of the accident, which is always farther inside one's own head than it is convenient to penetrate without galoshes.

8.
THE CORNFIELD

Up to the cornfield, old and curly,
I took Joe, who rises early.
Joe my yearling, on my shoulder,
Observed the old corn growing older.
And I could feel the simple awe
He felt at seeing what he saw:
Yellow light and cool day
And cornstalks stretching far away.
My son, too young and wise to speak,
Clung with one hand to my cheek,
While in his head were slowly born
Important mysteries of the corn.
And being present at the birth
Of my child's wonderment at earth,
I felt my own life stir again
By the still graveyard of the grain.

Appendix E

READERS' RESPONSES

PERSONAL

One of the first reader responses to *Charlotte's Web* is described by White himself: "My first fan mail on Charlotte was a long letter from a California vegetarian, who feels that my book shows that I am ripe to take the veil and live on grain, fruit, and nuts. I guess I'll never lack for nuts, anyway."[1]

REVIEWS

The very week I write this, the distinguished novelist Jane Langton has declared *Charlotte's Web* to be "possibly the greatest children's book ever written in the English language."[2] She's not alone.

Except for the lukewarm reception in *The Booklist* and Anne Carroll Moore's dour greeting in *The Horn Book* (both following), almost all early reviews of *Charlotte's Web* were favorable. M. F. Kieran wrote in *The Atlantic Monthly*:

> Though I am not usually attracted by stories that personify animals, this one is absolutely delicious. I warn you it may be wise to have two copies in the house—one for children and one for their parents.[3]

In the same issue of *The Saturday Review* in which Mary Gould Davis termed *Charlotte's Web* "a fantasy that has the beauty and delicacy of the web itself," Bennett Cerf made it a point to write in his "Trade Winds" column that no book of the season would delight him more than *Charlotte's Web*, "embellished" with illustrations by Garth Williams. Cerf expressed pleasure especially in the fact that Wilbur would be saved the humiliating fate of gracing a Christmas dinner "with a candied apple jammed into his mouth."[4]

The New Yorker greeted the book as "high caprice on a farm, handled with wit and wisdom, [that] serves to put an imperfect world back into joint . . ."[5] and P. L. Travers, writing in the *New York Herald Tribune*, observed that "such tangible

magic is the proper element of childhood and any grown up who can still dip into it—even with only so much as a toe—is certain at least of dying young even if he lives to be ninety."[6] Later, she noted poetically that White's is a story whose magic glows like a lamp within it, and that it has "an absorbed and dreamlike air such as one sometimes surprises in a child playing alone."[7]

But, as said at the outset, the praise was not unanimous. Since, it's been said, even Homer nods, we should not respond too haughtily to the gaffe in *The Booklist*:

> Like *Stuart Little* . . . this fable will have an ostensible appeal for children by virtue of its simple style, nature lore, and realistic juvenile characters; the younger readers, however, are likely to lose interest as the story moves on, leaving it to adults who enjoy the author's symbolic and philosophic implications. . . .[8]

However, the notice by the influential Anne Carroll Moore, in *The Horn Book*, deserves to be pondered in its entirety:

> From picture books I step into real trouble and I may as well confess that I find E. B. White's *Charlotte's Web*, illustrated by Garth Williams (Harper $2.50), hard to take from so masterly a hand. There is no one whose writing I more deeply regard in the adult field. *Stuart Little* disappointed me but thousands of people liked it. *Stuart Little* was a dream story. *Charlotte's Web* is born of real life in the wonderful countryside of my own childhood. I grew up on a large farm in Maine. There are chapters of great beauty and rare understanding of the life of farm animals in *Charlotte's Web*. They moved me very deeply as I read them without Garth Williams' fine pictorial interpretation, but as a children's book it never came clear from the preoccupation of an adult who had not spent a childhood on a farm. The story got off to a fine start. Fern was as living a girl as one could wish when she rescued the runt pig from her father's ax, but no such country child would have spent day after day beside the manure pile to which the pig was consigned and repeated afterward to as dumb a mother as a parent's page ever invoked what the animals told her in their language. Fern, the real center of the book, is never developed. The animals never talk. They speculate. As to Charlotte, her magic and mystery require a different technique to create that lasting interest in spiders which controls childish impulse to do away with them.[9]

Best, now, to end with the huzzah of a writer whose joy must surely have gladdened White's heart. Wrote Eudora Welty:

What the book is about is friendship on earth, affection, and protection, adventure and miracle, life and death, trust and treachery, pleasure and pain, and the passing of time. As a piece of work it is just about perfect, and just about magical in the way it is done. What it all proves—in the words of the minister in the story which he hands down to his congregation after Charlotte writes "Some Pig" in her web—is "that human beings must always be on the watch for the coming of wonders. . . . "

"At-at-at, at the risk of repeating myself," as the goose says, *Charlotte's Web* is an adorable book.[10]

Appendix F

CRITICAL APPRAISALS

Although the American academic subculture appears to demonstrate respect for literature by the prodigious amassment of commentary, such a profusion of exegesis is not our goal. Our own goal is *not* to amass as much commentary as possible. Indeed, I could compile a literary-critical pantheon by naming merely the critics I have omitted. Here, I wish merely to suggest the range of responses elicited by a book that has been a cornerstone in the emotional development of millions of Americans under the age of fifty.

Children's books, the distinguished critic Roger Sale has pointed out, need little explicating[1]—an inconvenient truth for those who deem it their professional duty to explicate. That fact may have spared White's book some of the most intimidating contemporary academic fire breathing. Nonetheless, as we'll see, even the pig and the spider have not escaped unsinged.

The difference between the samples in this section and those in the previous one is that the previous reviews were ostensibly to tell teachers, parents, librarians (significantly, not children, who, after all, do not normally read book reviews), whether they should want to acquire the then-new book. What follows here is, allegedly, sober rumination some time after the fact of *Charlotte's* publication.

The critical response to *Charlotte's Web* has been interpretative rather than evaluative. And occasionally, a critic has dropped a stitch. Several engaging and forgivable bloopers appeared in England, where Margaret Blount alluded to "Wilberforce the pig"[2]; and Fred Inglis has the story taking place "on a quiet farm in a Midwestern state," and—astonishingly—considers the film "a faithful version of the book."[3] It's difficult to believe that, if Inglis read the book, he also saw the film.*

In the U.S., in the "Twayne United States

*Almost by definition, significant aspects of a profound novel may be untranslatable into film. Of the death of Charlotte, Roger Sale noted that "White gives Charlotte the knowledge that she is dying, but retains the simple dignity of which consciousness usually deprives us [and which is a quality animals retain]."[4]

Authors Series" volume on White, Edward C. Sampson refers to "Fern Zuckerman,"[5] and a distinguished critic, perhaps following the error in an easily available secondary source, makes White a native of Brooklyn, rather than a transplant to Brooklin, Maine.

As for critics who seem to have been distinctly cool to the book, Anne Carroll Moore's is really the only recognizable name. We've included part of her *Horn Book* review in the previous section, but a few paragraphs from a hitherto unpublished and strangely mixed letter from Moore to Ursula Nordstrom fills in the picture:

> June 2, 1952
>
> Dear Ursula,
>
> I find Charlotte's Web entrancing. I've read it twice for the sheer beauty of the parts I like best both for what is on the page and for all it evokes for one whose childhood was spent on a Maine farm with real barns and swings one jumped to from hay mows (?) It is an idyll from which I find it uncommonly (?) difficult to detach myself as a critic. He has created a living girl in Fern but he leaves her in limbo. Few children are going to believe such a live wire will spend hours on end in the barn cellar. Fern never justifies the bright promise of her first appearance and I simply cannot bear her telling over again to her mother in so many words all she has gathered from the hours she has spent listening to long speeches from Charlotte and others (?) in very far from barnyard terms.
>
> Charlottes Web holds, as (or?) I think, some of the best writing E. B. White has done. Only the children's reaction to what I feel is far too much talk and explanation will determine its place as a children's book whatever the hold on their parents in their relation to E. B. White of the New Yorker.
>
> To me it presents a very different problem from that presented by Stuart Little—Charlotte's Web is not a dream story—it is life itself and while I may be wrong, I could wish E. B. White had edited it to a point of longtime survival. He may not feel concerned with its future in children's literature but I am, for it seems to me he held a classic in his hand and I have such great admiration for his work that I would like to have no reservations. I've no doubt Garth Williams will make a fascinating book out of it. . . . *[6]

Beyond that, not really negative but eminently thought-provoking is the view of Joseph Epstein, who took a sober retrospective view of White in 1986 and concluded that "the one thing that can be unequivocally said about him is that one has to search very sedulously indeed to find a

*This unsigned, poorly typed letter has inked parentheses around occasional phrases, with penned question marks in the margin, next to some of the more enigmatic pronouncements. This suggests that our text is a transcription, likely from an original handwritten letter, and perhaps retyped by Nordstrom herself, as was occasionally her custom.

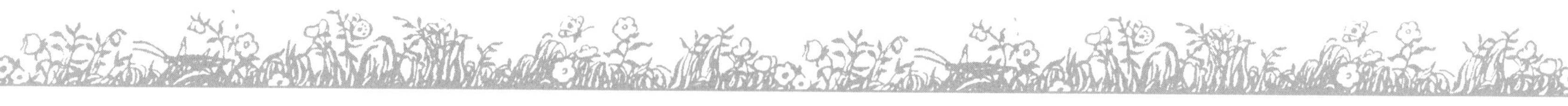

gloomier writer than E. B. White. The gloom is not merely incidental but pervasive in his writing."[7]

Epstein acknowledged the seemingly positive endings of all White's novels. He granted that children see them as happy, for "children have this advantage over adults: they are permitted to love things they do not understand."[8] But approaching the novels with full awareness of the life of E. B. White, and deeming White to have been "a man writing out of his obsessions," Epstein saw each novel as, in a way, a novel of terror, and of rescue. "[C]oming at these books as an adult, and loaded down with knowledge of their author's life, with its longings and fears, one cannot avoid reading them as fables about E. B. White's own life"—a life Epstein termed "a tragedy with a putatively happy ending."[9]

White's general writing *style* has been addressed primarily in relation to the essays[10], and I've touched on the matter in relation to the novels.[11] Epstein again puts it pithily:

> White wrote in what, technically, is known as the plain style. His specialty was the declarative sentence: subject, predicate, direct object, indirect object, in that order. His sentences contained few subordinate clauses, inversions, semicolons, or dashes. His vocabulary was also plain: no foreign words, no arcane words, almost no abstract words, only occasionally a slang word like "dippy" or "loopy" that has its own charm. For the most part, an E. B. White essay is composed of plain words arrayed in plain syntax forming plain declarative sentences, one after another, back to back, on and on.[12]

Then Epstein cites White's own analysis of the process (from *ES*): "[T]he truth is I write by ear, always with difficulty and seldom with any exact notion of what is taking place under the hood."[13]

Barbara Rogers is one of the most astute and overlooked observers of E. B. White. Besides interweaving details from White's life seamlessly with commentary on the novels,* Rogers notes the basic Whitean conviction that style is inseparable from the man (indeed, this is the cornerstone of White's own views in Chapter V of *ES*), and then goes on to state, more specifically, that it was White's practice "to eliminate needless connective words and to use punctuation marks instead. In doing so, he allows relationships between things to emerge of themselves, without being forced out by his own linguistic manipulation."[14] This is a true and accurate observation.

Marion Glastonbury amusingly observed

*And sharing my own preference for *Stuart Little*, confessed only here, in this note that nobody can see.

that *The New Yorker* was like Charlotte's web, both in being influential and in being renewed at regular intervals. Closer to the actual text, Glastonbury cited Walter Benjamin's view that "an orientation towards practical interests is characteristic of many born storytellers," and noted White's passion for the specific:

> . . . You could stock your farm from his inventory and go away on holiday with the bags he packs. You could also choose your car from his traffic jam: "Fords and Chevvies and Buick roadmasters and GMC pickups and Plymouths and Studebakers and Packards and De Sotos with gyromatic transmissions and Oldsmobiles with rocket engines and Jeep station wagons and Pontiacs." Actuality is a brand name; even *things* have a history, a past and a future.[15]

Other critics, especially early ones, began by helping readers obtain a basic orientation to the book. Thus, Eleanor Cameron:

> E. B. White has not only given us a revelation of farm life as much from the point of view of his animals as from that of his human beings, but has also created his protagonists with absolute truthfulness, each to his kind. These animals and people illustrate to perfection Elizabeth Bowen's statement that characterless action is not action at all, for the act cannot be divided from the actor, nor the qualities and likelihood of an act from a particular actor.
>
> Wilbur, the runt pig, who is saved in the beginning by Fern's love for him, never ceases throughout the progress of the story to be anything but naïve and ingenuous, completely unsophisticated in a plump, pig-like way, dependent upon others for comfort and spiritual sustenance and upon plenty of food and sleep and sunny weather for day-to-day happiness. Like many a naïve and ingenuous person, he is deeply influenced by the opinions and moods of others; he is always the innocent who is acted upon in order that he shall be saved, rather than the hero who acts independently and with assurance to save himself.
>
> The real hero of the book is Charlotte, the spider, "brilliant, beautiful, and loyal"—so Wilbur characterizes her: controlled in the face of Wilbur's hysterics and desperation, acutely perceptive of the nature of mankind (as shown in her awareness that Wilbur's salvation lies in her one chance of working upon the gullibility of human beings), patient as spiders have need to be, and completely unsentimental when it comes to the prospect of her own death at the peak of her forces. All this is in marked contrast to Wilbur's own behavior under the same circumstances. Female spiders always die after they

have hatched their eggs, and there is nothing to do—Charlotte knows—but to accept the fact with dignity. Yet E. B. White does not hesitate for a moment to tell the complete truth about his appealing heroine: that in addition to possessing the above excellences, she is bloodthirsty. Wilbur cannot bear this, but "'It's true,'" Charlotte tells him, "'and I have to say what is true.'"

Nor does White hesitate to tell the truth about Fern, even though it may not show her in a very favorable light. After the story opens, with Fern saving the piglet from being killed because he is the runt of the litter, Fern spends all her free time during the following months sitting at Wilbur's pen, listening to the animals' conversation, and watching Wilbur grow. Next to Charlotte, she is his most devoted friend. And yet, because Fern is human and a child, she changes. During the opening chapters, Fern's whole life is Wilbur and the events of the barn, for she is at that particular age when imaginative children quite easily convince themselves that not only do birds and animals talk, but that they themselves understand them. And it is a nice little detail that never once does Fern enter into these conversations among the animals, but only reports them afterwards, quite matter-of-factly, to her mother and father, seeing nothing unusual or surprising in her understanding of bird and animal talk. Thus the halcyon summer passes. But then something happens to Fern. For the first time in her childhood she becomes disturbingly aware of a member of the opposite sex, one Henry Fussy. And at the very moment when Wilbur is winning his prize at the county fair, when he has become that pig which long, long ago (in other words, three or four months ago) she had envisioned him becoming, she is off with Henry, aware only of Henry. Nor does she ever come regularly to the barn again because "She was growing up, and was careful to avoid childish things, like sitting on a milk stool near the pigpen."

On the other hand, Wilbur never forgets Charlotte, nor can his love for her children and grandchildren ever supplant his love for her nor his gratitude to her. And it was quite moving to me to find in a library copy of the book a heavy black pencil line, rather wobbly, which some child had felt compelled to draw around the words, "Charlotte died. . . . No one was with her when she died." I had an idea that, like Wilbur, that child would never forget Charlotte.

It is the burden of feeling and meaning in *Charlotte's Web* which makes it memorable, which will speak to all times and not just to our own time.[16]

Several critics have observed that the tale takes place on at least two levels, though not all agree as to what those levels may be. Thus, the distinguished English writer Aidan Chambers perceived an "inner" and "external" psychological "space" in the novel:

> E. B. White's *Charlotte's Web* . . . is about our exterior world, and is controlled by the Judaeo-Christian sense of an ending, in which continuity towards a possible . . . "happy" end is achieved by individual acts of sacrifice carried out in the consequential historic line, one generation to another, like runners in a relay race: good, let's say, running against evil, each runner handing on the baton of a good, or an evil, life to the next. Death . . . is used as the closing of a door, an end in itself, which by implication requires a beginning of equal character in the birth of a new person as one of the sacrificial acts of the old. The story and the storyteller remain earthbound in every sense.[17]

Sonia Landes contrasted *Charlotte's Web* to books that start in reality, slip into fantasy, and come back to reality (e.g., *The Adventures of Alice in Wonderland*). *Charlotte's Web* she found to be a book in which "fantasy so alternates with reality that the reader never really leaves home and experiences fantasy as a cognate of reality," and she aptly noted that this alternation raised difficult compositional problems for the writer who had to manage these transitions.[18]

The outstanding British critic John Rowe Townsend similarly noted two worlds—the barnyard world and another world that is "perhaps more real," thus giving us, now, six worlds of the story.

> . . . The point about loyal, intelligent Charlotte is that she is our kin, one of us. So is poor fat unheroic Wilbur, gulping and slurping in the warm slops or wallowing in the manure-heap; so are the gobble-obble-obbling geese and the greedy self-seeking rat Templeton. The death of Charlotte, which makes small girls weep, is the death of a person, made bearable by the continuance of life through her offspring. The barn and farmyard are a world. The passage of seasons, the round of nature, are unobtrusively indicated.
>
> Outside the life of the farmyard there is another world, not perhaps more real but on a different plane, which is that of commonplace human life; and perhaps the most poignant thing in the book is the passage of small girl Fern from involvement with the animals as people to a perfectly normal, but imaginatively regressive, preoccupation with the glittering actualities of the fairground. Fern has begun the

saving of Wilbur, but by the end she has forgotten him; that is life, too. Childhood passes. *Charlotte's Web*, though a short and apparently straightforward story, is astonishingly full and rich.[19]

Still other critics call our attention to specific *themes*. David Rees, speaking about children's books, termed the book "the one great modern classic about death."[20] And, in an excellent piece, Gerald Weales noted that "from the opening threat to Wilbur to Charlotte's lonely death toward the end, the book holds to the idea of death as a fact of life. . . ."[21]

The seasonal orientation of the book was eloquently expressed by Helen Solheim:

> The spring is Fern's season: the book opens with her story, in that time. The summer, radiantly, belongs to Wilbur, though his growth and development are a motif, if not more, throughout the whole. In the fall and the harvest fair, our attention, though not the crowd's, turns to Charlotte: autumn is, to borrow a metaphor from another part of the kingdom, Charlotte's swan song. In winter Fern has outgrown her interest in the barnyard, and so we lose interest in her. Wilbur is mature now and is taking on the uninteresting manners of parents. Charlotte is gone. And so, as the year comes full circle, we see here, too, that time is not circular at all. It is the time for new heroes, and for a new story.[22]

The rarefied world of academic publication has spawned some interpretations that could have prompted laconic response from E. B. White.

One author, although granting that White may have been unaware of the fact, claims that *Charlotte's Web* is a rendering of Erik Erikson's "eight developmental stages of man."[23] Another critic accommodates the story of Wilbur to "a Heideggerian model."[24]

Critics with even curiouser agendas, such as Lucy Rollin or Jack Zipes, transport us to worlds of which humble Wilbur surely never dreamed. Writes Rollin:

> The sac containing Charlotte's babies also becomes a representation of oedipal desire. . . . Wilbur's hyperbolic 514 babies not only occasion pride and possessiveness but totally diffuse any sibling rivalries. Moreover, while Wilbur ensures Charlotte's survival in her children, through those (female) children who stay with him he ensures his own survival as well. . . .
>
> Charlotte's complexity and the valorization of motherhood through her and her web must certainly provide comfort and even inspiration to

> readers, especially female ones. Moreover, this book focuses entirely on the domestic sphere, where the world of men gives way to women—to women's use of language and women's relationships. Furthermore, the main character, a male, is central to the web of the text because he is central to the web of female relationships that structure it.[25]

Jack Zipes re-articulates the feminist concerns more explicitly in a social-economic structure:

> Like Barrie's "fantasy" [*Peter Pan*], White's novel depicts male protagonists who are outsiders. Insofar as they do not assume productive roles within the power systems of their novels, which are symbolically connected to the power systems of their authors' societies, they implicitly critique the gender systems of their authors' societies.[26]

On the other hand, no critic anywhere has come to grips with the book in more comprehensive and enlightening fashion than White's tactful, indefatigable biographer Scott Elledge. Both perforce and voluntarily, Elledge exercised restraint in recounting details of the life of E. B. White. But when Elledge was free to focus his humane critical intelligence on the text, invariably he said that which is most important to say.* In his chapter on *Charlotte's Web*, Elledge tracks White's life during the writing, stresses the profound significance of the fact White was writing an introduction to a new edition of Don Marquis's comic masterpiece *archy & mehitabel*, and analyzes the book stylistically and thematically with insight and balance. Elledge has an appreciation for White's essential skepticism that has been expressed by no other critic except Epstein. Wrote Elledge:

> When Charlotte explains to Wilbur why she saved his life, she gives two reasons: she likes him, and "perhaps [she] was trying to lift up [her] life a little." Here, as the skeptical White comes close to the problem of moral imperatives, he is cautious. *Perhaps*, he says, she was trying to lift up her life a little—to transcend her genetic inheritance, or be a little better than she had to be; and when she adds, "Heaven knows anyone's life can stand a little of that," she carefully, as well as humorously, warns that a little concern for moral improvement goes a long way. . . .
>
> Charlotte lives and dies a free creature, intellectually as well as instinctively accepting her biologically determined fate. In laying her five

---

*Only when Elledge (E., p. 293) says that the "manuscripts and notes of *Charlotte's Web* do not reveal much about the stages of its composition," do I differ, using Appendix B (pages 204–9) as evidence.

hundred and fourteen eggs in her beautifully made sac she is not carrying out the wishes of spider society any more than she is doing it to please her mate. She's pretty sure why she creates her *magnum opus*, in the full knowledge that when it is finished she will die. . . .

Children's books in the past had seldom faced up so squarely as did *Charlotte's Web* to such truths of the human condition as fear of death and death itself; and they had not implied the courageous agnosticism that disclaimed any understanding of why life and the world are the way they are. In 1952 few children's books had made so clear as *Charlotte's Web* that the natural world of the barn does not exist to serve the world of the farmers who think they own it. And few children's books have so clearly embodied a love that can cure fear, make death seem a part of life, and be strong without being possessive. . . .

All of which is to suggest that *Charlotte's Web* was and probably will continue to be a modern book based on the integrity of a humble and skeptical view of the natural world and of the human beings in it. It gives no support to prejudice in favor of the superiority of human beings, or of one sex over another. It does celebrate a child's generous view of the world and a child's love of that world.[27]

Although generally acknowledged in the U.S. (but not in the U.K.) to be a masterpiece, *Charlotte's Web* has visibly strained the linguistic and analytic powers of most critics who have attempted to attend to it. Perhaps the critical scalpel is not the proper instrument, and, as the children's poet David McCord suggested, "no scholar-critic will ever tear apart the fabric of *Charlotte's Web* as were it something that never should have been put together in the first place. *Esto perpetua*."[28]

Appendix G
RECOMMENDED READING

The definitive biography of E. B. White is Scott Elledge's *E. B. White, A Biography.* Elledge assiduously gathered even elusive materials from White's life. More importantly, his commentary on White's works, including *Charlotte's Web*, may well be the most balanced that we have to date. Perhaps it is Elledge's longtime preoccupation with the monumental poet John Milton that allows him a broad perspective and a sense of proportion. In any case, Elledge's notion of what is worth saying makes a great deal of later critical writing on E. B. White appear distinctly eccentric.

White himself read Elledge's manuscript, and although he "neither approved nor disapproved of the biography itself"[1] White did straighten out a few facts and did extend to the entire project a sort of tacit, bemused approval.

A valuable, literate, comprehensive encyclopedia entry for White is that of Barbara Rogers cited on page 250.[2]

As for scholarly literary essays about *Charlotte's Web*, although some shed light, many are obfuscatory cases of special pleading. Especially in recent years, a number of these essays have taken on a strident tone as, in the guise of illuminating a heartrending children's novel, they stretch readers' patience and credulity while they argue political and surreally mandarin literary-critical theory.

From the universities, still the best general appreciation giving us both insight and understanding into the man he calls an endaemonist (a man happy with the life of reason) is Warren Beck's 1946 "E. B. White."[3] After Beck's sane and moving essay, one would be advised to hie oneself away full-speed from academic writing, looking first to the appreciative piece "E. B. White," in the "Talk of the Town" section of *The New Yorker* by White's stepson, Roger Angell.[4]

Significantly at odds with Angell's sunny assessment, and proving that human beings are nothing if not complex, Joseph Epstein's "E. B. White, Dark and Lite," is a persuasive and profound probing of what I, too, perceive as a darker side of White, the humorist and children's author—who, in fact, shrewdly covered his emo-

tional tracks with the considerable resources of his literary style.[5]

Finally, most recently, for the fortieth anniversary of *Charlotte's Web*, White's former *New Yorker* colleague Faith McNulty wrote a graceful homage that offers a quick summary of the life and a happy appreciation of the book.[6] Appropriately, McNulty's piece appeared in the very "Children's Books for Christmas" section that Katharine White was writing when E. B. White began to ruminate about composing a children's book.

NOTES

INTRODUCTION

1. Welty, *NYTBR*, October 19, 1952, p. 49.
2. "Children's Books 1930–1960 That Have Become Classics," in *Publishers Weekly*, November 14, 1960, p. 12.
3. Davis, 243; *L*, pp. 360, 423, 549, 550, 603, 618, 629 and *passim.*
4. Bantam Audio Publishing, three cassettes or three compact discs. 192 minutes each set.
5. E, pp. 30, 31.
6. Gherman, p. 45.
7. E, p. 102.
8. Hall, pp. 226, 231–32.
9. Kramer, p. 141. Also, E, pp. 122.
10. E, pp. 118–19.
11. *L*, p. 72.
12. The article first appeared in White's column "One Man's Meat," *Harper's Magazine*, Vol. 178 (January 1939), pp. 217–20, and is included in the collection *OMM*, pp. 27–35. See also page 236 herein.
13. *L*, p. 270.
14. *NYT*, March 6, 1966, p. X 19.
15. EBW sent the ms. to Oxford University Press and Viking; E, p. 254.
16. *NYT*, March 6, 1966, p. X 19.
17. L, p. 353.
18. *The Journal of Beatrix Potter*, 1881–1897, transcribed from her code writing by Leslie Linder, with an Appreciation by H. L. Cox, p. 207. London: Frederick Warne, 1966.
19. *SL*, p. 50.
20. *SL*, p. 129.
21. *L*, p. 406.
22. *L*, p. 651.
23. *SL*, p. 85.
24. *SL*, p. 92.
25. Folder A.
26. Manuscript page, in Box I, Folder A, Cornell University Library, Division of Rare & Manuscript Collections.
27. *CW*, p. 42.
28. *CW*, p. 60.

29. *L*, p. 305.
30. *L*, p. 406.
31. E, p. 215.
32. *L*, p. 516.
33. *L*, p. 375. See *ACW*, page 218, and compare *ACW*, page 239.
34. Unpublished letter to Judy Zuckerman, October 22 [no year], Cornell University Library, Division of Rare & Manuscript Collections.
35. "Death of a Pig," *Atlantic Monthly*, January 1948; collected in *ST*, pp. 243–53. See pages 228–35.
36. *ST*, p. 253.
37. E, p. 301.
38. *L*, pp. 353–54, 482.
39. *L*, p. 482.
40. E, p. 30.
41. *OMM*, p. 228. See also page 45.
42. *L*, p. 647. For further egg references, see the paragraphs on brooding hens in *ST*, p. 170.
43. *CW*, p. 13.
44. *OMM*, p. 236.
45. *ST*, p. 247.
46. *L*, p. 614. See *ACW*, page 224.
47. *CW*, p. 42.
48. *CW*, p. 113.
49. *CW*, p. 176.
50. *CW*, p. 179.
51. Unpublished letter from Ursula Nordstrom, April 10, 1952, in HarperCollins files.
52. *L*, p. 645.

TITLE, COVER, ENDPAPERS, FRONTISPIECE

1. *ST*, p. 185.
2. *L*, p. 361.
3. Unpublished letter to Ursula Nordstrom, July 13 [1952], in HarperCollins files.
4. Unpublished letter to Ursula Nordstrom, September 29 [no year], in HarperCollins files.
5. Unpublished letter to Ursula Nordstrom, June 23, 1952, in HarperCollins files.

CHAPTER I

1. Unpublished letter to annotator, June 17, 1980 (see page 208). For specimens of White's false starts, see Appendix B, p. 206–8.
2. E, pp. 251, 379.
3. *L*, p. 426.
4. *PC*, pp. 197, 198. See also Appendix D, pages 228–35.
5. *ST*, p. 235.
6. *PC*, pp. 132, 133.
7. *ES*, pp. 19, 21.
8. *TS*, p. 22.
9. E, p. 30.
10. *TNY*, February 5, 1944, p. 30; cited E, pp. 251, 379.

11. *L*, p. 349.
12. Mark Twain, "To the Gas Company."
13. *TS*, p. 210.
14. E, p. 300.
15. *ST*, pp. 228–29.

CHAPTER II

1. *TS*, p. 64. This manuscript page is not with the *CW* papers at Cornell, but with the *TS* manuscript at the Morgan Library, in New York.
2. Shohet, p. 105.
3. Facklam, pp. 72–81. Also, David Larsen, "This Little Piggy Can Come to Your House," in *Los Angeles Times*, June 1, 1989, part V, p. 1.
4. Appendix B, pages 207–8.
5. *ES*, p. 72.
6. *L*, p. 615. See page 224.

CHAPTER III

1. *L*, p. 615. See page 224.
2. E, p. 302; *OMM*, p. 212. See also *ACW*, page 41.
3. *L*, p. 614.
4. E, p. 301.
5. Panofsky, pp. 295–320.
6. *ES*, p. 21.
7. *ES*, p. 23.
8. *ES*, p. 2.
9. Unpublished letter to Ursula Nordstrom, June 23, 1952, in HarperCollins files.
10. Unpublished letter to Ursula Nordstrom, June 23, 1952, in HarperCollins files.
11. E, pp. 24–25, from the essay "A Boy I Knew."
12. *ST*, pp. 228–29.
13. Box II, Folder II, Cornell University Library, Division of Rare & Manuscript Collections. This box contains material for a discarded screenplay.
14. *S*, p. xviii.
15. *OMM*, pp. 302–11.
16. *SL*, p. 92.
17. Nodelman, p. 71. See also Appendix A, page 202.
18. *L*, p. 615. See also Appendix D, page 224.
19. William Shakespeare, *Hamlet*, Act IV, Scene iii, lines 17–30.

CHAPTER IV

1. *ES*, p. 15.
2. *ST*, p. 247. Appendix D, page 231. See also *ACW*, page 22.
3. McCord, p. 1326.
4. Grahame, p. 10.
5. Enright, p. 188.

6. E, p. 252; *TNY*, October 7, 1944, p. 22.
7. Personal communication, April 3, 1991.
8. *L*, p. 361. See page 214.
9. Unpublished letter to Ursula Nordstrom, June 23, 1952, in HarperCollins files. See also page 215.

CHAPTER V

1. *L*, p. 614.
2. Landes, p. 276.
3. *ES*, p. 76.
4. E, p. 293.
5. Egoff, p. 417.
6. Gertsch, p. 15.
7. *L*, p. 614. See also Appendix C, pages 210–17.
8. E, pp. 293, 294.
9. Personal communication from Norman I. Platnick, Chairman and Curator, Department of Entomology, American Museum of Natural History, October 27, 1992.
10. Gertsch, p. 23.
11. Comstock, pp. 185, 186; Gertsch, p. 124.
12. *L*, p. 614.
13. Gertsch, p. 15.
14. *WF*, p. 163.
15. *L*, p. 613. See *ACW*, page 223.
16. Gertsch, pp. 237, 238.
17. Sale, p. 261.

CHAPTER VI

1. *L*, p. 481. See *ACW*, page 219.
2. *L*, p. 614.
3. *The Lady Is Cold*, p. 15; quoted in E, p. 158.
4. Grahame, pp. 72–73.
5. E, pp. 291, 292. *L*, p. 613; see *ACW*, page 223.
6. *OMM*, p. 228. See *ACW*, page xxix.
7. *S*, p. xi.
8. *ES*, p. 84.
9. Potter, p. 45.
10. *SL*, p. 93.
11. *OMM*, pp. 313, 314.
12. *L*, p. 613. See *ACW*, page 223.
13. Unpublished letter to Ursula Nordstrom, April 10, 1952, in HarperCollins files.

[There are no notes to Chapters VII and VIII]

CHAPTER IX

1. Gertsch, p. 182, and "Spiders' Webs: Dew Processes," in *The Economist*, July 18, 1992, p. 101.
2. *L*, p. 614.
3. *ES*, p. 28.

4. Gertsch, p. 13.
5. "On Writing for Children," pp. 67–68. *The Paris Review*, No. 48 (Fall 1969), pp. 67, 68.
6. *ES*, p. 75.

CHAPTER X

1. John Milton, book VIII, line 374.
2. *ES*, p. 77.
3. *S*, p. xviii.
4. E, p. 20.
5. *OMM*, p. 291.
6. *SL*, p. 61.
7. Gertsch, p. 182.

CHAPTER XI

1. Gertsch, p. 5.
2. *ES*, p. 80.
3. Unpublished letter to Ursula Nordstrom, June 23, 1952, in HarperCollins files.
4. D, p. 243.
5. Glastonbury, p. 111. See also Appendix E, page 251.
6. *OMM*, pp. 230–33.

CHAPTER XII

1. *ES*, p. xiii.
2. *TNY*, March 21, 1953, "The Talk of the Town," p. 27.
3. Potter, p. 73. See *ACW*, page 202.
4. *SL*, p. 93. See *ACW*, page xxv.
5. *L*, p. 645.

CHAPTER XIII

1. Gertsch, p. 179.
2. Gertsch, pp. 2, 182.
3. Gertsch, pp. 56–58.
4. Landes, p. 275.
5. E, p. 102.
6. Unpublished letter to Ursula Nordstrom, in HarperCollins files.
7. *TS*, p. 201.
8. *L*, p. 11. For stylistic discussion, see Neumeyer (1987).
9. For examples, see *ES*, p. 26.
10. Comstock, p. 186.
11. Gertsch, p. 208.
12. *ES*, p. 80.
13. Comstock, p. 215.
14. Unpublished autobiographical sketch, in Harper-Collins files.

CHAPTER XIV

1. *L*, p. 614.
2. Landes, p. 278.
3. Landes, p. 276.
4. *ST*, pp. 97–103.
5. Gertsch, p. 5.

CHAPTER XV

1. For readers wishing to follow the thread of the pastoral in Western iconography, see Panofsky, pp. 295–320.

CHAPTER XVI

1. *PC*, p. 127.
2. *PC*, p. 128.
3. *L*, p. 646.
4. *ES*, p. 18.
5. *ES*, p. 51.
6. *L*, p. 485.
7. Unpublished letter from Garth Williams to annotator, October 2, 1983. See also *ACW*, page 200.
8. *ES*, p. 75.
9. *ST*, p. 185.

CHAPTER XVII

1. E, p. 268.
2. *OMM*, p. 314.
3. Unpublished letter from Ursula Nordstrom, June 20, 1952, in HarperCollins files.

CHAPTER XVIII

1. *OMM*, p. 312.
2. Gertsch, p. 88.

CHAPTER XIX

1. Personal communication, summer 1984. See also *ACW*, page xxvi.
2. *WF*, p. 53.
3. Unpublished letter to Elledge, 1977, Cornell University Library, Division of Rare & Manuscript Collections.
4. Kevin Williams, p. 11.
5. EBW, "The Manuscript Club," *The Cornell Era*, Vol. 53, No. 15, June 11, 1921; quoted in E, p. 56.
6. Ulrich Knoepflmacher, conversation with annotator.

CHAPTER XX

1. *L*, p. 320.
2. "Acceptance Message," p. 117.
3. *L*, pp. 293–96.

CHAPTER XXI

1. Unpublished letter from Ursula Nordstrom to Katharine White, April 10, 1952, in Harper-Collins files.
2. Unpublished letter to Ursula Nordstrom, 24 November [no year], in HarperCollins files.
3. Knoepflmacher, p. 134.
4. *L*, p. 634.

CHAPTER XXII

1. *PC*, p. 129.
2. Potter, p. 16.
3. Potter, p. 27.
4. *ES*, p. 76.
5. *L*, p. 613.
6. Comstock, pp. 215–16.
7. Unpublished letter from Ursula Nordstrom, June 20, 1952, in HarperCollins files.
8. *SL*, p. 131.
9. *L*, p. 406.
10. Gertsch, p. 29.
11. Personal communication from Norman I. Platnick, Chairman and Curator, Department of Entomology, American Museum of Natural History, October 27, 1992.
12. D, p. 140.
13. *S*, p. xxii.

APPENDIX A. GARTH WILLIAMS, THE ILLUSTRATOR

1. *L*, p. 591.
2. Unpublished letter from Garth Williams to annotator, October 2, 1983.
3. *L*, p. 265.
4. Unpublished letter from Eugene F. Saxton, April 28, 1938, in HarperCollins files.
5. Unpublished letter, October 3, 1945, in Harper-Collins files.
6. *L*, p. 354. See *ACW*, page 216.
7. *L*, p. 482. See page 219.
8. Nodelman, page 219.
9. Potter, p. 74.

APPENDIX B. THE MANUSCRIPTS

1. *ES*, p. 72
2. *L*, p. 559.
3. *L*, p. 518.
4. *L*, p. 331.
5. *L*, p. 608.
6. *L*, p. 331.
7. *L*, p. 331; see *ACW*, page 218.
8. See also Neumeyer, "Creation."
9. Unpublished letter to annotator, June 17, 1980. See also page 1.

APPENDIX C. SPIDERS

1. E, p. 295.
2. *L*, p. 354. See also *ACW*, page 216.
3. *L*, p. 353.
4. *L*, p. 354. See *ACW*, page 199.

APPENDIX D. E. B. WHITE'S LETTERS AND COMMENTS ABOUT *CHARLOTTE'S WEB*

1. *L*, p. 331.
2. *L*, p. 375.
3. *L*, pp. 481–83.
4. *L*, pp. 549, 550.
5. *L*, p. 584.
6. *L*, p. 585.
7. Hall, p. 116.
8. *L*, pp. 613–14.
9. *L*, p. 608.
10. *L*, p. 618.
11. *L*, p. 615.
12. *L*, p. 618.
13. *L*, pp. 644–45.
14. *ST*, pp. 243–53.
15. E, p. 270.
16. *OMM*, pp. 20–21.
17. "Pigs and Spiders." See also Hall, p. 448.
18. *L*, p. 375.
19. *OMM*, pp. 15–16.
20. "On Writing for Children," pp. 84–85.
21. Lewis, p. 208.
22. *ST*, pp. 160–61.
23. *The Fox of Peapack and Other Poems*. New York: Harper, 1938, p. 126.

APPENDIX E. READERS' RESPONSES

1. *L*, p. 365.
2. Langton, p. 21.

3. Kieran, p. 101.
4. See Cerf, p. 6.
5. Kinkead, p. 195.
6. Travers, "Tangible," p. 1.
7. Travers, "My Childhood," p. 639.
8. *The Booklist*, p. 2.
9. Moore, p. 394.
10. Welty, pp. 203–6.

APPENDIX F. CRITICAL APPRAISALS

1. Sale, p. 2
2. Blount, p. 256.
3. Inglis, p. 179.
4. Sale, p. 265.
5. Sampson, p. 100.
6. Unpublished letter from Anne Carroll Moore to Ursula Nordstrom, June 2, 1952, in Harper-Collins files.
7. Epstein, p. 49.
8. Epstein, p. 56.
9. Epstein, p. 56.
10. Fuller.
11. Neumeyer, "E. B. White."
12. Epstein, p. 55.
13. Epstein, p. 55.
14. Rogers, p. 670.
15. Glastonbury, p. 111.
16. Cameron, pp. 575–77.
17. Chambers, pp. 65–66.
18. Landes, p. 270.
19. Townsend, pp. 241–42.
20. Rees, p. 69.
21. Weales, p . 410.
22. Solheim, pp. 404–5.
23. Singer, p. 17.
24. Gagnon, p. 66.
25. Rollin, pp. 45, 50.
26. Zipes, p. 143.
27. Epstein, p. 304–5.
28. McCord, p. 1326.

APPENDIX G. RECOMMENDED READING

1. E, p. xv.
2. Rogers.
3. Beck, pp. 175–81.
4. Angell, p. 31.
5. Epstein, pp. 295–319.
6. McNulty, pp. 137–44.

WORKS CITED

BOOKS BY E. B. WHITE*

Charlotte's Web. New York: Harper, 1952.

The Elements of Style (by William Strunk, Jr., and E. B. White). 3rd ed. New York: Macmillan, 1979.

The Fox of Peapack and Other Poems. New York: Harper, 1938.

Is Sex Necessary? Or Why You Feel the Way You Do (by James Thurber and E. B. White). New York: Harper, 1929.

The Lady Is Cold: Poems by E. B. White. New York: Harper, 1929.

Letters of E. B. White. Ed. Dorothy Lobrano Guth. New York: Harper, 1976.

One Man's Meat. New York: Harper, 1942.

The Points of My Compass: Letters from the East, the West, the North, the South. New York: Harper, 1962.

*The bulk of White's papers are deposited at the Cornell University Library, Division of Rare & Manuscript Collections, Ithaca, New York. *American Literary Manuscripts* lists twenty-six other depositories.

The Second Tree from the Corner. New York: Harper, 1954.

Stuart Little. New York: Harper, 1945.

A Subtreasury of American Humor. Ed. E. B. White and Katharine S. White. New York: Coward, 1941.

The Trumpet of the Swan. New York: Harper, 1970.

The Wild Flag: Editorials from The New Yorker *on Federal World Government and Other Matters*. Boston: Houghton, 1946.

Writings from The New Yorker *1925–1976*. Ed. Rebecca M. Dale. New York: Harper, 1990.

INTERVIEW, PRINTED

"On Writing for Children." In "The Art of the Essay," *The Paris Review*, No. 48 (Fall 1969), pp. 65–88. (Reprinted in *Writers at Work, 8th series*. Ed. George Plimpton. Intro. Joyce Carol Oates. New York: Viking, 1988.)

OTHER

"Acceptance Message." Claremont Reading Conference, *Thirty-fourth Yearbook*. "Reading and School Life." Ed. Malcolm P. Douglass. Claremont (Calif.) Graduate School, 1937, p. 117.

"The Librarian Said It Was Bad for Children." *The New York Times*, Mar. 6, 1966, p. X 19.

"The Manuscript Club," in *The Cornell Era*, Vol. 53, No 15, June 1921. Quoted in E, p. 56.

"Pigs and Spiders." *McClurg's Book News*, January 1953, p. 49.

SECONDARY SOURCES BIBLIOGRAPHIES

Anderson, A. J. *E. B. White: A Bibliography*. Metuchen, N.J.: Scarecrow, 1978.

Hall, Katharine Romans, comp. *E. B. White: A Bibliographic Catalogue of Printed Materials in the Department of Rare Books, Cornell University Library*. New York: Garland, 1979. Lists not only all editions of White's books, but over 2,190 articles he contributed to periodicals.

BIOGRAPHIES

Davis, Linda H. *Onward and Upward: A Biography of Katharine S. White*. New York: Harper, 1987.

Elledge, Scott. *E. B. White, A Biography*. New York: Norton, 1984, 1985.

Russell, Isabel. *Katharine and E. B. White: An Affectionate Memoir*. New York: Norton, 1984, 1988.

Sampson, Edward. *E. B. White*. New York: Twayne, 1974.

OTHER WORKS CITED IN *THE ANNOTATED CHARLOTTE'S WEB*

Angell, Roger. "E. B. White." *The New Yorker*, "The Talk of the Town," Vol. 14 (Oct. 1985), p. 31.

Beardsley, Monroe. "Style and Good Style." In *New Rhetorics*. Ed. Martin Steinmann, Jr., pp. 191–213. New York: Scribner's, 1967.

Beck, Warren. "E. B. White." *English Journal*, Vol. 35 (1946), pp. 175–81.

Blount, Margaret. *Animal Land: The Creatures of Childhood*. New York: Morrow, 1975.

The Booklist, Vol. 49, Sept. 1, 1952, p. 2.

Burningham, John. *Come Away from the Water, Shirley*. New York: Crowell, 1977.

Burton, Virginia Lee. *The Little House*. Boston: Houghton, 1942.

Cerf, Bennett. "Trade Winds." *The Saturday*

Review, Nov. 15, 1952, pp. 6–7.

Cameron, Eleanor. "McLuhan, Youth, and Literature," Part II. *The Horn Book*, Dec. 1972, pp. 572–79.

Chambers, Aidan. *Booktalk: Occasional Writing on Literature and Children*. New York: Harper, 1986.

Comstock, John Henry. *The Spider Book: A Manual for the Study of the Spiders and Their Near Relatives, the Scorpions, Pseudoscorpions, Whip-Scorpions, Harvestmen, and Other Members of the Class Arachnida, Found in America North of Mexico, with Analytical Keys for Their Classification and Popular Accounts of Their Habits*. Rev. and Ed. W. J. Gertsch. Ph.D. Ithaca: Comstock, 1948.

Egoff, Sheila, G. T. Stubbs, and L. F. Ashley, eds. *Only Connect: Readings on Children's Literature*, 2nd ed. New York: Oxford University Press, 1980.

Enright, D. J. "A Mania for Sentences." In *Encounter*, Apr. 1978, pp. 70–75. (Reprinted as "Lifting Up One's Life a Trifle: On E. B. White," in *A Mania for Sentences*, pp. 185–92. London: Chatto, 1983.)

Epstein, Joseph. "E. B. White, Dark and Lite." *Commentary*, Apr. 1986, pp. 48–56. (Reprinted in *Partial Payments: Essays on Writers and Their Lives*, pp. 295–319. New York: Norton, 1989.)

Facklam, Margery. *Who Harnessed the Horse? The Story of Animal Domestication*. Ill. Steven Parton. Boston: Little, Brown, 1992.

Fuller, John Wesley. *Prose Styles in Essays of E. B. White*. Ph.D. diss., University of Washington, Seattle, 1959. (Reprint: Ann Arbor: UMI, 1979.)

Gagnon, Laurence. "Webs of Concern: *The Little Prince* and *Charlotte's Web*." In *Reflections on Literature for Children*. Ed. Francelia Butler and Richard Rotert, with a foreword by Leland B. Jacobs, pp. 66–71. Hamden, Conn.: Shoe String Press, 1984.

Gertsch, Willis J. *American Spiders*. New York: Van Nostrand, 1949.

Gherman, Beverly. *E. B. White: Some Writer!* New York: Atheneum, 1992.

Glastonbury, Marion. "E. B. White's Unexpected Items of Enchantment." *Children's Literature in Education*, May 1973, pp. 3–11. (Reprinted in *Writers, Critics, and Children*. Ed. Geoff Fox, pp. 104–15. New York: Agathon, 1976.)

Grahame, Kenneth. *The Wind in the Willows*. Illus. E. H. Shepard. New York: Scribner's, 1933, 1953.

Hemingway, Ernest. *The Green Hills of Africa*. New York: Scribner's, 1935.

Hoban, Russell. *The Mouse and His Child*. New York: Harper, 1967.

Inglis, Fred. *The Promise of Happiness: Value and Meaning in Children's Fiction*. Cambridge: Cambridge University Press, 1981.

Kieran, M. F. Review of *CW*. *The Altantic Monthly*, Vol. 190: Dec. 1952, p. 101.

Kinkead, Katherine. *The New Yorker*, Dec. 6, 1952, p. 195.

Knoepflmacher, Ulrich. "The Doubtful Marriage: A Critical Fantasy," in *Children's Literature 18*. Ed. Francelia Butler. New Haven: Yale University Press, 1990.

Kramer, Dale. *Ross and* The New Yorker. New York: Doubleday, 1951.

Landes, Sonia. "E. B. White's *Charlotte's Web*: Caught in the Web." In *Touchstones: Reflections on the Best in Children's Literature*. Ed. Perry Nodelman. West Lafayette, Ind.: Children's Literature Association, 1985.

Langton, Jane. "Shiloh," *NYTBR*, May 10, 1992, p. 21.

Lewis, C. S. "On Three Ways of Writing for Children." In *Only Connect: Readings on Children's Literature*. Ed. Sheila Egoff, G. T. Stubbs, and L. F. Ashley. 2nd ed., pp. 207–20. New York: Oxford University Press, 1980.

Marquis, Don. *archy & mehitabel*. New York: Doubleday, 1930.

McCord, David. "E. B. White." In *20th-Century Children's Writers*. Ed. D. L. Kirkpatrick, pp. 1322–26. New York: St. Martin's, 1978.

McNulty, Faith. "Children's Books for Christmas." *The New Yorker*, Nov. 25, 1991, pp. 137–44.

Moore, Anne Carroll. "The Three Owls' Notebook." *The Horn Book*, Dec. 1952, p. 394.

Neumeyer, Peter F. "The Creation of *Charlotte's Web*: From Drafts to Book." *The Horn Book*, Oct. 1982, pp. 489–97, and Dec. 1982, pp. 617–25.

———. *Donald and the . . .* Illus. Edward Gorey. Reading, Mass.: Addison-Wesley, 1969.

———. "E. B. White: Aspects of Style." *The Horn Book*, Sept./Oct. 1987, pp. 586–91.

——— and Edward Gorey. *Donald Has a Difficulty*. New York: Fantod, 1970.

Nodelman, Perry. *Words About Pictures: The Narrative Art of Children's Picture Books*. Athens: University of Georgia Press, 1988.

Panofsky, Erwin. "*Et in Arcadia Ego:* Poussin and the Elegiac Tradition." In *Meaning in the Visual Arts*, pp. 295–320. Garden City, N.Y.: Doubleday, 1955.

Potter, Beatrix. *The Tale of Peter Rabbit*. New York: Warne, 1903.

Prelutsky, Jack. *Under the Blue Umbrella*. Illus. Garth Williams. New York: Greenwillow, 1990.

Rees, David. "*Timor Mortis Conturbat Me*: E. B. White and Doris Buchanan Smith." In

The Marble in the Water: Essays on Contemporary Writers of Fiction for Children and Young Adults, pp. 68–77. Boston: Horn Book, 1980.

Rogers, Barbara. "E. B. White." In *American Writers: A Collection of Literary Biographies*, ed. Walton Litz. Supplement I, Part 2, pp. 651–81. New York: Scribner's, 1979.

Rollin, Lucy. "The Reproduction of Mothering in *Charlotte's Web*," in *Children's Literature 18*. Ed. Francelia Butler, pp. 42–52. New Haven: Yale University Press, 1990.

Sale, Roger. *Fairy Tales and After: From Snow White to E. B. White*. Cambridge, Mass.: Harvard University Press, 1978.

Selden, George. *The Cricket in Times Square*. New York: Farrar, Straus, 1960.

Sendak, Maurice. *Where the Wild Things Are*. New York: Harper, 1963.

Shohet, Richard M. *Functions of Voice in Children's Literature*. Ed.D. diss., Harvard University, 1971. (Reprint: Ann Arbor: UMI, 1971.)

Singer, Dorothy G. "*Charlotte's Web* and Erikson's Life Cycle." *School Library Journal*, Vol. 22, No. 3 (Nov. 1975), pp. 17–19.

Solheim, Helene. "Magic in the Web: Time, Pigs, and E. B. White." *South Atlantic Quarterly*, Vol. 80, No. 4 (Autumn 1981), pp. 391–405.

Townsend, John Rowe. *Written for Children: An Outline of English-Language Children's Literature*. New York: Lippincott, 1965, 1974.

Travers, P. L. "Tangible Magic." Review of *CW*. *New York Herald Tribune Book Review*. Part 2. Nov. 16, 1952, pp. 1, 38.

———. "My Childhood Bends Beside Me." *The New Statesman and Nation*, Vol. 44. Nov. 29, 1952, p. 639.

Twain, Mark. *The American Claimant*. New York: Charles Webster, 1892.

———. "To the Gas Company." In *Mark Twain's Notebook*. Ed. Albert Bigelow Paine, p. 212. New York: Harper, 1935. Also in *The Portable Mark Twain*. New York: Viking, 1946.

Weales, Gerald. "The Designs of E. B. White." In *Authors and Illustrators of Children's Books: Writings on Their Lives and Works*. Ed. Miriam Hoffman and Eva Samuels. Pp. 407–11. New York: Bowker, 1972. (Reprinted from *NYT*, May 24, 1970, sec. 7, part 2, p. 2ff.)

Welty, Eudora. *The Eye of the Story: Selected Essays and Reviews*. New York: Random, 1970. pp. 203–6. Originally published as "Life in the Barn Was Very Good" in *NYTBR*, Oct. 9, 1932, p. 49.

Weeks, Edward. "The Peripatetic Reviewer." *Atlantic Monthly*, Dec. 1952, pp. 88, 90.

White, Katherine S. *Onward and Upward in the Garden*. New York: Farrar, Straus, 1979.

Wilder, Laura Ingalls. The Little House books. New York: Harper, 1953.

Williams, Garth. *The Rabbits' Wedding*. New York: Harper, 1958.

Williams, Kevin. "Composition and Meaning in Selected Writings of E. B. White." Senior thesis, Amherst College, April 1988. (Copy in Department of Rare & Manuscript Collections, Cornell University.)

Zipes, Jack. "Negating History and Male Fantasies Through Psychoanalytical Criticism." *Children's Literature 18*. Ed. Francelia Butler, pp. 141–43. New Haven: Yale University Press, 1990.

INDEX

This is an index to the annotations, introductory material, and appendices to THE ANNOTATED CHARLOTTE'S WEB. The text of *Charlotte's Web* itself is not indexed.

Numbers in *italics* refer to illustrations.

action, 69, 70, 156, 208. *See also* rhythm; slapstick
Adams, Franklin P., xx
Addams, Charles, 214
Ade, George, 105
affirmation, xxiv, xxvi *(fn)*, 7, 39, 148, 176
alliteration, 42
American Claimant, The (Twain), 202
American Spiders (Gertsch). *See* Gertsch
amorality, 39, 223, 225, 255–56
analogies, 103, 129
Angell, Roger, 257
animals
  intelligence of, 67, 89, 123
  relations of, with humans, 42, 52, 106
  talking by, 16, 22, 29, 49, 54, 105, 199, 223, 224
  White's interest in, xxv–xxvi, 15, 223–24, 237–38, 239
  See also anthropomorphism; dogs; geese; mice; pigs; rats; sheep; spiders
anthropomorphism, 22, 30, 38, 58, 66, 81, 214, 220, 224
Arable, Avery, 6, 52, 68, 84, 112, 126–28
Arable, Fern
  ability of, to understand animals, 49, 52–53, 65, 104, 107, 149, 223, 252, 253
  absence of, at Wilbur's triumph, 156, 252
  changes in, 8, 85, 105, 107, 119, 128, 133, 139, 149, 154, 156, 219, 252–54
  illustrations of, 9, 15, 46, 202–3, 215
  importance of, in *Charlotte's Web*, 225, 246, 249
  late inclusion of, in drafts, 52, 133, 204, 205, 206, 226
  names of, xxix, 1
Arable, Mr., xxix, 1, 5, 49, 54
Arable, Mrs.
  depiction of, xxxii, 54, 84, 106, 137, 143, 246
  illustration of, 108, 200, 215
  name of, xxix, 1
Araneus cavaticus, 37, 182, 216, 237
Arcady. *See* pastoral tradition
archy & mehitabel. See lives and times of archy & mehitabel
Atlantic Monthly, The, xxviii, 227, 245
Austen, Jane, 226

bacon, 3, 6, 22
barns, *14*, *185*
  Charlotte's Web as hymn to, 13, 219, 223, 224
  community in, 33, 57, 148, 224
  illustrations of, 15, 83
  smells of, xxix, 13, 41
  White's, 83, 203 *(fn)*, 225
  White's feelings for, xxv–xxvi, xxix, 12, 13, 15, 39, 71, 107, 183, 224, 239
  See also animals; farm; manure; rural world
Barrie, J. M., 255
Beardsley, Monroe, 127
Beck, Warren, 257

Bemelmans, Ludwig, 205, 222
Beneath a Blue Umbrella (Prelutsky), 197–98
birth, xxiii, 1–2. *See also* life
Blount, Margaret, 248
Blue Hill (Maine) Congregational Church, 90
 Blue Hill Fair, 118, 130
Booklist, The, 246, 246
bottle feeding, 6, 8, 206
Bowen, Elizabeth, 251
Bronx Zoo, 7, 15
Burningham, John, 202
Burton, Virginia Lee, 176

Cameron, Eleanor, 7, 251–52
Camus, Albert, 17
Canfield, Cass, Sr., xxiii*(fn)*, 30, 214
cars, 83–84, 130
catch phrases, 82
Cerf, Bennett, xix, 245
Chambers, Aidan, 253
characterization. *See* voice; *specific characters*
Charlotte
 anthropomorphizing of, 22, 30, 66, 214, 220, 224
 character of, 36, 38, 41, 44, 48, 134, 223, 251–55
 characteristics of, 24, 37, 38, 48, 140, 252, 255–56
 children of, xxxi, 158, 170, 180, 238, 254
 as contrast to Wilbur, 50, 165, 251
 death of, xxx–xxxi, 81, 167, 170, 176, 219–21, 253
 first appearance of, 31
 as hero, 36, 251–52
 illustrations of, xxix, 15, 22, 30, 66, 199, 214–15, 220, 221
 language used by, 35, 38, 44, 48, 53, 104, 175
 prophecies of, 164, 172
 roles of, 35, 40, 47, 50, 51, 61, 64, 104, 116, 145, 175
 sounds connected with, 31
 Templeton's salvation of, 72–73, 164
Charlotte's Web (White)
 annotating of, xvii–xviii
 beginning of, 1, 13, 52, 204, 205, 208, 218
 cover of, xxxii–xxxiv
 endpapers of, xxxiii
 film versions of, xix, 83, 111, 118, 170–71, 203, 208-9, 248
  projected, 208–9, 219–21, 222–25
 frontispiece, xxxiii–xxxiv
 origins of, xxii, xxvii–xxviii, 218, 225, 227, 237–38, 239
 responses to, 246–56
 sales of, xix
 setting of, 43
 sound recordings of, xix
 standing of in children's literature, xix
 title of, xxxii, 157
 translations of, xix, xxxii, 157
 White on, 218–42
 See also drafts; fantasy; illustrations; pastoral tradition; themes; *specific characters in*
"Children's Books" (White), 236
children's literature, xviii, 248
 Charlotte's Web's standing in, xix
 death in, 256
 White's knowledge of, 215, 227
 writing of, 227, 236, 242
collections as revealing character, 45. *See also* lists
Come Away from the Water, Shirley (Burningham), 202
comedy, xix
community, 33, 57, 148, 224. *See also* friendship; world government
Comstock, John Henry, 38, 103, 178, 210
Connelly, Marc, xxi
Consolidated Edison Company, 5–6
Cornell University, xxviii
 Cornell Daily Sun, xx
 Strunk at, 2
 White, Andrew D., at, xx
 White archives at, xvii, xx*(fn)*, 1, 28, 144, 204. *See also* drafts of *Charlotte's Web*
 White's attendance at, xx, 150
"Cornfield" (White), 227, 244
"creeping," 45, 90
Cricket in Times Square, The (Selden), 197
crying, 22, 30, 150
"cute," 10
cycles
 as theme in *Charlotte's Web*, xxvii, xxx–xxxi, 138, 176, 180, 247
 as theme in other works, 176, 227, 244
 See also recycling; seasons

Dartmouth College, 160
Daugherty, James, 198
Davis, Linda H., xx*(fn)*, xxvi, 203*(fn)*
Davis, Mary Gould, 245
de Rochemont, Louis, 42, 219–20
"Dear Reader" (White), 227, 239–40
death
  animals' discussion of, 48–49
  Charlotte's, xxx–xxxi, 81, 167, 170, 176, 219–21, 253
  in pastoral tradition, 13, 113
  as theme in *Charlotte's Web*, xix, xxx–xxxi, 91, 209, 225, 247, 253, 254, 255–56
  of White's pig, xxviii–xxix, 2, 227, 228–35, 239
  See also life; salvation
"Death of a Pig" (White), xxviii–xxix, 2, 227, 228–35
Deitch, Gene
  Charlotte's Web screenplay projected by, 205, 225
  White's letters to, 12, 13, 22, 38, 39, 42, 46, 175, 222–24
description, 3, 51, 139, 163, 202
diction, 5. *See also* language; voice
Disney, Walt, 222, 223–24
distance, 31, 63, 70, 78, 144–45
dogs, xxviii, 20, 97
Donald and the… and *Donald Has a Difficulty* (Neumeyer), 202*(fn)*
Donne, John, xxviii
Dorian, Dr., 9, 12, 119
  illustration of, 109
  name of, 105–6
  views of, 42, 54, 145, 157, 178
double entendre, 61
drafts of *Charlotte's Web*, *188*, *190*, *191*, *192*, *193*, *196*, 204–9
  barn in, xxv, 13, 96, 183, 208
  chapter title changes in, 130, 138, 155, 163
  Fern's late inclusion in, 52, 133, 149, 204, 205, 206, 226
  location of, xvii, 1, 204
  missing, 133, 206–7
  names in, 6, 18
  omission of commentary from, 96, 156, 163
  omniscient narrator in, 41, 50, 153
  reuse of scenes from, 8
  for screenplay, 6, 205, 208–9, 225
  shifting of characters in, 20, 97
  simplification in, 3, 49, 56, 127, 136, 138, 139, 140, 156, 163
  Templeton in, 29, 139, 164, 175
  web words in, 97, 98
  Wilbur in, 4, 11, 72, 153, 164, 206-8
  word changes in, 61, 120, 125, 126, 127, 155, 164, 165, 170, 174, 175, 179

"E. B. White" (Angell), 257
"E. B. White" (Beck), 257
E. B. White: A Biography. *See* Elledge
"E. B. White, Dark and Lite" (Epstein), xxvi*(fn)*, 12, 249–50, 255, 257–58
Eclogues (Virgil), 8
eggs, xxix, 72, 73
  spider, xxix, 145, *146*, 237–38, 252
Elements of Style, The (Strunk and White), xx, 2, 69, 101, 120. *See also* White, E. B., on writing
Elledge, Scott
  on *Charlotte's Web*, 255–56, 257
  as White's biographer, xvii, xx*(fn)*, xxi, xxvi, xxvii, 13, 71, 116, 227, 257
  White's letters to, 145
Enright, D. J., 28
Epstein, Joseph, xxvi*(fn)*, 12, 249–50, 255, 257–58
Erikson, Erik, 254

fairs, 118, 130, 139, 227
"Fall" (White), 139
fantasy, 42, 81, 219, 223, 226, 242, 245, 253
farm (White's), xxvii, 19, 7, *44*, *146*, *185*, 237–38. *See also* animals; barns
farmers, 120
fathers, 4, 5, 79
Fern. *See* Arable, Fern
Ferris wheels, xxvi, 139, 173, 241
film versions of *Charlotte's Web*, xix, 83, 111, 118, 170–71, 203, 208–9, 248
  projected, 208–9, 219–21, 222–25
folktale styles, 19, 94
foreshadowing, 23, 31, 67, 72, 79
Forster, E. M., 237
Fox of Peapack and Other Poems, The (White), 104

Frascino, Edward, 221
freedom, 17, 19, 23
Freud, Sigmund, 109
friendship, xxvi, 27, 31, 41, 91, 114, 163, 209, 224, 225, 239, 247
Fryeburg Fair, 118, 130
Fuller, John Wesley, 48
Fussy, Henry, 111, 139, 149, 203*(fn)*, 252
"Future of Reading, The" (White), 227, 243

Gagnon, Laurence, 254
geese, *44*, 45, 86, 214
  language of, 17, 29, 34, 86, 253
  White's feelings about, xxix, 220
gender, 4, 8, 10, 52, 68, 112, 126–28, 246, 254–55, 256
Gertsch, Willis J., 38, 40, 92, 102, 109, 140, 147, 179, 199, 210, 216, 217, 237
Glastonbury, Marion, 83, 250–51
"Good-bye to 48th Street" (White), 118
Gorey, Edward, 202*(fn)*
Grahame, Kenneth, 8, 26, 43
grammar, 69, 120. *See also Elements of Style;* White, E. B., on writing
Greenstein, Milton, 222
Gude, J. G., 170–71, 221, 224–25
gullibility of human beings, 79, 80, 84, 89, 96, 106, 151, 157–58, 251
Gulliver's Travels (Swift), 45
Guth, Dorothy Lobrano, xx*(fn)*, xxvi

Hamilton, Hamish, xxiii*(fn)*
Hamner, Earl, 209
Hanna-Barbera–Sagittarius Productions. *See Charlotte's Web*, film versions of
Harper & Brothers, (publishers), xxiii, xxiv, 30, 198, 215, 227, 239–40. *See also* Nordstrom
Harper's Magazine, xxii, xxiv, xxviii, 227
Harvard Crimson, The, 159
Hemingway, Ernest, 5
Hesiod, 8
Hoban, Russell, 90
hogs, 40, 128
Homer, 12, 14, 106, 246
Horn Book, The, 245, 246, 249
Hubley, John and Faith, 220–21, 222
humor, 184
  in *Charlotte's Web*, 28, 47, 60, 70, 74, 84, 101, 120
  difficulty of explaining, xxxii, 17, 129
  language as key to White's, 5–6, 28, 60, 61, 84, 120
  parody, xxi

illustrations, 198–200
  of barns, 15, 83
  as collaboration between authors and illustrators, 66, 88, 95, 100, 198, 199, 202
  of Charlotte, 15, 66, *192*, 199, 214–15, 221
  of Dr. Dorian, 109
  of fair, 132
  of farmyard chase, 21
  of Fern, 9, 15, 46, 202–3, 215
  of geese, 214
  of Mrs. Arable, 108, 200, 215
  passing of time shown by, 9
  of spiders and webs, xxix, xxxiv, 15, 22, 30, 36, 59, 66, *192*, 199, 214–15, 220, 221
  of Templeton, xxxiii–xxxiv, 58, 147, 169, 202
  of Wilbur, 202, 215
  See also Frascino; Williams, Garth
immortality, 145, 154
Inglis, Fred, 248
insects, 37
intertextuality, 43
irony, 4, 24, 49, 63, 74
Is Sex Necessary? (Thurber and White), 114

Johnson, Samuel, xv, xviii
joy, xxvi*(fn)*, xxxi, 224, 225

Kaston, Mrs., 218
Katharine & E. B. White (Russell), 114, 203*(fn)*, 204*(fn)*
Kieran, M. F., 245
"kill," 48–49, 126. *See also* "murder"
Knoepflmacher, Ulrich, 154, 170
Krauss, Ruth, xxiv

Landes, Sonia, 34, 94, 106, 109, 253
Langton, Jane, 245
language, 46, 75, 102
  and characterization in White's works, 4, 5, 17, 35, 44, 45, 47, 49, 65, 82

as theme of *Charlotte's Web*, 49, 158
White's humor tied to, 5–6, 28, 60, 61, 74, 84, 120
White's use of concrete, 2, 14, 48, 61, 83, 120, 125, 126, 127, 136, 138, 144, 155, 164, 165, 170, 174, 175, 179, 251
See also drafts; grammar; voice
Lawson, Robert, 198
Leaf, Munro, 236
Less than Nothing (White), 28, *187*
letters. *See* Deitch; Elledge; Guth; Neumeyer; Nordstrom; White, E. B.; White, Katharine; Williams
Letters of E. B. White (ed. Guth), xx*(fn)*, xxvi
Lewis, C. S., 227
life
brevity of, 43, 113, 164
Charlotte's Web as paean to, xix, xxx, 13, 42, 105, 224
as theme in *Charlotte's Web*, xxxi, 39, 91, 223–25, 247, 249.
what is important in, xxv–xxvi, 7, 18
See also birth; death; pastoral tradition
Lindey, Alexander, 220–21
lists, 14, 25, 26, 29, 75, 97, 123, 125, 251. *See also* collections
Little, Mr. and Mrs., 200
Little House, The (Burton), 176
Little Women (Alcott), 163
lives and times of archy & mehitabel, the (Marquis), xxxii, 38–39, 44, 175, 223, 255
loneliness, 27
Lurie, Alison, xxviii
Lurvy, 18, 23, 74, 108, 205
lyrical passages, 8, 42, 51, 62, 113. *See also* pastoral tradition; rhythm

McCook, H. C., 210, 216
McCord, David, xix, 26, 256
McNulty, Faith, 258
Madeline (Bemelmans), 205, 222
"magnum opus," xxvi–xxvii, 144, 256
Maine, 246
White's life in, xxvi–xxix, 7, 60, 90, 118, 130, 225, 240
manure, xxv, xxix, xxx, 13, 96, 206, 207, 224. *See also* recycling
Marquis, Don, xxxii, 38, 44, 175, 255
mice, xxix, 4–5, 29. *See also Stuart Little*
Milton, John, 17, 67, 257
miracles
as theme of *Charlotte's Web*, 209, 223, 247
web as, xxxii, 77, 109–10, 129, 145, 178, 225
web writing as, 87, 157
White on, 77
See also gullibility; triumph
money, xix, 203*(fn)*, 226
Moore, Anne Carroll, xxiv, 176, 245, 246, 249
morality, 39, 223, 225 , 255–56
Mount Vernon (New York), 71
Mouse and His Child, The (Hoban), 90
Mozart, Wolfgang Amadeus, 170–71
"murder," 2, 48–49, 228, 232, 237. *See also* violence
music, 170–71, 223, 225. *See also* rhythm

names
Arable family's, xxix, 1
Avery's, 206
of Charlotte's children, 158
Charlotte's Latin species, 37, 182, 216, 237
Dr. Dorian's, 105–6
Fern's, 1
Homer Zuckerman's, 12, 106
Lurvy's, 18, 205
in *Stuart Little*, 105
Templeton's, 26
narrative strategies, 4–5, 12, 19, 87, 94, 113, 117, 131
narrator, 209, 219
omniscient, 5, 9, 39, 41, 43, 45, 50, 52, 56, 66, 117, 153
reliability of, 52, 53
stance of, 31, 63, 78
Neumeyer, Peter, 204*(fn)*
opinion of *Stuart Little*, 250*(fn)*
White's letters to, 1, 114, 144, 208
Williams' letter to, 66, 121, 199, *200–1*
works by, 48, 202*(fn)*
New England, 43, 134, 223. *See also* Maine
New York City, xxvi, xxvii, 60
New York Evening Post, xx
New York Herald Tribune, 245–46

New York Public Library, xxiv, 210, 216
New York Times, The, xxiii*(fn)*, 184
New York World, xx
New Yorker, The, 250–51
  biographical sketches of White in, 257, 258
  Charlotte's Web reviewed in, 245
  children's book columns in, xxii, 227, 258
  White's work for, xx–xxii, xxiii, xxv*(fn)*, xxviii, 1, 90, 99, 118, 227
  Williams' work for, 197
Nielsen, Aage, 1
Nodelman, Perry, 21, 202
Nordstrom, Ursula, 249
  suggestions for changes in *Charlotte's Web* by, xxxi, 132, 163, 179
  as White's editor at Harper, xxiv, 101, 167, 202, 205, 218
  White's letters to regarding illustrations, xxxii, xxxiv, 15, 30, 46, 83, 199, 214–16, 221–22
  and Williams, xxxiv, 198, 210, 221
north. *See* quests
North Brooklin, Maine. *See* Maine

"On Writing for Children" (White), 227, 242
"Once More to the Lake" (White), 18
One Man's Meat (White), 130, 227
Onward and Upward (Davis). *See* Davis, Linda H.
Our Town (Wilder), 220

pace. *See* rhythm
paean, 105. *See also* life, *Charlotte's Web* as paean to
Paradise Lost (Milton), 67
paragraph, 25, 33, 69, 123
Paris Review, 227
parody, xxi. *See also* humor
pastoral tradition, *Charlotte's Web* in, xix, 8–9, 13, 42, 43, 62, 105–6, 113, 171, 219
Philosophy of Style (Spencer), 14
pigs
  birth of, 1–2
  care of, 30, 96, 120
  death of, xxviii–xxix, 2, 49, 228, 235, 237
  life expectancy of, 40, 134
  as pets, 10
  spring, 11, 67, 228
  weight of, 128, 134
  See also "Death of a Pig"; Wilbur
"Pigs and Spiders" (White), 227, 237–38
plenitude, 13
politics, xxv*(fn)*, xxxiii*(fn)*, 90, 224
Potter, Beatrix, xxiv, 17, 41, 46, 88, 174, 202
praise, 96
Prelutsky, Jack, 197–98
protagonists, 12
Publishers Weekly poll, xix
punctuation, 15, *186*, 250
"put to sleep," 48–49

quests, xxv–xxvii, 179, 226

Rabbits' Wedding, The (Williams), 197
rats, xxix, 4, 29, 45, 74. *See also* Templeton
reading, 227, 243
realism, 226
recapitulation, 87, 113
recycling (of food), xxx–xxxi, 22–23, 25, 231. *See also* manure
Rees, David, 254
repetition, 17, 29, 34, 86, 131
resurrection. *See* cycles; recycling
rhythm of White's writing, 23, 27, 33, 48, 50, 62, 65, 101, 124, 138, 176, 184. *See also* action; lyrical passages
Robert the Bruce, 215
Rogers, Barbara, 250, 257
Rollin, Lucy, 254–55
Rose and the Ring, The (Thackeray), 5
Ross, Harold, xx, xxi, xxii, xxiii*(fn)*
runts, 2, 12
rural world
  and Arable family name, 1
  White's love for, xxix, 7, 18, 39, 62, 223, 256
  See also animals; barns; farm; Maine; manure
Russell, Isabel, 114, 203*(fn)*, 204*(fn)*

St. Nicholas Magazine, xx
Sale, Roger, 41, 248
salvation, xxvi, xxviii, 91, 153, 218, 225, 237, 239, 251
Sampson, Edward C., 249
San Francisco, xxv*(fn)*, 90
"Sanitation" (White), 45

Saturday Review, The, 227, 245
Saxton, Eugene, xxiii, 30
seasons, xxx, xxxi, 8, 39, 42, 113–14, 138, 176, 219, 223, 253, 254. *See also* cycles
"Second Tree from the Corner, The" (White), 109
"Security" (White), 227, 241
Selden, George, 197
self-mockery, xxvi, 144
Sendak, Maurice, xxiv, 53
sentimentality, lack of, in *Charlotte's Web*, 38, 40, 45, 251
"setting forth," 179. *See also* quests
Shakespeare, William, 4, 14, 22–23
"Shape of Television, The" (White), 1–2
sheep, 49, 123
Shepard, Ernest H., 198
Shohet, Richard M., 8–9
Silverstein, Shel, xxiv
Singer, Dorothy G., 254
Skowhegan (Maine) Fair, 130
slapstick, 21, 68, 126, 228. *See also* action, humor
Solheim, Helen, 254
song sparrows, xxi, 43, 99
Sophocles, 17
Speck, Dr., 6
Spencer, Herbert, 14
spiders
  as aeronauts, 103, 178, 179
  characteristics of, 37, 48, 63, 76, 77, 81, 92, 102, 109–10, 140
  illustrations of, xxix, 15, 22, 30, 66, 199, 214–15, 220, 221
  White's observations of, xxviii, xxix, *146*, 210, 215–16, 220, 223, 225, 237–38
  White's research on, xvii, 37, 38, 40, 55, 102, 147, *189*, *194*, *195*, 210, *211–13*, 214–16, *217*, 225, 251–52
  See also Charlotte; eggs; webs
Spiders and Their Spinningwork (McCook), 210, 216
Stevenson, Adlai, xxxiii*(fn)*
Strunk, William, Jr., xx, 2, 86, 56
Stuart Little (White), 46, 51, 57, 90, 246, 249
  ending of, xxiii*(fn)*
  illustrating of, 121, 197, 198, 221, 227
  linearity of, 176
  lists in, 75
  mouselike appearance of protagonist in, 12, 242
  Neumeyer's opinion of, 250*(fn)*
  origins of, xxiii, 4, 239
  quest in, xxv–xxvi, 179, 226
  response to, xxiii*(fn)*, xxiv, 246, 263–64
  sales of, xxv
  sentiments in, 18
  themes of, xxv
  as White's first children's book, xix–xx, xxii, xxxiv
  word changes in, xxiii*(fn)*
style, 45. *See also* language; voice
subtext, 43
Subtreasury of American Humor, A (ed. E. B. & K. White), 70, 105
suspense, 67, 76. *See also* foreshadowing
Swift, Jonathan, 45
swineherds, 2
symbolism, 224
syntax, 48. *See also* rhythm

Tale of Peter Rabbit, The (Potter), 17, 88, 202, 174
"tantony pig," 2
television, 1–2, 209
Templeton
  Charlotte's salvation by, 72–73, 164
  illustrations of, xxxiii–xxxiv, 58, 169, 202
  lists involving, 14, 29
  name of, 26
  sounds associated with, 26, 30, 45, 90
  White's depiction of, xxix, 17, 29–30, 45–47, 90, 139, 148, 175, 223, 253
Thackeray, William, 5
themes
  in *Charlotte's Web*, xix, xxv–xxvii, xxix, xxx, 17, 26, 254. *See also* affirmation; cycles; death; freedom; friendship; immortality; joy; life; loneliness; miracles; salvation; triumph
  in *Stuart Little*, xxv, 17
  in *Trumpet of the Swan*, 17
Thoreau, Henry David, xxvi, xxviii, 115
Thurber, James, 114
town meetings, 90
Townsend, John Rowe, 253
Travers, P. L., xix, 245–46

triumph, xxxi, 155, 157. *See also* miracles
Trumpet of the Swan, The (White), xxiv, 104
  bottle feeding in, 8, 206
  characters in, 4, 12, 79, 107, 198
  ending of, 7
  humor in, 101
  illustrator of, 202, 221–22
  writing of, 208, 210, 226, 239
Twain, Mark, 5–6, 51, 101, 115, 202
"Twins" (White), 7, 15

understatement, 63, 122
Ungerer, Tomi, xxiv
United Nations, xxv*(fn)*, 90
University of California—San Diego, 30, 120

"Vermin" (White), 29
violence in White's works, 226, 237. *See also* "kill"; "murder"
Virgil, 8
voice, 17, 47. *See also* narrator, omniscient
voices
  Charlotte's, 31, 35, 44, 48, 49, 53, 89, 175
  of cob in *Trumpet of the Swan*, 4, 79
  Dr. Dorian's, 108
  of farmers, 23, 82
  of geese, 17, 29, 34, 86, 253
  Mr. Arable's, 5, 49
  of sheep, 49
  Templeton's, 30, 45, 47
  Wilbur's, 34, 35, 48–49

Walden (Thoreau), 115
Weales, Gerald, 254
webs
  facts about, 55, 92, 124
  illustrations of, xxxiv, 36, 59, 214–15
  as miracle, xxxii, 77, 109–10, 129, 178, 225
  words for Charlotte's, 20, 97, 98, *193*, 218
  See also spiders
Webster's Unabridged Dictionary, 116
Welty, Eudora, xix, 246–47
Where the Wild Things Are (Sendak), 53
White, Albert (White's brother), xxvi, 101, 116
White, Allene (Joel White's wife), 30, 105
White, Andrew D. (mentor of E. B. White at Cornell, source of nickname "Andy"), xx
White, E(lwyn) B(rooks) ("Andy")
  on *Charlotte's Web*, xv, 218–27
  depiction of children's feelings by, 44, 256
  health of, xxiii, xxvi*(fn)*, xxviii, 29, 228
  honors bestowed on, 159–60
  letters of
    to Cass Canfield, 30
    to Gene Deitch, 12, 13, 22, 38, 39, 42, 46, 175, 222–24
    to Louis de Rochemont, 42, 219–20
    to Scott Elledge, 145
    to J. G. Gude, 170–71
    to Peter Neumeyer, 1, 114, 144, 208
    to Ursula Nordstrom, xxxii–xxxiv, 15, 30, 46, 83, 101, 167, 198, 199, 202, 205, 210, 214–16, 218, 221–22
  life of, xx–xxxi, 90, 104, 114, 116
  likeness of, in *Stuart Little*, 200
  and literature, 114, 115, 215, 227, 236
  manuscript reproductions of, *188*, *190*, *191*, *192*, *193*, *196*
  personal characteristics of, xxiii, xxvi*(fn)*, 12, 19, 64, 70, 90, 144–45, 159–60, 221, 239–40, 249–50, 255–58
  photographs of, *xxvii*, *44*
  poems by, xx, xxix, 1, 4–5, 15, 29, 42, 104, 210, 227, 244
  as professional writer, xx–xxii, 239
  recording of *Charlotte's Web* by, xix
  on writing, 2, 11, 14, 15, 25, 35, 45, 48, 60, 65, 69, 78, 101, 103, 120, 127, 150, 174, 175, 204
  writing habits of, xxiii, 208, 250
  writing skills of, xvii, xxi, 11, 18, 35, 48, 56, 87, 101, 150, 163, 250. *See also* description; drafts; language; narrative strategies; narrator; paragraph; punctuation; rhythm; voice
  See also barns; farm; rural world; spiders; *titles of works by*
White, Joel (White's son), 130, 227, 244

White, Katharine (White's wife), 144
 children's-book columns of, xxii, 227, 258
 death of, 145
 on film version of *Charlotte's Web*, 83, 203*(fn)*
 letters to, xxiv, 163
 as model for Mrs. Arable, 108, 200
 New York Times letter from, 184
 White's life with, xx, xxi–xxii, xxvi, 114
 White's poems for, 42, 210
White, Samuel (White's father), xxvi, 116
Wiggins, James Russell, 90
Wilbur
 age of, 67, 83
 anthropomorphism of, 8, 22, 30
 character development of, 23, 50, 117, 143, 145–46, 164–66, 168, 170, 251–53
 Charlotte contrasted with, 50, 165, 251
 in early drafts, 4, 72, 164, 206-8
 illustrations of, 202, 215
 language used by, 34, 35, 47, 48
 naïveté of, 34, 35, 40, 47, 49, 251
 as runt, 2, 12
 See also salvation
Wild Flag, The (White), 38
Wilder, Laura Ingalls, xxiv, 197
Wilder, Thornton, 219
Williams, Fiona, 198
Williams, Garth
 as illustrator, 197–203, 249
 letter to Peter Neumeyer from, 66, 121, 199, *200–1*
 Nordstrom as link between White and, xxiv, xxxiv, 132, 210, 214–16
 reviewers on, 245, 246
 White's interest in illustrations of, xxxiii, 15, 30, 46, 81, 197–99, 214–16, 220, 221
 See also illustrations
Williams, Kevin, 145
Wind in the Willows, The (Grahame), 8–9, 26, 43
"winking," 5
Winnie-the-Pooh (Milne), xxxiii
Woman's Home Companion, xx, 4
Works and Days (Hesiod), 8
world government, xxv*(fn)*, 90
writing, "truth" of, 80, 89, 96, 151, 157–58. *See also* White, E. B., on writing

Zipes, Jack, 254, 255
"Zoo Revisited" (White), 15
Zuckerman, Homer, 12
Zuckerman, Judy, xxviii

Underwood